THE PROPOSITIONAL LOGIC OF AVICENNA

NABIL SHEHABY

THE PROPOSITIONAL LOGIC OF AVICENNA

A Translation from *al-Shifā': al-Qiyās*
with Introduction, Commentary and Glossary

D. REIDEL PUBLISHING COMPANY

DORDRECHT-HOLLAND / BOSTON-U.S.A.

First printing: December 1973

Library of Congress Catalog Card Number 73–75642

ISBN 90 277 0360 4

Published by D. Reidel Publishing Company,
P.O. Box 17, Dordrecht, Holland

Sold and distributed in the U.S.A., Canada, and Mexico
by D. Reidel Publishing Company, Inc.
306 Dartmouth Street, Boston,
Mass. 02116, U.S.A.

To My Parents

TABLE OF CONTENTS

ACKNOWLEDGEMENTS   XIII

INTRODUCTION   1

LIST OF ABBREVIATIONS   29

TRANSLATION – *AL-QIYĀS*

BOOK V

CHAPTER ONE / On Conditional Propositions and Their Types   35

The kinds of syllogisms which lead to predicative conclusions and those leading to conditional conclusions – A general definition of conditional propositions – The two kinds of conditional propositions – Complete and incomplete connection – Complete and incomplete conflict – Different views on conditional propositions – The two kinds of following: (a) implication; (b) chance connection – The restricted conditional – The different senses of the particles used in connective propositions – The antecedent and the consequent of the connective proposition are not statement-making sentences – The restricted and the unrestricted connective proposition – An implication is true when both its parts are false – And when the antecedent is false and the consequent is true – It is false when the antecedent is true and the consequent is false.

CHAPTER TWO / On Separative-Conditional Propositions   44

The different ways of expressing conflict – A separative proposition expresses (1) real conflict and the particle it takes is 'It is exclusively' – (2) The case where both its parts may be false – (3) The case where both its parts may be true – Other usages of 'either' – The antecedent and the consequent of the separative proposition are interchangeable, but not so in the connective – An analysis of (1), (2) and (3) are compared with each other – A comparison between (1) on the one hand and (2) and (3) on the other – There is no separative proposition in which the meanings of the antecedent and the consequent are not related – Other forms of conditional propositions.

CHAPTER THREE / On the Kinds of Combinations in Pure Conditional Propositions and in the Conditional Compounded of Predicative and Conditional Propositions   53

The different forms the antecedent and the consequent of a conditional proposition take – The separative can have more than two parts; but the connective
has only two – The subject and/or the predicate of the parts of a conditional can
be identical – The reduction of conditionals to predicative propositions – 'If'
and 'Either' etc. can be put after or before the subject of the antecedent; and in
the first case the proposition would be indeterminable – The view that the connective is an affirmative statement and the separative a negative one. His view
on what affirmation and negation in conditional propositions are – The truth-
conditions of the connective and the separative.

CHAPTER FOUR / On Explaining the Meaning of the Universal,
the Particular, the Indefinite and the Singular [Connective-]
Conditional Proposition   61

A certain view on how to determine the quantity of a connective proposition.
His view on this issue – When is a conditional considered universal or indefinite?
– When is the conditional regarded as singular? – A criticism of the view that a
universal connective is equal to a universal predicative – The universal affirmative connective proposition – Can a connective expressing chance connection be
universally affirmed? – Is 'Always: when every donkey talks, then every man
brays' true in either one of the senses of following? – An objection and an answer related to the above issue – A proposition expressing chance connection is
true when the consequent is true – The antecedent of a connective proposition
is not a statement-making sentence – A return to the discussion of universal affirmative connective propositions – Would they be affected if impossible conditions are added to their antecedents?
Particular Connective Propositions: The first kind of particular connective
propositions – The second kind of particular connective propositions – Is it
possible for the particular connective to have universal parts?

CHAPTER FIVE / On the Universal Negative in [Connective-]
Conditional Propositions   76

The universal negative connective proposition – The two kinds of negation in
connective propositions – (1) The universal negation of chance connection –
(2) The universal negation of implication – Can a connective with a false antecedent and consequent be universally negated?
The Four Forms of Separative Propositions: The universal affirmative separative proposition – The universal negative separative proposition – Can the
separative have universal parts? – The particular affirmative separative proposition – Modal conditional propositions.

BOOK VI

CHAPTER ONE / On the Syllogisms Compounded of Connective-
Conditional Propositions Arranged in Three Figures   91

The three figures of the syllogisms compounded of connective premisses – The
first figure – Its moods – An objection against the first figure and an answer to it –
The second figure – Its moods – The third figure – Its moods.

CHAPTER TWO / On the Syllogisms Compounded of Connective
and Separative Propositions   101

When the minor is connective and the major a real separative; and the middle
part is the consequent of the minor and the antecedent of the major – IA/I –
AI/– – It is productive when either one of the premisses is particular – No
production when the separative is negative – No production from two negative
or two particular premisses – When the minor is connective and the major is
unreal separative; and the middle part is the consequent of the first and the
antecedent of the second – Sterile moods – The connective is particular – The
separative is particular – No production when the separative is negative – No
production when the premisses are particular – The same figure but the middle
is negative – When the premisses are affirmative and one of them is universal it
will be sterile – and when one of them is particular it will be sterile – When the
separative is negative it is sterile – When the parts of the separative are negative
– When the separative is real and the middle part is the antecedent of both
premisses – When either one of the premisses is particular – When the separative
is particular – When the separative is unreal and the middle part in the same
position and it is affirmative – The separative is particular – The connective is
particular – No production when the separative is negative – Now the middle
part is negative – One of the premisses is particular – When the connective is
negative and one of the premisses is particular – No production when the separative is negative – The separative with both parts negative – When the connective is the major premiss and the middle part is the antecedent of both – The
separative is particular – The connective is particular – The connective is particular negative – When the separative is unreal and the middle is in the same
position – The separative is particular – No production when the connective is
particular – No production when the separative is negative – The separative is
particular – No production when the connective is particular – When the middle
is negative and it is the consequent of the first and the antecedent of the second –
The separative is particular – No production when the connective is particular –
No production when the separative is negative – The separative is particular
negative – No production when the connective is particular negative – When
the separative is real and the middle is the consequent of both premisses – The
separative is particular – The connective is particular – No production when the
separative is negative – The separative is particular negative – The connective is
particular negative – When the separative is unreal and the middle is the consequent of both premisses and it is affirmative – The separative is particular –
The connective is particular.

CHAPTER THREE / On the Syllogisms Compounded of Separative
Propositions   118

Syllogisms from two separative premisses and the conditions for their produc-

tion – II/– – There are no figures in this kind of syllogism – The mood where
both premisses are affirmative one of which has a negative part – There is no
production if the premiss with the negative part is negative – There is no production if one of the premisses is particular; or when the negative premiss has
affirmative parts – No production if one premiss is a real separative – When
both premisses are unreal separative and the middle part is affirmative, the conclusion is not affirmative – When the premisses are particular, the conclusion
would be a connective proposition – When the premisses are unreal and the
middle is negative – When the premisses are affirmative – When one premiss is
particular – When one premiss is negative there will be no production – No
production when both premisses are particular or when one of them has two
negative parts. If between them they have three negative parts they produce
when the middle is negative – Other combinations.

CHAPTER FOUR / On the Syllogisms Compounded of Predicative
and Conditional Propositions 124

Syllogisms from a conditional and a predicative premiss; – (i) the predicative is
the major premiss and the middle term occurs in the consequent of the conditional and the predicative – The first figure and the conditions for its production
– When the connective is universal affirmative – When the connective is particular affirmative – When the connective is universal negative – When the connective is particular negative – The second figure – When the connective is universal
affirmative – When the connective is particular affirmative – When the connective is universal negative – The third figure – When the connective is universal
affirmative – When the connective is particular affirmative – When the connective is universal negative – When the connective is particular negative – (ii) When
the connective is the major premiss – The first figure – When the connective is
universal affirmative – When the connective is particular affirmative – When it
is universal negative – When it is particular negative – The second figure – When
the connective is univérsal affirmative – When the connective is particular affirmative – When it is universal negative – When it is particular negative – The
third figure – When the premisses are universal affirmative – When the connective is universal negative – When the connective is particular negative.

CHAPTER FIVE / On the Three Figures of the Syllogisms Compounded of a Predicative and a Conditional Proposition Where
the Predicative Shares [Either Its Subject or Its Predicate] with
[the Subject or the Predicate] of the Antecedent (of the Conditional Proposition) 138

(iii) When the middle term occurs in the antecedent of the conditional and the
predicative – The first figure – When the connective is universal affirmative –
When the connective is universal negative – When the connective is particular
affirmative – When the connective is particular negative – When the connective

is universal affirmative – When the connective is universal negative – The second figure – When the connective is universal affirmative – When the connective is universal negative – When the connective is universal affirmative – When the connective is universal negative – The connective is universal affirmative – The connective is universal affirmative – The connective is universal affirmative – When the connective is universal affirmative – The connective is universal negative – When the connective is universal affirmative – When the connective is universal negative – The third figure – When the connective is universal affirmative – When the connective is universal negative – The connective is particular affirmative – When the connective is universal affirmative – When the connective is universal negative – (iv) When the predicative is the major premiss – The first figure – The connective is universal affirmative – The second figure – When the connective is universal affirmative – The third figure – When the connective is universal affirmative.

CHAPTER SIX / On the Three Figures of the Divided Syllogism   152

The difference between the divided syllogism and induction – A separative and several predicative premisses which share their predicates. The first figure – The second figure – The third figure – A separative premiss and several predicatives not sharing their predicates – The first figure – The second figure – The third figure – One separative and one predicative premiss – The first figure – The second and the third figures – Two separative premisses – The first figure – The second figure – The connective is the minor and the separative is the major premiss – The first figure – The second figure.

BOOK VII

CHAPTER ONE / On Equipollence and Opposition Between Connective-Conditional Propositions   163

Immediate inference in conditional propositions – Universal connective propositions – Particular connective propositions.

CHAPTER TWO / On the Opposition Between Separative-Conditional Propositions and Separative- and Connective-Conditional Propositions and the State of Their Equipollence   171

Inferences from separatives to connectives and vice versa – Inferences involving separative propositions – Back to the subject of immediate inference from separative to connective propositions and vice versa.

CHAPTER THREE / On the Conversion of the Connective Proposition   180

BOOK VIII

CHAPTER ONE / On the Definition of the Exceptive Syllogism   183

The difference between exceptive and conjunctive syllogisms – When the connective expresses complete implication; (i) we assert the antecedent deducing the consequent – When the connective is incomplete implication; (i) we assert the antecedent deducing the consequent – The connective is complete implication; (ii) we assert the consequent deducing the antecedent – The connection is complete implication; (ii) we deny the consequent deducing the denial of the antecedent – The connective is incomplete implication. No production when the antecedent is denied – Or when the consequent is asserted – The connective is complete implication; (iii) we deny the antecedent deducing the denial of the consequent – (iv) we deny the consequent deducing the denial of the antecedent.

CHAPTER TWO / On the Enumeration of the Exceptive Syllogisms [which have a Separative-Conditional Premiss]   193

When the conditional is separative expressing complete conflict; (i) we assert any part deducing the denial of the other – (ii) or denying any part deducing the other – When the real separative has more than two parts, then (i) if we assert one part we (a) deny everyone of the others or (b) deny the separative consisting of the others – (ii) If we deny one of the parts, we produce a separative consisting of the others – Both parts of the separative may be true. If one of the parts is denied the other must be asserted – Both parts of the separative may be false – When one of the parts is asserted, the other must be denied.

BOOK IX

CHAPTER ONE / On Explaining that Exceptive Syllogisms Cannot Be Completed Except by Conjunctive Syllogisms   203

COMMENTARY

BOOK V   215
BOOK VI   258
BOOK VII   266
BOOK VIII   270
BOOK IX   277

GLOSSARY   283
BIBLIOGRAPHY   287
INDEX   291

ACKNOWLEDGEMENTS

I wish to express my gratitude to the Warburg Institute for the award of a three-year fellowship during which a large part of this work was written. I would like to acknowledge my debt to Professor A. I. Sabra who during that period offered me his earnest supervision, and to Professor Sir Karl R. Popper for his unfailing help and encouragement. I am also grateful to Professor Raymond Klibansky who kindly checked my Greek in some places. My thanks are due to the Canada Council and the McGill Grants Committee who provided me with grants to consult and obtain microfilm copies of many manuscripts in Europe and the Middle East needed in my work. Finally I wish to thank Professor Norman Kretzmann, editor of Synthese Historical Library, for his useful suggestions.

INTRODUCTION

The main purpose of this work is to provide an English translation of and commentary on a recently published Arabic text dealing with conditional propositions and syllogisms. The text is that of Avicenna (Abū ʿAlī ibn Sīnā, 980–1037); and it appears as part of the *Analytics* of his major work *al-Shifāʾ*.[1] This part of *al-Shifāʾ* has never been translated into any European language before; nor was it studied by modern scholars in the East or in the West. The absence of a translation and a reliable study in addition to other internal difficulties concerning the book's style and sources confront us with a rather complicated, if not forbidding, task. However, important as it is in understanding Avicenna's thought in particular and the development of Arabic logic at a crucial stage in general, the student of Arabic philosophy cannot shy away from trying to find his way through this maze. I do not wish to claim an exhaustive study of the text. Apart from the translation I tried, however, to explain Avicenna's main ideas on conditional propositions and syllogisms. In this introduction I shall first treat the question of the text's sources; and later give an outline of Avicenna's theory of conditionals. It goes without saying that Avicenna's treatment of conditional propositions and syllogisms in *al-Shifāʾ* represents his views on the subject as they were held throughout his life. The brief account we find in *al-Najāt*, a book which belongs to the same period as *al-Shifāʾ*, and in the much later work *al-Ishārāt* show no change of opinion. The details as well as the general outlook are the same; except that the last two works are much shorter versions of *al-Shifāʾ*.[2]

In a short introduction to *al-Shifāʾ*, Avicenna's student Abū ʿUbayd al-Jūzjānī described the circumstances in which the book was written. He tells the reader that he first asked his master to write a commentary on Artistotle's works. Avicenna replied that he had no time for this kind of work, but he was ready to write a book which would avoid the tedious work of explaining the meaning of terms and in which he would arrange his ideas in the order he liked.[3]

Intermittently and in about six years' time (approximately between 1014–20)[4] Avicenna completed his most important work in philosophy and science called *al-Shifā'* (known in Latin as *Sufficientia*). It came out in the form of an encyclopaedia which, as Avicenna himself says in his preface to the book, contains the gist of the philosophical knowledge attributed to the Ancients, i.e. the Greeks.[5] Many a writer in Arabic before him conceived an account of Greek philosophy as a more or less faithful summary or explanation of one standard work or another by a Greek author. Avicenna, in contrast with such an attitude, not only quotes and explains conflicting Greek views without committing himself to one work; but he also criticizes these works and sometimes introduces new viewpoints. After a long period in which Arabic writers were acquainted with Greek philosophy through translations (which in their later stages had reached a high standard of accuracy), paraphrases and commentaries, it was natural for a man of Avicenna's standing to be dissatisfied with the passive task of merely recording and explaining other people's views – a task which occupied him at the beginning of his intellectual development[6] – and rather to enter into dialogue with Greek thinkers either in the form of criticism or by bringing forward positive ideas which, he imagined, could solve some of the philosophical issues discussed by these thinkers. This attitude, I think, is a sign of a mind confident of its understanding of what it reads and which finds no satisfaction in views that do not answer the problems posed by the growing civilization to which it belongs. His preface to *al-Shifā'* shows that this new approach was a conscious act of mind. There he makes it clear that the book contains new ideas which are the product of his own thinking on Greek philosophy. To be precise, Avicenna adds that his contributions are mainly in the fields of physics, metaphysics and logic.[7]

I should perhaps say a few words on the method Avicenna had chosen to compose his book. Roughly speaking he starts describing a point by giving what he thinks to be the right explanation of it. At this stage he usually does not tell us whether what he says represents his own views or those of some other philosopher(s). Sometimes this exposition is developed by bringing into it other ideas in the form of quotations from other writers. Then he refers to or quotes counterviews on the same subject. These counterviews are usually followed by his answer, which is in harmony with the explanations given at the beginning. Most of the time Avicenna raises what he calls 'objections', *shukūk*, against a certain point in his theme. His formulation of these objections show that he is anticipating them rather than recording an already established problem. This means that the Muslim philosopher is trying to create new problems in a position which is either his own or one he advocates. The aim of these objections is to point out an apparent contradiction in Avicenna's standpoint. It is always followed by an answer followed by another objection and so forth. This objection-answer form of writing sometimes occupies the major part of the chapter in which it occurs, especially when developed into a conversation between Avicenna and his imaginary critics. There is no point in trying to trace this method back to previous Arabic philosophical writings, I mean writings that were exclusively concerned with analysing Greek philosophy. As I said before Arabic philosophers before Avicenna were busily engaged in producing treatises, establishing faithful translations of Greek (or Syriac translations of Greek) works and in writing paraphrases and commentaries on standard Greek texts.[8] These philosophers were mostly Christians who received encouragement from Muslim patrons to continue the same tradition that started in Syria long before Islam.[9] There is no evidence that these philosophers ever sought to change their limited approach. As one reads throughout *al-Shifā'* and becomes familiar with the method described above in its multifarious applications that cover all the branches of Ancient philosophy, the real intention of the author no longer remains hidden. For, compared with the methods of presentation used by previous writers in philosophy, Avicenna's method resembles in many ways the one Aristotle had chosen for expounding his own philosophy. We have no evidence from Avicenna's writings that he wanted to assume the role of Aristotle, who criticized and in a sense integrated the philosophies of his predecessors. It should also be made clear that we do not claim that Avicenna, even if he tried to assume such a role, is another Aristotle. All that concerns us here is to record Avicenna's new approach, which is no doubt an important turning point in Islamic philosophy.

From what I have already said it is clear that the reader of *al-Shifā'* is faced with various views on one and the same topic. Some of these views are the author's. Others are the result of Avicenna's wide reading which includes Greek works that represent different schools of philosophy. Almost all of these are left with no reference to their authorship. It is therefore of primary importance to try to find out what Greek works Avicenna must have consulted when writing his book.

One thing must be pointed out before we proceed to the subject of Avicenna's sources, namely that when the author quotes some philosopher or a school of philosophy he does not tell us, except in very few places, who or which school held this or that view. We must also add here that al-Jūzjānī, in introducing al-Shifā', said that Avicenna had written the logical section at a time when he got back his library and that this section of al-Shifā' is much influenced by his readings at that time. This is an important remark, especially because it comes from the student and companion to whom Avicenna dictated the whole book. It is, therefore, plausible to assume that the reported views in the logic of al-Shifā' are formulations of opinions held by writers whose books were available to Avicenna.

SOURCES

In discussing the sources of the logical part of al-Shifā' I shall limit myself to works which are most likely to have treated the subject of conditional propositions and syllogisms and which, therefore, might have influenced Avicenna's study of this subject. The inquiry into the sources of the book as a whole will be pursued to the extent that it will help to shed light on the main problem of conditional reasoning. There are three kinds of works that should be examined. First, al-Shifā' itself and in particular the part which deals with conditional propositions and syllogisms, since this part indicates, though vaguely, its own sources. Second, Avicenna's other works and letters in which he speaks of his readings in philosophy. Third, the main Arabic bio-bibliographies – al-Fihrist of Ibn al-Nadīm, the Ta'rīkh of Ibn al-Qiftī and Ibn Abī Usaybi'a's Ṭabaqāt al-Aṭibbā'. The above three works, though of much help to the historian of Arabic thought do not give the full story. We shall consult them on whatever information they could provide on Arabic translations, commentaries and epitomes of works related to our subject. Some gaps in their picture will be filled with the aid of some other Arabic books.

The one person who is frequently referred to in al-Shifā' is Aristotle. However, this fact will not be of much help to us. For Aristotle, who is called by the Muslim philosopher ṣāḥibu 'l-manṭiq (the author of the logic), did not treat of conditional propositions and syllogisms in his works.

In the *Prior Analytics* Aristotle mentions conditional syllogisms and promises to write on the subject[10], but his promise, so far as we know, was not carried out. This, of course, does not rule out the possibility that Avicenna might have relied on a pseudo-Aristotelian work on conditional syllogisms. That this in fact was not the case is shown by the only reference to Aristotle in the text which is directly related to the treatment of conditional syllogisms. At the end of a chapter in which Avicenna begins to survey what he calls 'exceptive syllogism' (*al-qiyās al-istithnā'ī*), namely the inference carried out by means similar to those applied in Chrysippus' five indemonstrables, he says that Aristotle had written a book on conditional syllogisms[11], but the book is lost.[12] In the same place Avicenna speaks of a school or group of logicians who, according to him, refused to treat conditional syllogisms in the same way as Aristotle had treated predicative (categorical) syllogisms (*al-qiyās al-ḥamlī*). He criticizes these people saying that they sought to widen the gap between their logic and that of Aristotle by contradicting his methods.[13] To explain this critical remark, we refer the reader to the two different approaches to conditional syllogisms mentioned in Avicenna's book. The first simply uses the Stoic inference-schemas as they are exemplified by Chrysippus' indemonstrables.[14] The second applies the idea of the middle term borrowed from Aristotle with some changes.[15] Whatever the demerits of applying the idea of the middle term are, Avicenna is certainly following here a Peripatetic practice which started with Theophrastus.[16] Thus, the only possible interpretation of Avicenna's criticism mentioned above is that the author is in favour of the Peripatetic method, which applies Aristotle's theory of the categorical syllogism to conditional inferences, and that he does not see the point behind the Stoic innovation. One therefore expects that whenever a matter of principle is disputed, Avicenna will side with Aristotle's followers rather than with the Stoics.[17]

At another point of his discussion of exceptive syllogisms Avicenna refers to a dispute between, on the one hand, those who side with Aristotle and on the other, a man "who is strong in medicine but weak in logic".[18] Though the disputed point is trivial and does not touch any fundamental issue, the identity of the people involved deserves our attention. There is more than one indication that the man who is strong in medicine and weak in logic is Galen.[19] Avicenna never mentions Galen by name. More than once he refers to him as "the most excellent among physicians" or sometimes "the excellent physician".[20] The Arabs knew Galen both as a medical writer and as a logician. His logical works received the same attention from Arabic translators as his work on medicine. We can only state here the fact that his medical works were as influential in the Arabic world as Aristotle's philosophical writings. Galen's ideas on logic, however, were not received with the same enthusiasm. Avicenna, and al-Fārābī before him, attacked Galen for his stand against the syllogisms compounded of possible premises.[21] Galen's views on this matter and perhaps other logical matters seem to be the reason behind calling him "a weak logician". I should say here that this criticism of Galen does not diminish Avicenna's debt to the Greek physician. For, as will be shown later[22], there are close similarities between Avicenna's ideas on conditional propositions and syllogisms and those of Galen which we find in the only extant logical work of his – the *Institutio Logica*.

As far as exceptive syllogisms are concerned Avicenna adds nothing to the above remarks. Two conclusions can be drawn from them. (1) That Avicenna rightly emphasizes the difference between exceptive syllogisms and those conditional syllogisms which are formulated according to the Aristotelian idea of the middle term (called by him 'conjunctive-conditional', *shartī iqtirānī*); and that he attributes the first kind to an anti-Aristotelian school. (2) That he clearly disagrees with this anti-Aristotelian school though he gives no reasons for his disagreement. It is, perhaps, not rash to say that Avicenna would have ignored exceptive syllogisms altogether but for the fact that his original plan was to discuss all that is of any importance in Greek thinking.[23]

There is one last thing he said on his sources. In a long and carefully worked out passage which comes at the end of his treatment of conjunctive-conditional syllogisms he mentions two books which he read on these syllogisms. One of them is, to quote his own words, "attributed to the most excellent among later (scholars)"[24]. This book, he adds,

seems to be wrongly imputed to him. It is neither clear nor reliable. It neither gives an extensive survey of the subject nor does it achieve its purpose. It gives a mistaken exposition of conditional propositions, of a large number of syllogisms which accompany them, of the reasons for productiveness and sterility, and of the number of moods in the figures. The student should not pay any attention to it – it is distracting and misleading.[25]

Avicenna then goes on to describe the difference between his own approach and that of the author of this work. "The author", he says, did not know what makes conditional propositions affirmative, negative, universal, particular and indefinite; nor did he know how conditional propositions oppose or contradict each other. He also did not know how one conditional proposition can be the subaltern of the other. For he thought that all these characteristics are determined by the parts of the conditional proposition.[26]

In other words, according to Avicenna, the author of the book thought that the quality and quantity of the antecedent and consequent of the conditional proposition determine the quality and quantity of the conditional statement compounded of them. Avicenna's approach is the opposite of this. For he held the view that the conditional proposition is a statement-making sentence whose parts are in themselves not statement-making sentences. In the Commentary I try to explain how this doctrine was based on Avicenna's view that the conditional sentence itself can be asserted categorically, i.e. unconditionally. This enabled Avicenna to analyse it in terms of affirmation, negation, ... etc. It is important to note that all Avicenna's criticisms and attacks in the part devoted to conjunctive-conditional syllogisms are directed against the approach held by the author of the above work, whom Avicenna calls "the most excellent among later (scholars)". This phrase recurs several times in al-Shifā'[27], but nowhere is the man's name mentioned. I. Madkour[28] suggests that he is Alexander of Aphrodisias, which is a quite reasonable suggestion, especially because in al-Najāt (pp. 23–24), after mentioning Alexander by name, Avicenna describes him as the most scholarly among later scholars (muḥaṣṣilīn). (See below). But we should add that there is no independent evidence for the attribution of a book on conditional (or hypothetical) syllogisms to Alexander. Avicenna himself casts doubt on this attribution, but he gives no reason for his doubt apart from the weakness of the author's arguments, which Avicenna might have considered unworthy of Alexander.[29] In any case whether the book is by Alexander or not, it must have contained Greek views that Avicenna thought could not be ignored. There is also the question whether Avicenna's approach was really initiated by him. What makes this question all the more problematic is what he himself says in the same place where he refers to the above work. He says that he had read a long annotated book on the same subject eighteen years before and that that was in his native home (which must be Bukhārā). He says nothing more except that he has not seen the book since he left the city.[30]

These are the only references to sources that one finds in Avicenna's treatment of conditionals. As might be expected the other parts of the logic contain very few references to books or writers on logic. Porphyry is mentioned several times, but all the references to him occur in the *Introduction (al-Madkhal)* which is supposed to parallel his *Isagoge.*[31] There are also many references to the person identified above as Alexander of Aphrodisias. The most significant references to Alexander is the one in which he is described as the "excellent (scholar) to whom I address myself in the main", *al-fāḍil al-ladhī aktharu ishtighālī bi-mukhāṭabatihi.*[32] In the *Analytics* of *al-Shifāʾ* Avicenna describes someone as *shaykhu 'l-naṣārā*[33] (the master of the Christians). There is no way of knowing who this man is, but he might well be the Christian philosopher John Philoponus. The names of both Alexander and Philoponus occur in a letter which Avicenna had previously written to Abū Jaʿfar al-Kiyā. In the letter he told Abū Jaʿfar that he was occupied at the time with the works of people like Alexander, Themistius and John Philoponus[34], rather than those of the Christian School of Baghdad.[35] Themistius' name together with Alexander's and Theophrastus' appear in the logical part of Avicenna's short work *al-Najāt* (p. 23), though not in the context of his discussion of conditionals. In the same work (p. 7) he speaks of the literalists (*al-ẓāhiriyyūn*) among logicians which could be a reference to the Stoics. No less relevant is al-Shahrastānī's report. In *al-Milal wa'l-Niḥal* (ed. by W. Cureton, Leipzig, 1923), he talks of Avicenna's dependence on Themistius and says that Avicenna "defends him, backs his doctrine and does not rely on any of the Ancients but him" (p. 326, see also p. 312). All this, however, is said in the context of al-Shahrastānī's account of Aristotle's views in the *Metaphysics, Physics* and *Ethics* (pp. 312–26).

From Ibn al-Nadīm and Ibn al-Qifṭī we learn that Alexander of Aphrodisias wrote two commentaries on the *Prior Analytics* (to the end of I, VII).[36] But we are not told whether Arabic translations of these works were available. Ibn al-Nadīm, however, tells us that Alexander's commentary on the *Topics* included part of Book I and Books V–VIII; and that the commentary by Yaḥyā ibn ʿAdiyy on the same work depends on it.[37] Both Arabic sources mention also a commentary on the *De Interpretatione* by Alexander, though they add that it was not extant.[38] The same sources again say that Porphyry wrote an *Isagoge to Categorical Syllogisms,* which was translated by Abū ʿUthmān al-Dimashqī[39] and a commentary on the *De Interpretatione.*[40] They mention a commentary on the *Prior Analytics* by Themistius[41] and also one by John Philoponus[42], but this time remain silent about any translations of these works into Arabic. Themistius'[43] and Philoponus'[44] commentaries on the *Topics* together with the latter's commentary on the *De Interpretatione*[45] are also referred to by the same bio-bibliographers. No Arabic translations of these works are mentioned, and no mention is made of any Arabic translations of what they described as a commentary on the *De Interpretatione* by Theophrastus.[46] Al-Qifṭī says that Galen had written a commentary on the *De Interpretatione*.[47] Ibn Abī Uṣaybiʿa repeats[48] al-Qifṭī's report and adds that Ḥunayn ibn Isḥāq had found an incomplete copy of this work.[49] There are four other logical works which several Arabic sources attributed to Galen: the *Institutio Logica, On the Number of Syllogisms, On Hypothetical Syllogisms (Fī al-Qiyāsāt al-Waḍʿiyya)*, and the *Apodeictics*. From Ḥunayn ibn Isḥāq's list of Galen's works which are said to be translated into Arabic by Ḥunayn and his school, we know that the first two works and more than half of the last were translated into Arabic.[50]

Arabic logicians before Avicenna were not solely occupied with translating Greek logical works into Arabic. Their works include also epitomes of and commentaries on Aristotle's *Organon*. Though Avicenna does not mention any Arabic logicians in his works, we must assume that some of these must have influenced him in one way or another, at least in the early stages of his philosophical development.[51] For an account of the epitomes and commentaries written by these logicians, who were in most cases the translators themselves, we will again consult the usual sources. Ibn al-Nadīm and Ibn al-Qifṭī attribute the following books to Abū Bishr Mattā ibn Yūnus: a commentary on the *De Interpretatione*, another on the *Prior Analytics* and a third on the *Topics* which includes Book I only.[52] They also attribute to Abū Bishr a book *On Conditional Syllogisms (al-Maqāyīs al-Sharṭiyya)*[53] which might be nothing but an extract of his commentary on the *Prior Analytics*. Epitomes of the *De Interpretatione* are also said to have been written by Ḥabīb ibn Bahrīz[54], Ḥunayn ibn Isḥāq[55], Isḥāq ibn Ḥunayn[56] and Ibn al-Muqaffaʿ.[57] We are also informed that al-Fārābī had written epitomes of all the logical works of Aristotle.[58] Al-Fārābī's *al-Qiyās al-Ṣaghīr*[59] together with his long commentary on the *De Interpretatione*[60] and the *Prior Analytics*[61] in addition to the *Utterances Employed in Logic* (ed. by M. Mahdi, Beyrouth 1968) and the *Topics* seem to be the only extant logical works of this great Aristotelian commentator. The same Arabic bio-bibliographers say that al-Kindī had written an epitome of the *De Interpretatione*[62] and a commentary on the *Prior Analytics*.[63] Both Aristotelian works had been commented on by Quwayrī.[64] Al-Rāzī[65], al-Sarakhsī[66] and Thābit[67] are said to have epitomized the same two Aristotelian works mentioned above; while a book called *Risāla fī'l-Manṭiq* (*A Treatise on Logic*) and another called *al-Burhān* (*Apodeictics*) are attributed to al-Rāzī.[68] A commentary on the *Topics* and a treatise *On the Analysis of Syllogisms* are said to be among Yaḥyā ibn ʿAdiyy's works.[69] Excepting al-Fārābī's five works mentioned before, none of these works has survived. Thus, on the face of it, this list cannot be of much help to us. But it does give a fairly detailed picture of the active work on books which could have touched the problem of conditionals in one way or another.

To go back to al-Fārābī's extant works on logic. In *al-Qiyās al-Ṣaghīr* there is a brief account of what our text calls exceptive syllogisms, which are based on Chrysippus' indemonstrables. These are inference-schemas in which the major premiss is a connective proposition (if ... then). In the first we assert the antecedent of the connective to produce the consequent; and in the second we assert the negation of the consequent to produce the negation of the antecedent. Then al-Fārābī talks of inferences in which the major premiss is a separative proposition (either ... or). A separative proposition, he says, expresses either complete or defective conflict. The one expressing complete conflict is the exclusive disjunctive, i.e. whose parts cannot be all true or all false. Defective conflict is that in which all the parts can be false. The inference-schemas we get when the major premiss expresses complete conflict are those in which we assert any part and produce the negation of the other or we assert the negation of one to produce the other. If the major premiss in this case consists of more than two parts, then we produce one part after negating all the others, al-Fārābī says. When the major premiss expresses defective conflict, then the only kind of inferences we get are those in which we assert one of the parts to produce the negation of the other(s). (See *al-Qiyās al-Ṣaghīr*, pp. 257–60, and in the English translation pp. 74–80.) The terminology used here is very similar to Avicenna's. But Avicenna differs from al-Fārābī in that he distinguishes also between complete and incomplete connective propositions (the first is the equivalence and the second is the implication) in addition to his treatment of a third kind of separative propositions in which all parts can be true. Not to speak of Avicenna's truth-functional analysis of all these propositions and his treatment among conditional syllogisms those he named conjunctive-conditionals. There are differences between them even on some of the above issues as we shall see. Neither al-Fārābī's long commentary on the *De Interpretatione* nor that on the *Prior Analytics* treat of conditionals. In the *Utterances Employed in Logic* he does not say anything worth considering.

AVICENNA'S THEORY OF CONDITIONAL PROPOSITIONS AND SYLLOGISMS

In the remaining pages of the Introduction I shall try to give an outline of Avicenna's theory of conditional propositions and syllogisms based on his systematic and uninterrupted text. A proposition is called 'conditional' (*shartiyya*) if what it states is (a) a relation of following (*ittibāʿ*), or (b) a relation of conflict (*ʿinād*). The proposition expressing the first relation is called 'connective-conditional' (*shartiyya muttasila*); and the one expressing the second relation is called 'separative-conditional' (*shartiyya munfasila*). The literal forms in which these relations appear are fixed. The relation of following appears as an 'If ... then' ('*in ... fa*') sentence; while the 'Either ... or' ('*immā ... wa immā*') sentence reveals the relation of conflict.[70]

But what does Avicenna mean by 'following' and 'conflict'? He distinguishes between two kinds of following.[71] A sentence follows another (a) if their meanings are so connected that whenever the antecedent is true the consequent must also be true; or (b) if both the antecedent and the consequent are true without their meanings being connected in any way. If a sentence follows another in sense (a), the compound sentence expressing their relation of following is said to express the relation of implication (*luzūm*). When (b) is what we mean by following, the connective-conditional proposition will express chance connection (*ittifāq*). Avicenna then states the truth conditions of both kinds of connective propositions in terms of the truth-value (truth or falsity) of the antecendent and the consequent. A connective-conditional proposition which expresses the relation of implication is true if both its parts are true or if both are false or if the antecedent is false and the consequent true. It is false in the remaining case, namely when the antecedent is true and the consequent false.[72] When the connective proposition expresses chance connection, it will be true when both its antecedent and consequent are true; and false in the three remaining cases.[73]

Avicenna introduces another classification of connective propositions. He remarks that when the antecedent and the consequent in an 'If ... then' sentence are true, the compound sentence will be true regardless of whether it expresses implication or chance connection. Thus, when a connective-conditional proposition is considered true because it has true antecedent and consequent, it is called 'unrestricted' (*'lā 'l-iṭlāq*). If, on the other hand, a connective proposition is viewed as one in which the consequent is implied by the antecedent, then it should be called 'restricted' (*'lā 'l-taḥqīq*).[74]

There remains one important kind of conditional proposition which we have not yet discussed: the connective proposition which reveals 'complete connection' (*ittiṣāl tāmm*). Complete connection obtains when the antecedent implies the consequent and the consequent the antecedent (in the sense of implication explained above).[75] Accordingly, when the antecedent implies the consequent, but not vice versa, this is called 'incomplete connection' (*ittiṣāl ghayr tāmm*).[76] Though the connective proposition expressing complete connection is not defined in terms of the truth-values of its component parts, it is obvious that it is true when both its component parts are true and when both are false, and it is false otherwise. This is the same as the equivalence described by modern logicians.[77] There is from a formalistic point of view a difference between Avicenna's complete connection and the equivalence of modern logic. Modern logicians use a special kind of functor when they express equivalence, but in Avicenna's logic complete connection is expressed in two implications thus: If *p*, then *q* and if *q*, then *p*.[78]

Conflict, to use Avicenna's definition, is the relation in which the antecedent and the consequent cannot be true together (244, 13 and 247, 8). He calls conflict 'complete' if one of the component parts is true and the other false. He calls it 'incomplete' or 'defective' if both of the component parts are false.[79] However, when Avicenna lists separative propositions he mentions three kinds.[80] In the first, which he sometimes calls 'real separative' (*al-munfaṣila al-ḥaqīqiyya*), one of the component parts must be true and the other false. This of course means that the real separative proposition is true if one of the parts is true and the other false; and false if both component parts are true or if both are false. In the second kind, both the antecedent and the consequent can be false. Thus, in this case, the separative proposition will be true if both of the component parts are false or if one is true and the other false; but it is false when both are true. In the third kind, the antecedent and the consequent can be true. This means that the proposition will be true if both of the antecedent and the consequent are true or if one is true and the other is false; while it is false if both parts are false. The second and the third kinds are sometimes grouped together and called 'unreal separative' (al-munfaṣila ghayr al-ḥaqīqiyya). The curious thing is that the examples Avicenna gives of the third kind are all of a proposition whose antecedent and consequent are negative sentences.[81] It seems that he was thinking of this particular case when he formed this kind of separative proposition; since immediately after discussing the above three kinds of propositions, he gives an example of a separative proposition whose antecedent and consequent may be true but this time having affirmative component parts.[82] He speaks of this proposition as though it belongs to another kind of separative propositions which he neither includes in his division of separative propositions nor refers to afterwards.

The author of al-Shifā' refers also to the case of the separative proposition expressing complete conflict when it has more than two parts.[83] Galen before him[84] said that this particular case (which Avicenna calls real separative) will be true if one of its component parts is true and every one of the remaining parts (which may be two or more) is false. If in the proposition 'Either p or q or r', p is asserted, then q and r must be denied. When q and r are denied, then p is asserted. Thus, the relation between p on the one hand and q and r on the other must be a relation of complete conflict. (This is identical with al-Fārābī's account; see p. 10.)

Avicenna's account differs in more than one detail. He no doubt regards a proposition like 'Either p or q or r' when it expresses complete conflict as do Galen and al-Fārābī, that is as a proposition in which one of the parts is true and the rest are false. But see what he does when inference-schemas are constructed with the help of these propositions. First of all when one part is asserted, then the denial of every one of the other parts is produced. Or, he adds, we can take all these parts as a separative proposition and deny that. That is when we assert p we produce either

Not-q and Not-r or Not-$(q \, v \, r)$.[85] If, on the other hand, we deny one of the parts, then we produce a separative proposition in which another part is to be denied. That is when we deny p, we produce q or r one part of which is to be denied to produce the other.

To the above account of separative propositions one thing must be added in order that we may fully appreciate Avicenna's understanding of the way these propositions in particular and logic in general should be treated. This is his view that logic is concerned with facts rather than words. In Galen's *Institutio Logica* there is a short report of two different terminologies used for analysing separative propositions which reveal two different approaches in logic. One of these, according to Galen, is held by those who attend to words; and the other by those who attend to the nature of things.[86] From what Galen says and from what we know from sources like Sextus, Diogenes and Alexander of Aphrodisias, it has been assumed that the Peripatetics were concerned with facts while the Stoics attended to words.[87] Avicenna, for his part, stresses this Peripatetic thesis saying that words are only a means for communication and that logic should be concerned with meanings acquired by the intellect from the external world.[88] We can thus see the reason behind Avicenna's concern with the facts that the separative proposition reveals, which makes him pay little attention to the nature of the functor. In fact, most of the examples he gives of separative propositions are of the kind whose component parts have one common subject, like the proposition 'The body either moves or is at rest'. In other words, he sees the separative proposition as revealing more than one possibility for an existing object.

Until now all conditional propositions referred to are compounded of what Avicenna calls 'predicative propositions' (*qaḍāyā ḥamliyya*). He mentions, however, the possibility for the conditional proposition to be compounded of conditional propositions.[89] He first distinguishes between the main statement, whose functor dominates the rest, and the conditional statements which are the antecedent and the consequent of the first, and whose functors are subordinate to the functor of the main statement. Thus, the conditional proposition will be called 'connective' or 'separative' according to whether the main statement is connective or separative. Avicenna then discussed the different ways in which these conditional components can be combined to form the compound conditional proposition. He considers the possibility of the main proposition having as component parts connective or separative or both kinds of conditional propositions. He further notes that one of the component parts might be a predicative proposition while the other is either a connective or a separative proposition.

To complete this sketch of Avicenna's views on conditional propositions I want to explain briefly the view, expressed in the part of *al-Shifā'* called *On Propositions (al-'Ibāra)*, that the conditional proposition should be treated as a single statement-making sentence.[90] In contrast with some modern logicians who regard the conditional proposition 'If *p*, then *q*', whose antecedent and consequent are themselves propositions, as a compound sentence consisting of three propositions, Avicenna treats it as though it contains one statement and thus classifies it with predicative propositions.[91] In both *On Propositions*[92] and the *Analytics*[93] he points out that the parts of a conditional proposition, when considered as parts of a conditional proposition, are neither true nor false because they are not complete statements. He explains this view by saying that the antecedent 'If the sun rises' is neither true nor false since it is not a complete statement; neither is the consequent 'then it is day'. The only statement which he recognizes is the one which states that the consequent follows (in any of the senses of following described above) or is in conflict with the antecedent. Starting from here it is quite obvious for him that the conditional statement itself can be stated unconditionally, i.e. categorically. This leads him to the analysis of conditional propositions in terms of quality (*kayf*) and quantity (*kamm*) in the same way as categorical propositions. He classifies connective and separative propositions under four general divisions: universal affirmative, universal negative, particular affirmative and particular negative.[94] For every one of these divisions he introduces a special quantifier (*sūr*); 'always: when' (*kullamā*) and 'always: either' (*dā'iman immā*) for the first division, 'never' (*laysa 'l-battata*) for the second, 'sometimes' (*qad yakūnu*) for the third, and 'sometimes not' (*qad lā yakūnu*), 'not always: when' (*laysa kullamā*) and 'not always: either' (*laysa dā'iman*) for the fourth. A quantifier is supposed to indicate two things. (a) The time at which the statement is true and (b) whether the statement is absolutely true or true under certain conditions (other than the temporal condition (a)).[95] In Avicenna's view the quantifier in the connective proposition 'Always: when the sun rises, then it is day' indicates not only that the above proposition is true at all times, but also that the consequent follows the antecendent whatever qualification or conditions we may add to the antecedent. On the other hand, the quantifier of the connective proposition 'Never: when the sun rises, then it is dark' indicates that whatever conditions we may add to the antecedent there is no time in which the consequent will follow it. In the same way Avicenna interprets the quantifier in the connective proposition 'Sometimes: when the sun rises, then it is cloudy' saying that this statement is true at certain times and under some conditions which we may add to the antecedent.

According to Aristotle immediate inference and the syllogism are the only means by which inferences from categorical premisses can be carried out. Avicenna applies both methods to premisses among which at least one is a conditional premiss.[96] He also applies the Chrysippian inference-schemas in inferences which have a conditional proposition of any type as a premiss. Avicenna's use of the word syllogism is wider than the particular case in which the idea of the middle term is applied.[97] He labels the conditional inference in which the idea of the middle term is applied 'conjunctive-conditional syllogism' (qiyās sharṭī iqtirānī), while he calls the Chrysippian inference-schema 'exceptive conditional syllogism' (qiyās sharṭī istithnā'ī).[98] There is also a third kind of conditional syllogism discussed in the same text called the 'divided syllogism' (al-qiyās al-muqassam). I shall discuss every one of these inferences in the order given above.

By discovering what inferences can validly be made from one proposition to other propositions having the same parts, we discover at the same time the different kinds of immediate inference. Avicenna first tries to establish what he calls 'mutual implication' or 'equipollence' (talāzum) between certain conditional propositions. First of all he considers the case of connective propositions which are related in the above way. He finds that the universal affirmative and the universal negative propositions whose antecedents and consequents are constituted of the same parts become equipollent when their consequents are made to be contrary to each other.[99] For example, he says that there is an equipollence between the proposition 'Always: when every A is B, then every C is not D' and 'Never: when every A is B, then every C is D.'[100] Also, he notices that among conditional propositions of the same kind the particular affirmative and the particular negative which have their antecedent and consequent constituted of similar parts become equipollent when their consequents are made to be contrary to each other.[101] For example, the proposition 'Sometimes: when every A is B, then every C is not D' is equipollent to 'Not always: when every A is B, then every C is D'. Considering, on the other hand, separative-conditional propositions, he observes that the universal affirmative implies the universal negative proposition (whose antecedent and consequent have similar parts) when their antecedents are contrary to each other.[102] The same is true of the particular affirmative and the particular negative, namely that the first implies the second when their antecedents are contrary to each other.[103] For example, 'Always: either every A is B or every C is D' implies 'Never: either every A is not B or every C is D'; and in the other case the proposition 'Sometimes: either every A is B or every C is D' implies 'Not always: either every A is not B or every C is D'. Avicenna also asserts that a real separative proposition which has affirmative parts implies the connective proposition which has the same quality and quantity as the separative proposition but whose antecedent is the contrary of that part of the separative which is similar to it, provided that the two propositions are compounded of the same terms. It also implies the connective proposition which agrees with it in quantity and quality, but whose consequent is the contrary of the corresponding part in the separative proposition, again provided that the two are compounded of the same terms.[104] For example, the proposition 'Always: either every A is B or every C is D' implies 'Always: when every C is not D, then every A is B'; and also implies the proposition 'Always: when every A is B, then every C is not D'. He again says that the separative proposition in which at least one of the parts is negative implies the connective proposition which has the same quantity and quality as the separative but whose antecedent is the contradictory of that part of the separative proposition similar to it.[105] For example, the proposition 'Always: either nothing of A is B or nothing of C is D' implies the proposition 'Always: when some C is D, then nothing of A is B' and the proposition 'Always: when some A is B, then nothing of C is D'. The connective proposition, on the other hand, implies the separative which has the same quality but a different quantity.[106] In this case, Avicenna goes on, the antecedents and the consequents must have the same quantity and quality. For example, the proposition 'Always: when some A is B, then nothing of C is D' implies 'Never: either some A is B or nothing of C is D'. Also the universal negative among connective propositions implies the universal negative separative proposition with its antecedent negated. E.g. 'Never: when every A is B, then every C is D' implies 'Never: either every A is not B or every C is D'.

We turn now to inferences which Avicenna considers to be syllogistic. As we said before, for Avicenna conditional syllogisms are of three kinds. (1) The conjunctive-conditional in which at least one of the premisses is a conditional proposition.[107] In case one or both premisses are conditional propositions, the conclusion will be a conditional proposition. In this kind of syllogism the antecedent and the consequent of the conclusion are related by a middle part (hadd awsaṭ) shared by both premisses. If the middle part is the consequent of the minor premiss and the antecedent of the major, this will be called the 'first figure'.[108] It is called the 'second figure' if the middle part is the consequent of both premisses. And it is called the 'third figure' if the middle part is the antecedent of both premisses. These figures are divided into moods according to the quantity and quality of the premisses. The premisses of such syllogisms can be either connective or separative propositions or a combination of both. Each one of these cases is divided into figures as described above and accompanied by the appropriate moods. There is no need to go through all these figures and moods since Avicenna explains them in detail in his text.[109] But to give the reader an example of what Avicenna had in mind, I shall present here the first mood of the first figure when the premisses are connective propositions.

> Always: when A is B, then C is D
> and always: when C is D, then H is Z,
> therefore always: when A is B, then H is Z.

Conjunctive-conditional syllogisms may also consist of one connective and one predicative premiss. In this case either the antecedent or the consequent of the connective premiss shares its subject (or predicate) with the subject (or predicate) of the predicative premiss. In the first figure the middle term will be the predicate of the antecedent and the subject of the predicative premiss. In the second figure, the middle term will be the predicate of both the antecedent of the connective premiss and the predicative premiss. The middle term in the third figure will be the subject of both. There are also another three figures when a middle term exists between the consequent of the connective premiss and the predicative premiss. These figures are again divided into moods according to the quantity and the quality of the premisses involved. The following example, taken from Avicenna, may perhaps clarify this:

> Always; when H is Z, then every C is D,
> and every D is A,
> therefore always: when H is Z, then every C is A.

(2) This kind is called the 'exceptive syllogism'.[110] It is in fact an inference-schema which consists of a conditional premiss and a predicative premiss that, to use Avicenna's words, asserts or denies the antecedent or the consequent of the conditional premiss. Avicenna devides these inferences or syllogisms into twelve productive moods. The division is based on his previous distinction between connective propositions which express complete or incomplete connection on the one hand; and on the other, the distinction between 'real' and 'unreal' separative propositions. There are, for him, four schemas when the conditional premiss expresses complete connection. In the first we infer the consequent of the conditional premiss when we assert the antecedent. In the second we assert the negation of the antecedent to infer the negation of the consequent. In the third we assert the consequent and infer the antecedent of the conditional premiss. In the fourth we infer the negation of the antecedent when asserting the negation of the consequent. When the conditional premiss expresses incomplete connection, the result will be only two inference-schemas: one leads to the consequent when the antecedent of the conditional premiss is asserted, and the other to the negation of the antecedent when the negation of the consequent is asserted. In case the conditional premiss is a real separative which consists of two parts, then by denying either of the parts we produce the other; and when either of the parts is asserted, we produce the negation of the other. Avicenna counts these as two moods. There are two more moods when the real separative consists of more than two parts. In the first we assert any of the parts producing the negation of each of the other parts, or the negation of the rest taken as a separative proposition. In the second we deny one of the parts producing, he says, a separative proposition consisting of the rest. From this we deny one part ... etc. until at the end we produce the last part. There are two kinds of unreal separative propositions. The first is the one in which both parts may be true. Here we get one mood in which

when either of the parts is denied, the other part is produced. The second may have both its parts false. In such a case we get a conclusive mood when we assert any of the parts to produce the negation of the other. The inference-schema can be exemplified by the following:

If A is B, then C is D,
but A is B,
therefore, C is D.

(3) This is what Avicenna calls the 'divided syllogism'.[111] In this kind of conditional syllogism one of the premisses must always be a separative proposition whose component parts (which are always predicative propositions) share their subject or their predicate. The other premiss or premisses can be either (a) a group of predicative premisses which, again, share their subject or predicate; (b) a group of predicative premisses which share neither their subjects nor their predicate; (c) one predicative proposition; (d) one connective proposition; or (e) a separative proposition. In order that such combinations be conclusive, there must be a middle part which the premisses share between themselves. In (a) the syllogism is divided into the three following figures:

B is either C or H or Z
C and H and Z are A
———————————
B is A

and

B is either C or H or Z
A is C and H and Z
———————————
B is A

and

C or H or Z is B
C and H and Z are A
———————————
B is A

(b) is also divided into three figures:

D is either C or B
C is H and B is Z
———————————
D is either H or Z

and

> D is either C or B
> H is C and Z is B
> ───────────────
> D is either H or Z

and

> C or B is D
> C is H and B is Z
> ───────────────
> D is either H or Z

There are only two figures in case (c):

> C is B
> B is either H or Z
> ───────────────
> C is H or Z

and

> B is C
> B is either H or Z
> ───────────────
> C is H or Z

In (d) there are also two figures:

> If C is B, then H is Z
> Z is either D or A
> ───────────────────
> If C is B, then H is either D or A

and

> If C is B, then H is either Z or D
> A is either Z or D
> ───────────────────
> If C is B, then H is A.[112]

Though there is much that can be said against Avicenna's ideas on the subject of conditional propositions and syllogisms, there is no doubt as to their historical significance. The vivid picture which the text reveals of the Peripatetic doctrines in addition to many of the Galenic views will be of much interest to the historian of late Greek logic. The most important aspect of this picture is perhaps the role which the Peripatetics played in diverting the attention of philosophers from the worthy step which Stoic thinkers had taken. This Peripatetic influence is clear in Avicenna's case. But we should not forget that, in his turn, Avicenna

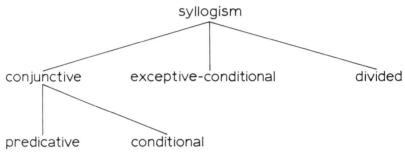

Fig. A.   Avicenna's division of the syllogism.

influenced all Arabic logicians after him. The works of the two eminent Arabic logicians, Qutb al-Dīn al-Shīrazī and Ibn Sahlān al-Sāwī, are careful elaborations of Avicenna's views. The authority which a work like *al-Shifā'* had on Arabic thought might be explained in part by the fact that it is, comparatively speaking, the most comprehensive work on Greek philosophy in Arabic.[113] Nothing of Avicenna's lengthy discussion can be found in al-Fārābī's section on conditional syllogisms.[114] Though the historian of Arabic thought regrets the loss of most of the early Arabic logical writings, nevertheless, Avicenna's *al-Shifā'* provides him with a condensed material that includes conflicting views with the acumen and understanding that never fails the author.

In this summary of Avicenna's main ideas on conditional propositions and syllogisms we have tried to define the key terms which he used in expounding his theory.[115] Avicenna's ideas bear the influence of both Peripatetic and Stoic theories on conditionals; but it would be an unwarranted simplification to assume that Avicenna had direct access to Stoic writings. The ideas and terminology of both schools were already mixed together in later Greek writings, and the mixture became common knowledge to Peripatetic authors. In fact, the tendency to compare the two sets of ideas and terms goes back to Galen, whose writings, as we have seen, must have had a significant influence on Avicenna.[116] Also, the fact that the writings of later commentators were more or less stereotyped and repetitious makes it more difficult for us to tell from the mere analysis of terminology which commentary (or commentaries) was the

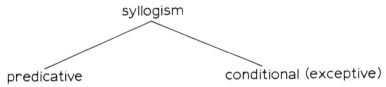

Fig. B.   Al-Fārābī's division of the syllogism.

direct source of *al-Shifā'*. But, it may be said again, it is more likely than not that Stoic ideas and terminology percolated to Avicenna through Peripatetic works.

A last word on the translation. In translating Avicenna's work I tried to bring out his meaning as clearly as possible and at the same time remain faithful to the original text. How far I succeeded in this is for the reader who is acquainted with Avicenna's style to judge. To facilitate references I have added transliterations of Arabic words in brackets, and indicated in the margin the page and line numbers of the Arabic edition. In most cases I modified the punctuation and the paragraph divisions which the editor had supplied. I also recorded any deviations from the text and the editorial readings. All the notes accompanying the text are mine.

NOTES

[1] Abū ʿAlī ibn Sīnā, *al-Shifā'*, *al-Qiyās* (ed. by S. Zayed), Cairo 1964, pp. 229–425. The lithographed edition of *al-Shifā'*, published in Tehran in H. 1303 (A.D. 1886), includes only the *Physics* and the *Metaphysics* (in two volumes).
[2] In contrast with *al-Shifā'*, neither *al-Najāt* nor *al-Ishārāt* discusses the different views of other philosophers on the subject of conditionals. Nor is there any detailed explanation of the author's own views on the subject such as the one we find in *al-Shifā'*. For example, the moods of the so-called conjunctive conditional syllogisms are not mentioned in either *al-Najāt* or *al-Ishārāt*. These two works neglect also the different kinds of connective and separative propositions to which Avicenna devotes a lengthy discussion in *al-Shifā'*. As a result of this negligence the number of exceptive syllogisms, which goes up to 12 moods in *al-Shifā'*, is in these works only four. Neither *al-Najāt* nor *al-Ishārāt* refers to what Avicenna calls the divided syllogism. The fragment which has reached us of Avicenna's *The Logic of*

the Orientals (*Manṭiq al-Mashriqiyyīn*, Cairo 1910), explains in a few pages (pp. 60–63) the two kinds of conditional propositions, and very briefly refers to the four forms of these propositions: the universal affirmative, the universal negative, the particular affirmative and the particular negative. There are also a few lines on p. 80 where he talks of the contradictory of the universal affirmative in connective-conditional propositions. The book is of no importance except for its controversial introduction, in which Avicenna makes it clear that he will depart from what the commentators on Greek works have been occupied with. Cf. *Manṭiq al-Mashriqiyyīn*, pp. 2–4; and *al-Madkhal* of *al-Shifāʾ* (ed. by C. Anawati and others), Cairo 1952, p. 10. Avicenna's claim that the so-called Oriental philosophy represents a departure from Peripatetic teaching has no support either in what is left of the *Manṭiq al-Mashriqiyyīn*, which is in harmony with his other views expressed in *al-Shifāʾ*, *al-Najāt* and *al-Ishārāt*, or in his *Notes* to Aristotle's *De Anima* [cf. *Aristū ʿInda ʾl-ʿArab* (ed. by A. Badawi), Cairo 1947, pp. 75–116]. In these notes Avicenna repeatedly quotes 'the Orientals'. But the views so quoted are in agreement with those expressed in *al-Shifāʾ*. [See Avicenna's *De Anima* (ed. by F. Rahman), London, 1959.] For a recent discussion of Avicenna's Oriental philosophy in the light of the text published by Badawi in *Aristū ʿInda ʾl-ʿArab* see S. Pines, 'La Philosophie orientale d'Avicenne et sa polémique contre les bagdadiens', *Archives d'histoire doctrinale et littéraire du moyen-âge* **XIX** (1952) 5–37.

[3] *Al-Madkhal*, p. 2. See also Ibn al-Qifṭī, *Taʾrīkh al-Ḥukamāʾ* (ed. by J. Lippert), Leipzig 1903, pp. 419–20.

[4] Al-Jūzjānī says that he met Avicenna when the latter was 32 years old (Ibn al-Qifṭī, *op. cit.*, pp. 422 and 426) and that a few years later Avicenna started writing *al-Shifāʾ* and finished it at the age of forty. (See *al-Madkhal*, pp. 1–3.) Cp. I. Madkour's view in his introduction to *al-Madkhal*, p. 4, that the book was written in more than ten years.

[5] *Al-Madkhal*, p. 9.

[6] *Ibid.*, p. 2.

[7] "There is nothing that is of importance in the works of Ancient (philosophers) which we have not included in this book. If (the ideas) are not found in the place where these books usually deal with them, they will be found in another place which we thought is more appropriate. We also added to these (ideas) what we grasped through our own understanding and gathered by our own thought, especially in the fields of physics, metaphysics and logic." *Al-Madkhal*, pp. 9–10.

[8] The question-answer method can be found in *Kalām*. However, I am convinced that Avicenna was following not the *mutakallimīn* but Aristotle. See below.

[9] In a letter to Abū Jaʿfar al-Kiyā (published in A. Badawi's *Aristū ʿInda ʾl-ʿArab*) Avicenna talks of their "weakness and ignorance" (p. 122). See also what he says in p. 120 in the same letter.

[10] Aristotle, *Prior Analytics* (ed. and trans. by H. Tredennick), the Loeb Classical Library, London and Cambridge, Mass., 1938, 50b1–5. As a matter of fact Aristotle talks about hypothetical rather than conditional syllogisms. See the Commentary below pp. 215–16.

[11] This remark may be simply based on the passage in Aristotle mentioned above. However, the quotation in al-Fārābī's *al-Jamʿ bayna Raʾyayy al-Ḥakīmayn* (ed. by A. N. Nader), Beyrouth 1960, p. 86, from a book by Aristotle on *al-Qiyāsāt al-Sharṭiyya* (*Conditional Syllogisms*) at least shows that independently of Aristotle's remark Muslim philosophers had some evidence to convince them that Aristotle did write such a book. Cp. al-Fārābī's *Sharḥ Kitāb al-ʿIbāra* (ed. by W. Kutsch and S. Marrow), Beyrouth 1960, p. 53, where he speaks of the claim that Aristotle had written "books on conditional syllogisms".

[12] *Al-Qiyās*, 397, 4–9.

[13] *Ibid.*

[14] See pp. 19–20 and the Commentary, pp. 270–75.

[15] See pp. 18–19.

[16] See the Commentary, pp. 218–19.

[17] Avicenna, in his preface to al-Shifā', describes the book in general as "more in support of the Peripatetics". Al-Madkhal, p. 10. See also his criticism of the four Stoic categories [al-Muqūlāt (ed. by M. el-Khodeiri and others), Cairo 1959, pp. 66–69].

[18] Al-Qiyās, 398, 11–12.

[19] A remark to the same effect is attributed to Abū al-Faraj ibn al-Ṭayyib by Ibn al-Ṣalāḥ, who says that the remark occurs in Ibn al-Ṭayyib's commentary on Avicenna's al-Qiyās; and that the context is Ibn al-Ṭayyib's criticism of the so-called fourth Galenian figure. Ibn al-Ṣalāḥ's quotation shows that Ibn al-Ṭayyib mentioned Galen by name. See N. Rescher's Galen and the Syllogism, Pittsburgh 1966, p. 76.

[20] Al-Qiyās, 107 and 161. In the first reference the context is the fourth figure of the syllogism.

[21] Ibid., 161. Al-Fārābī says that Galen's ideas on this subject are mentioned in the latter's Apodeictic (now lost); see al-Fārābī's Sharḥ Kitāb al-ʿIbāra, p. 193.

[22] See the Commentary, pp. 223–26; 234; 273–75 and 278.

[23] See note 7.

[24] Al-Qiyās, 356, 11.

[25] Ibid., 356, 11–15.

[26] Ibid., 356, 15–17 and 357, 1.

[27] See, for example, al-Qiyās, 14, 81, 90, 148 and 481.

[28] I. Madkour, L'Organon d'Aristote dans le monde arabe, Paris 1934, p. 37.

[29] Al-Qiyās, 356, 11.

[30] Though Avicenna does not say so, it seems that he approves of the book's approach to conditionals. Part of my discussion below (pp. 8–9) is devoted to the Arabic translations of Greek logical writings. There is more than one difficulty in trying to identify the book. First, the lists of Arabic translations found in the Arabic bio-bibliographies are not complete (cf. R. Walzer, Greek into Arabic, Oxford 1962, pp. 60–113). Secondly, we cannot be sure whether the book is an extract from a Greek commentary or an independent work by a Greek writer.

[31] Al-Madkhal, pp. 77, 80, 96 and 91.

[32] Al-Qiyās, 148, 9.

[33] Ibid., 481, 14–15.

[34] The letter is included in a book by Avicenna called al-Mubāḥathāt published by A. Badawi in Arisṭū ʿInda'l-ʿArab. The reference occurs in p. 122.

[35] See Pine's article referred to in note 2.

[36] Ibn al-Nadīm, al-Fihrist (ed. by C. Flügel), Leipzig 1871, p. 249. Ibn al-Qifṭī, Ta'rīkh, p. 36. Both references say that "one of the commentaries is more elaborate than the other".

[37] Al-Fihrist, p. 249; see Ta'rīkh, p. 37. The same sources say that Yaḥyā ibn ʿAdiyy relied in his commentary on the Topics on Ammonius' commentary, which includes Books I–IV of the Topics.

[38] Al-Fihrist, p. 249. Ta'rīkh, p. 35.

[39] Al-Fihrist, p. 253. Ta'rīkh, p. 257.

[40] Al-Fihrist, p. 249. Ta'rīkh, p. 35.

[41] Al-Fihrist, p. 249. Ta'rīkh, p. 36.

[42] Al-Fihrist, p. 249. Ta'rīkh, p. 36.

[43] Al-Fihrist, p. 249. Ta'rīkh, p. 37.

[44] Ibn Abī Uṣaybiʿa, Ṭabaqāt al-Aṭibbā' (ed. by August Müller), Cairo 1882, Vol. I, p. 105.

[45] *Al-Fihrist*, p. 249. *Taʾrīkh*, p. 35.

[46] *Al-Fihrist*, p. 249. *Taʾrīkh*, p. 36.

[47] *Taʾrīkh*, p. 35.

[48] Ibn Abi Uṣaybiʿa, as Nallino pointed out, relies on Ibn al-Qifṭī's *Taʾrīkh*. See Carlo Nallino, *Arabian Astronomy, Its History During the Medieval Times*, Rome 1911, p. 70.

[49] *Tabaqāt*, Vol. I, p. 101. Cp. *Ḥunain Ibn Isḥāq, Über die syrischen und arabischen Galen-Übersetzungen* (ed. and trans. into German by C. Bergsträsser), Leipzig 1925, p. 51.

[50] *Ḥunain Ibn Isḥāq, Über die syrischen und arabischen Galen-Übersetzungen*, pp. 47–48 and p. 51. Ḥunayn lists *On Hypothetical Syllogisms*, but says that he saw only one book of this work which he did not examine well. He does not refer to any Arabic translations of this part. Cp. Ibn al-Ṣalāḥ's statement that the only logical works of Galen that he saw are *On Demonstration* and *On the Number of Syllogisms*. (N. Rescher, *Galen and the Syllogism*, p. 76.)

[51] Avicenna tells us that he studied logic with ʿAbd Allāh al-Nātilī before the age of sixteen. He also says that he read several books and commentaries on physics, medicine, logic and metaphysics by himself after al-Nātilī had left Bukhārā. He says nothing to identify these works except that he used al-Fārābī's commentary on Aristotle's *Metaphysics* to help him understand the book. See *Taʾrīkh*, pp. 414–16. (There is an English translation of Avicenna's biography in A. J. Arberry's *Avicenna on Theology*, London 1951. The relevant passage occurs in pp. 9–12 of Arberry's translation.)

[52] *Al-Fihrist*, p. 249. *Taʾrīkh*, pp. 36–37.

[53] *Al-Fihrist*, p. 264. *Taʾrīkh*, p. 323.

[54] *Al-Fihrist*, p. 249. *Taʾrīkh*, p. 36.

[55] *Al-Fihrist*, p. 249. *Taʾrīkh*, p. 36.

[56] *Taʾrīkh*, p. 36.

[57] *Al-Fihrist*, p. 249. *Taʾrīkh*, p. 36.

[58] *Al-Fihrist*, p. 263. *Taʾrīkh*, p. 280.

[59] Edited and translated into Turkish with other works of al-Fārābī by Mubahat Türker under the title 'Fārābī'nin Bazi Mantik Eserleri', *Revue de la Faculté des Langues, d'Histoire et de Géographie de l'Université d'Ankara* XVI (1958) 165–286; English translation by N. Rescher, *Al-Fārābī's Short Commentary on Aristotle's Prior Analytics*, Pittsburgh 1963.

[60] *Sharḥ Kitāb al-ʿIbāra* (ed. by W. Kutsch and S. Marrow), Beyrouth 1960.

[61] The work is not yet published.

[62] *Al-Fihrist*, p. 249. *Taʾrīkh*, p. 36.

[63] *Al-Fihrist*, p. 249. *Taʾrīkh*, p. 36.

[64] *Al-Fihrist*, p. 249. His commentary on the *Prior Analytics* is to the end of I, VII.

[65] *Al-Fihrist*, p. 249 and p. 299. *Taʾrīkh*, p. 36 and p. 273.

[66] *Al-Fihrist*, p. 249 and p. 262. *Taʾrīkh*, p. 36.

[67] *Taʾrīkh*, p. 36 and p. 120.

[68] *Al-Fihrist*, p. 301–02 and p. 299.

[69] *Taʾrīkh*, pp. 362–63.

[70] Avicenna refers to other forms of conditional propositions, for example, 'A is not B unless (*ḥattā*) C is D' and 'A is B and (*wa*) C is not D'. However, these forms, he says, can be reduced to either a connective- or a separative-conditional proposition. See *al-Qiyā*, 251, 12–17, and 252.

[71] *Ibid.*, 233, 12–17, and 234.

[72] *Ibid.*, 260, 16–17 and 261.

[73] *Ibid.*, 238.

[74] *Ibid.*, 237, 13–16.

[75] This is probably the first time the concept of equivalence is mentioned in the history of logic.

[76] *Ibid.*, 232, 12–16.

[77] Cp. *al-Qiyās*, 390–91 and 396–97 where it becomes clear that 'complete connection' is the same as the equivalence of modern logic.

[78] Sometimes he expresses it in the form 'If p, then q', but he always adds that the conditional statement is to be understood as expressing complete connection.

[79] *Ibid.*, 232, 17–18, and 233, 1–4.

[80] *Ibid.*, 242–44.

[81] *Ibid.*, 244.

[82] *Ibid.*, 245, 5.

[83] *Ibid.*, 401, 7–15 to 404.

[84] *Galeni Institutio Logica* (ed. by Carlos Kalbfleisch), Leipzig 1896, V, 4.

[85] Avicenna realizes that the two conclusions are equivalent when $q \vee r$ has true parts.

[86] *Ibid.*, III, 5.

[87] J. S. Kieffer, *Galen's Institutio Logica, English translation, Introduction and Commentary*, Baltimore 1964, p. 76; and pp. 130–33.

[88] *Al-Madkhal*, pp. 22–24. See the Commentary to Book V, note 28.

[89] *Al-Qiyās*, 253–54.

[90] *Al-Shifāʾ, al-ʿIbāra*, British Museum MS., Or. 7500, fol. 40ʳ, lines 5–42.

[91] See Commentary, pp. 220–21.

[92] *Loc. cit.*

[93] *Al-Qiyās*, 235, 12–16; 236; 270, 14–17 and 271, 1–2.

[94] See the Commentary, pp. 242–54.

[95] *Al-Qiyās*, 272, 13–18, 273; 274 and also 263.

[96] Avicenna, like Alexander of Aphrodisias, regards the conditional (Alexander's hypothetical) syllogism as one which is compounded of at least one conditional premise. See *al-Qiyās*, 231, 11–12.

[97] Like Aristotle, Avicenna defines the syllogism as a discourse in which from certain propositions that are laid down something other that what is stated follows necessarily. See *al-Qiyās*, 54, 6–7.

[98] In many places in *al-Qiyās* the name 'conditional syllogism' is given by Avicenna to the first kind. Sometimes it is called 'conjunctive syllogism'. The last name is misleading because predicative syllogisms are also called 'conjunctive'. At one place in the same book Avicenna asserts that "The majority (of logicians) call it [i.e. the exceptive syllogism] conditional. I did not call it conditional because some conditional (syllogisms) are conjunctive." See *al-Qiyās*, 106.

[99] *Al-Qiyās*, 366.

[100] It should be noted that the antecedents and/or the consequents can be universal affirmative, universal negative, particular affirmative or particular negative.

[101] *Al-Qiyās*, 371.

[102] *Al-Qiyās*, 379, 17–18 *and* 380.

[103] *Ibid.*, 381, 3–10.

[104] *Ibid.*, 376, 6–16 *and* 377, 1–9.

[105] *Ibid.*, 378, 7–9.

[106] *Ibid.*, 382, 5–12.

[107] It is not clear why the word 'conjunctive' is used to refer to this kind of conditional syllogisms, unless the word is meant to refer to the conjunctive 'and' which connects the premisses in all conjunctive-conditional syllogisms. Note that the predicative syllogisms,

whose premisses are connected in the same way, are also called 'conjunctive'. Cp. note 110.
[108] Avicenna puts the minor premiss before the major.
[109] Al-Qiyās, 295–348.
[110] Al-Qiyās, 389. The Arabic word istithnā'ī means literally 'exceptive'. Avicenna, however, explains istithnā' as meaning the assertion that something exists (see al-Qiyās, 269, 11–12). This use of the word is certainly odd, and the only possible explanation in our view is that this syllogism gets its name from the word 'but' which precedes the major premiss in the istithnā'ī syllogism. As we said before (cf. note 107) the iqtirānī syllogism also seems to have got its name from the conjunctive 'and' which precedes its major premiss. In al-Qiyās, 389 and 390. Avicenna distinguishes between the conjunctive and the exceptive syllogism saying that in the first the premisses potentially contain either the affirmation or the negation of the quaesitum; while in the second the premisses actually contain them. J. S. Kieffer (Galen's Institutio Logica, p. 129) says that Alexander of Aphrodisias distinguishes between the terms metalêpsis and proslêpsis. The first, term is "used by Aristotle and the Peripatetics for the minor (Avicenna's major) premiss of a hypothetical syllogism, called by the Stoics ... proslêpsis". Alexander, Kieffer continues, understands the distinction to be that a metalêpsis repeats a clause contained in the hypothetical major premiss, but only stating it as an assertion instead of as a hypothesis. While the Aristotlian usage of proslêpsis denotes a premiss that is not contained actually in the major. (See Commentary to Book V, note 68.) The original meaning of πρόσληψις and μετάληψις is nearly the same: the first means 'taking in addition', 'additional assumption'; and the second 'participation', 'concurrence', 'taking something instead of another'. (See Liddell and Scott, A Greek-English Lexicon.) It is plausible to assume that the Arabic translator desired to distinguish between these terms for logical and historical reasons, and that the particles "and" and "but" used in the second premiss of the conjunctive and exceptive syllogisms respectively made him opt for iqtirānī and istithnā'ī. Cp. Tadhārī's translation of the Prior Analytics in Manṭiq Arisṭū, ed. by A. Badawi, vol. 1, Cairo 1948, where μεταλαμ βανόμενον (ἀξίωμα) (An. Pr. 41a, 40) is rendered al-muqaddama al-muhawwala, and ἐν δὲ τοῖς ἄλλοις συλλογισμοῖς τοῖς ἐξ ὑποθέσεως, οἷον οἴσοι κατα μετάληψιν is rendered wa ammā fī sā'ir al-maqāyīs al-shartiyya mithl al-latī takūnu bitahwīl al-qawl (An. Pr. 45b, 17). See also Isḥāq ibn Ḥunayn's translation of the De Interpretatione where προστίθημι is rendered yastathnī in 16a 15, 17a 12, and 17a 35. [I. Pollak, (ed.), Die Hermeneutik des Aristoteles in der arabischen Übersetzung des Ishāk Ibn Honain, Leipzig 1913.]
[111] Al-Qiyās, 349–56, 1–6.
[112] There is another combination (e) where the major premiss is a separative proposition. There are two figures here the second of which is not clear at all to me. I will give the first figure only:

> Either C is D or H is D
> D is either B or A
> _____
> Either C is D or H is B or A

For the second figure, see al-Qiyās, 355, 5–7.

[113] Al-Madkhal, p. 11.
[114] 'Fārābī'nin Bazi Mantik Eserleri', pp. 256–60.
[115] See the Commentary below.
[116] See above and the Commentary.

LIST OF ABBREVIATIONS

A   Azhar MS. 3415 (331 private).
B   Margin of Azhar MS.
C   Dār al-Kutub MS. 894
D   Dāmād MS. 824
E   Dāmād MS. 822
F   ʿĀshir MS. 207
G   ʿAlī Amīrī MS. 1504
H   British Museum MS. 7500
I   Nūr ʿUthmāniyya MS. 2708
J   India Office MS. 4752
K   Yeni Jāmiʿ MS. 772

TRANSLATION

Al-Qiyās

BOOK V[1]

ON CONDITIONAL PROPOSITIONS [2]
AND THEIR TYPES

5

[*The kinds of syllogisms which lead to predicative conclusions and those leading to conditional conclusions*]

Just as some premisses are predicative (*hamliyya*) and others are conditional (*shartiyya*), so also with *quaesita*: some are predicative and others are conditional. And just as some predicative propositions are asserted without a syllogistic reasoning and others require such a reasoning to be asserted, so also with conditionals. Many theses in mathematics, physics, and metaphysics are connective-(*muttasila*) or separative-(*munfasila*) con-

10

ditionals. Predicative propositions can be shown by predicative or conditional syllogisms; whereas conditional propositions are deduced either from pure (*sirfa*) or mixed (*mukhtalata*) conditional syllogisms as we shall explain [3], but never, as you know, from predicative syllogisms.

[*A general definition of conditional propositions*]

The conditional proposition agrees with the predicative in being a statement-making sentence subject to be truthfully or falsely asserted, and in which a meaning together with a relation of correspondence with

2] the external world are conceived. Every proposition is conceived first in itself. But it will be truthfully asserted if it corresponds with the external world. The conditional proposition is compounded necessarily of parts joined together to make a declaration. In spite of this it is different from the predicative in that the affirmative relation between its parts is not a relation in which the first part is said to be the second – as when one says 'Man is a creature-that-writes' where the first thing is taken to be the second. What is in common between it and the predicative is that it

5 expresses a judgement which relates one part to the other; and the difference between them is in the form of this judgement.

[*The two kinds of conditional propositions*]

Conditional propositions are also different from each other in respect of this relation. If taken in the affirmative, some have (their parts) affir-

matively related by following (*ittibāʿ*) and others by conflict (*ʿinād*).When
you say 'If the sun rises, then it is day', the affirmative coupling (*irtibāṭ*)
10   is by following; and when you say 'Either it is so or it is so', it is by conflict.

Let us start with an accurate account of what has been said on connection (*ittiṣāl*) and conflict.

[*Complete and incomplete connection*]

They said: Connection is either complete (*tāmm*) or incomplete (*ghayr
tāmm*); and so also is conflict: it is either complete or incomplete. They
took complete connection to be that in which the antecedent is implied
by (*yalzam*) the consequent as well as the consequent is implied by the
antecedent – as when they say 'Always: when the sun rises, then it is day;
15   and always: when it is day, then the sun rises'. Incomplete connection is
that in which the consequent is implied by the antecedent but not vice
versa – as when you say 'Always: when this is a man, then he is an animal'.
Since it is not always the case that if something is an animal, then it is
a man.

[*Complete and incomplete conflict*]

They also said: Conflict is either complete or defective (*nāqiṣ*). Complete conflict is that in which each part (of the proposition) is in conflict
[*233*]   with the other and the contradictory (*naqīḍ*) of each of them is the other
itself – as when we say 'Every number is either even or odd'. It is defective
when there is conflict but the contradictory of any one of the parts is not
the other itself – as when we say 'Six is either perfect or over-perfect'
without adding anything more. For if it is not over-perfect it need not be
perfect; it may be defective.[4]

[*Different views on conditional propositions*]

5   *Some said:* Connection stands for affirmation and separation (*infiṣāl*)
for negation. *Others said:* The conditional (proposition) on the whole
takes neither affirmation nor negation.[5] Besides, they may include among
the separative propositions like these: 'Zayd is either not a plant or
he is not an animal' and 'Zayd is either not writing or he is moving his
hand'. Also, they treated with conditionals indeterminable (*mutaraddi-
datu'l-aḥwāl*) propositions which we shall mention later on.[6] Some

10   thought that the connective-conditional is conditional because its antecedent is doubtful. Others thought that propositions like 'Always: when
this is a man, then he is an animal' are predicative and not connective,
as if one said 'Every man is an animal'.[7]

[*The two kinds of following:* (a) *implication;* (b) *chance connection*]
It is more appropriate for us now to first examine (the kinds of) following in connective propositions. We say: These are (a) the following in
which the posited antecedent that we relate to, which is a protasis (*shart*)

15   that takes the word 'if' and needs an apodosis (*jazā'*), requires *per se* that
the consequent should follow it. This (following) is self-evident – as they
say 'If the sun rises, then it is day'. When we posit the rising of the sun, this
will imply both in existence and in thought that it is day. Either because
the implicance (*malzūm*) is the cause which brings the second [i.e. the im-

34]   plicate] into existence – as is the case in the previous example; or because
it is an inseparable (*ghayr mufāriq*) effect – as when we say 'If it is day, then
the sun has risen'; or because it is a correlate (*mudāyif*); or because both
the implicance and the implicate are effects of one cause which implies
them together – for example, thunder and lightning are [affected by] the
movement of wind in the clouds; or because of other reasons which are

5   not needed here. The antecedent, however, may imply the consequent in
existence and not in immediate thought (*badīhati 'l-'aql*), in which
case the antecedent will not occur without being accompanied by the
consequent because they are related in existence in such a way that the
antecedent can never come into existence without the consequent. Either
because the antecedent is necessitated by the consequent or the consequent by the antecedent; or because both are necessitated by one cause;
or because they are correlative; or for some other reason of this kind if

10   there is any. (b) Following may differ from what we described before:
The antecedent and the consequent may be true without being connected
by any relation that we may notice – though there are relations between
them which are necessary Ideas existing in a realm that neither immediate of thought nor reasoning can make us aware of. When we say
'If man exists, then horse also exists', the following (of the consequent)
here is not stated as something necessary in existence itself. Nor did we

15   state that the existence of humanity makes it [i.e. the following] necessary
or impossible. What is stated is that [the parts are connected together] by

chance (*ittafaqa ittifāqan*) but not necessarily so, since they are not [ultimately] connected by chance and since this is not so in the nature of things.

[*The restricted conditional*]
The [connective-]conditional statement in general takes necessarily all the above (meanings of following). But if the posited antecedent of the connective-conditional statement is stated as a protasis and the consequent as an apodosis which follows by implication from the protasis, then the conditional statement should be called 'restricted (*ḥaqīqī*) conditional'. We need not worry about this. What we should do is to discuss what is peculiar to each kind.[8]

[235]

[*The different senses of the particles used in connective propositions*]
Some conditional words which are used in connective-conditional propositions indicate the above mentioned implication and others do not. Take the word 'if' (*in*). You do not say '*If* the day of resurrection comes, then people will be judged' because the consequent is not implied
5   by the posited antecedent. For (the consequent) is not something necessary but depends on God's will. Rather you say '*When* (*idhā*) the day of resurrection comes, people will be judged'. Moreover, you do not say 'If man exists, then two is even' or 'then void is non-existent'. You say '*Whenever* (*matā*) man exists, then two is also even' or 'then void is non-existent'. It seems that the word 'if' is very strong in showing implication, while 'whenever' is weak in this respect and 'when' is in between. The utterance
10   '*Since* (*idh*)[9] it is so, it is so' does not indicate an implication at all. Again, the words 'Always: when' (*Kullamā*) do not indicate an implication. But the word 'whereas' (*lammā*) fits both (the implicative and the non-implicative usages) and does not necessarily mean the one or the other – as when we say '*Whereas* it is so, it is so'.

[*The antecedent and the consequent of the connective proposition are not statement-making sentences*]
The antecedent of the connective-conditional proposition is a posited thesis which does not state whether what we posit exists or not. When
15   we say 'If it is so, then it is so', we are not saying that so is to be and together with it so is to be, that the antecedent is in itself a true proposi-

36]

5

10

15

tion and the consequent in itself is true, that they were uttered together, and that the antecedent, taken by itself, is a complete statement. Further, the antecedent does not say that 'So, with which so exists, also exists'. This is a situation-describing (*mahalliyya*) proposition which asserts that so exists with the existence of so without stating any condition at all. When a condition is stated, the parts will no longer be propositions. When you say 'If it is so' it is neither true nor false; and when you say 'then it is so' it is also neither true nor false provided that 'then' fulfills its real function of indicating that something follows from another. But if we speak in a language in which the consequent as a consequent has no (distinctive) sign but that it comes after something else, then it should be in itself either true or false. For in this case the consequent is not stated in full; and therefore its full meaning is not revealed. But to give the sentence its full meaning you should add 'then' to it; and if 'then' is added you would say 'then it is so' or 'together with what we said, it is so' which is neither true nor false until we know the posited thesis. However, the statement 'It is so'[10] is by itself either true or false. The antecedent as an antecedent should not also be treated as something to be doubted or asserted but something which implies or does not imply the consequent. It [i.e. the antecedent] can be undoubtedly false – as they say 'If ten is odd, then it is not divisible into two equal integers'; or it can be posited as something permanent and true in itself so that the consequent (which is implied by it) becomes a true proposition. But if taken as parts of a conditional proposition, neither the antecedent nor the consequent will be true or false; for neither one is to be taken as true when it is an antecedent or a consequent. And what cannot be taken thus cannot be subject to doubt. However, if we inspect them from outside (*min khārij*) we will perhaps doubt the consequent if the intention is to produce it; or the antecedent if the intention is to show that it is false.

[*The restricted and the unrestricted connective proposition*]

37]

5

We say: A statement which indicates that something is true with another, and whenever the first is true the other is true, is a proposition which is necessarily not predicative. Therefore, it is necessarily conditional and of the kind called 'connective'. The real nature of the protasis and the apodosis makes it necessary that the posited antecedent must imply the consequent in existence; either because they are related together by a relation of belonging, or by an explicit relation of real attribution (*nisbatu ṣarīhi iḍāfatin ḥaqīqiyya*), or by a relation of inseparable attribution (*nisbatu iḍāfatin lāzima*) in which they are either a cause or an effect, a whole or a part, a universal or a particular, or things of this sort of which you know that the relation they have (with each other) is something inseparable and not a constituent element of their substance, whether the relation is known or it is not known, in which case it should be known. The first [i.e. the kind in which both the antecedent and the consequent are true without the antecedent implying the consequent]

10   also can in one sense be divided in the above way, since the concomitance (*maʿiyya*)[11] of true propositions in existence is a kind of relation. But if the mind already knew that the consequent corresponds with reality and did not move to it either a priori or by reasoning from the first posited part [i.e. the antecedent], then there will be no use in positing the antecedent to move from it to the consequent. Let the connective proposition be either 'unrestricted' (*ʿalā 'l-iṭlāq*), namely where we claim that the consequent is true with the antecedent; or 'restricted' (*ʿalā 'l-taḥqīq*) in which

15   case the true consequent must be implied by the antecedent. The first is more general than the second, since it includes both implicative concomitance and chance concomitance.

[An implication is true when both its parts are false]

Some aspects of this division raise certain objections. Take for instance

[238]   the case in which an impossible is literally implied by an impossible – for example, when we say 'If man is not animal, then he is not sensitive'. Is this statement accepted or not? If the connection is not implicative, then it should not be accepted. Someone may say: If it is assumed that the

5   statement 'Man is not animal' is true how can 'Man is not sensitive', which is not implied by it, be connected with it by chance?[12] (To consider it a chance connection) what is required is that there should be a judgement, [the antecedent], which is assumed (to be true) and another, [the consequent], which is true and which is not implied by the first. But the statement 'Man is not sensitive' is not true. How can it be true and how can we say that it is connected by chance with that other thing which we assume (to be true) unless it is implied by it? For in such a case [i.e. when it is implied by the antecedent] we can say that, though (the consequent) is not true in itself in order to be connected by chance with (the

10 antecedent which is assumed to be true), it is implied by it. In answering
this one can say that the implication of a true statement is a specific case
of the more general one in which two true statements are connected by
chance. Therefore, if we have true statements connected by implication,
then they will be connected by chance. But if they are connected by
chance, then they may or may not be connected by implication. But (in
the above example) the consequent cannot be true with the first [i.e. the
antecedent] except when it is implied by it. For if the first is assumed to
15 be true, the second [i.e. the consequent] will only be true by implication,
because both cannot be together true. If the connection is not implicative,
then it will be true when both the antecedent and the consequent are true.
For a true statement does not exclude another true statement. But if one
of them is false, then it may or may not exclude the other.

239]   The statement 'If man is a creature-that-caws[13], then the raven is a
creature-that-talks' is false in both senses (of following). For (a) both
parts are false and therefore the statement does not express a true chance
connection; and (b) (the consequent) is not implied by the antecedent.
The statement 'If man exists, then void does not exist' is true in the first
5 sense [i.e. when it expresses chance connection] and false in the second
sense [i.e. when it expresses implication]; for both parts of the statement
are true [and therefore it expresses a true chance connection]; and (the
consequent) is not implied by (the antecedent). In restricted (connective
propositions) the implication is part of the consequent; but it is not so
in the unrestricted conditional (proposition). The word 'if' is used to indicate this [namely that implication is part of the consequent], and you
already knew what the other words indicate.

[*And when the antecedent is false and the consequent is true;*]
      You must know that the statement 'If five is even, then it is a number'
10 is true in one sense and false in another. It is true if the person who stated
it deduced its consequent necessarily (from the antecedent and another
proposition he already accepted); but it is not true in itself. For if it were
true in itself, then the consequent would necessarily be implied by the
first [i.e. the antecedent, alone]. The proposition 'If five is even, then it is
a number' and all similar propositions become true when we consider
their consequents as necessary (conclusions) of a syllogism in which one
of the premisses is omitted. Here is an analysis of this case: If (the state-

15   ment) 'Five is even' is assumed to be true, and it is also true in itself that 'Every even is a number', then we necessarily conclude that 'Five is a number'. However, we reached this conclusion because we conceded a true and a false premiss [at the same time], and one must not concede that false (statement) when he concedes the one which is true. When we

[240]   posit the thesis 'Five is even', we must not concede that 'Every even is a number'.[14] One of the premisses must not be conceded, and this should be (the first one). The assumption that 'Five is even' makes it necessary in itself that the other premiss must not be conceded. Therefore, if you

5   assume that 'Five is even', you must concede that 'Not every even is a number'. For no objection can be raised if the case is that of an impossible being implied by another impossible. If a false statement is conceded, then we should not concede a true statement. But if what we concede is an impossible, then what we should concede with it must be an impossible that follows necessarily from it. Here is a proof that when we concede that ['Five is even'] we should concede ['Not every even is a number']. No number is five-even; therefore, nothing which is five-even is a number. If we concede that 'Five is even' and 'This five is not a number', it will follow that 'Not every even is a number'. Only the person who posits this thesis [namely 'Five is even'] is committed to this [namely the statement that 'Not every even is a number']. However, he took a false thesis and

10   mixed it with a statement which is true in itself, from which he reached a conclusion that would not follow necessarily if the true premiss was not conceded with the one which is false. If we are looking for truth, then it will be necessary to deny the false (premiss) and to concede the one which is true. But if we want to pursue what is wrong, then it is necessary or possible to affirm the false premiss and to concede the contradictory of the one which is true. If the statement 'If five is even, then it is a number' is true in itself, then it will be true to say that what is five-even is a number.

15   Since this is false, the connective statement, which is equivalent to it in force (*fī quwwatihi*)[15], will also be false. And if the above predicative [i.e. 'Every five-even is a number'] is true, its coverse, namely 'Some numbers are five-even', will be true.

You have known the truth-conditions of the restricted connective proposition, or[16] the implication, when the antecedent alone is false and when the consequent and the antecedent are together false.

[it is false when the antecedent is true and the consequent false]

It is not possible for the antecedent to be true and the consequent to
be false because false statements cannot be implied by true statements.
[A connective] proposition can be false though its parts are true – for
example, 'Always: when man is a creature-that-rests, then he is a creature-that-moves'. (The above antecedent and consequent) correspond
with reality and therefore both are true propositions. The statement
'Never: if man is an animal, then he is a body' is false, for it denies what
is necessarily true.

1]

NOTES

[1] All the *Maqāla's* translated here are specified by the author as being "of the fourth Section
of the first Part which is the logic". Avicenna divided *al-Shifāʾ* into four Parts (*Jumal*):
logic, physics, mathematics and metaphysics. A Part (*Jumla*) is divided into Sections (*Funūn*)
for example, logic is divided into the Introduction, the Categories ... etc.; which are in turn
divided into Books (*Maqālāt*) whose subdivisions are the Chapters (*Fuṣūl*).

[2] The text reads 'syllogisms' for 'propositions'. The suggested reading is supported by the
fact that the whole chapter deals with conditional propositions.

[3] Book VI and VIII, i–ii.

[4] Euclid defines the perfect number as that which is equal to the sum of its own parts, i.e.
submultiples. Theon of Smyrna and Nichomachus add the definition of the two other kinds
of numbers in contrast with the perfect (i) the over-perfect, the sum of whose parts are greater
than the number itself and (ii) the defective, the sum of whose parts is less than the whole.
See *The Thirteen Books of Euclid's Elements*, tr. with intr. and comment, by T. L. Heath,
New York 1956 (2nd ed.), Vol. II, pp. 293–94.

[5] Cf. 258, 13–19; 259 and 260.

[6] See 256, 11–17; 257 and 258, 1–12.

[7] Cf. 264.

[8] See 237.

[9] Reading *idh* with C. The other MSS. read *idhā*.

[10] Reading with D *yakūnu kadhā*.

[11] Reading with D and E *al-maʿiyya* instead of *al-muʿayyana*.

[12] For a connective proposition which expresses chance connection is true only if both its
parts are true. And in the case in question only the antecedent is true, for this is what we
assumed, But the consequent is not, except if we say that it is formally implied by the
antecedent in which case it will be true by implication.

[13] Reading with D and E *nāʿiqan* instead of *nāṭiqan* (the other MSS.)

[14] Reading with the majority of MSS. *kullu zawj ʿadad*.

[15] Possibly a translation of δύναμαι which occurs in Galen's *Institutio Logica*, II, 5.

[16] Reading with C, D, I and J *aw*.

ON SEPARATIVE-CONDITIONAL PROPOSITIONS

[*The different ways of expressing conflict*]

Now we must examine the other kind (of relation expressed in conditional propositions), i.e. conflict. We say: A proposition which expresses conflict by merely talking of conflict as in saying 'This statement is in conflict with that' is not conditional. Also, a conditional proposition which expresses conflict may not be necessarily separative, since it is possible for a connective proposition to express conflict. What expresses conflict in a (separative) sentence is its literal form, namely the word 'either'.

[*A separative proposition expresses (1) real conflict and the particle it takes is 'It is exclusively'*]

The word 'either' is used univocally to express the following three cases: (1) The case of real (*ḥaqīqī*) conflict; which is what you indicate when you say for example, 'It is exclusively (*lā yakhlū*) one of the cases'. This is the same as saying 'Either this number is even or it is odd'. In this case your aim is to indicate that these [namely even and odd] are conflicting things and the thing [i.e. the number] is exclusively one of them. When we use the word 'either' in this sense, it is improper to divide conflict into
[243] complete and defective. For the defective is in this case false. When you say 'This number is exclusively either perfect or over-perfect' without adding anything to that, your statement will be false.

[(2) *The case where both its parts may be false*]

(2) The second case is a modification (*muḥarraf*) of what the former case indicates, for an additional consideration is implicitly taken into account. Let me explain this. If someone says: 'This thing is inanimate and[1] animal', we answer him saying: 'Either it is inanimate or animal'; and by this we mean that these two are in conflict with each other and, therefore, the thing cannot be both. We did not explicitly say that the thing is exclusively one of them. This is implicitly stated. As if you say:

if, as someone claims, the thing is one of these descriptions or the other, then you must understand that the thing cannot be both in the sense that the thing and the two descriptions are inseparable; but it is the one or the other: not both. For both are in conflict with each other and, therefore, cannot be said of one thing. In other words, both are in conflict with each other and, as someone claims, the thing is exclusively one of them. Like (1), it indicates the same kind of conflict (between the parts of the proposition) and that the thing is exclusively one of them. Except that when we say here 'The thing is exclusively one of the two things' our statement is not absolutely true but only relative to what the man we are addressing says. For he (only) mentions these two things and asserts them and their existence without saying that they are in conflict with each other; and we add to this that they are, and that they cannot exist together though the thing must be the one or the other. When 'either' is used in this sense it cannot express both complete and defective conflict but one of them.

[(3) The case where both its parts may be true]

(3) In the same situation described above conflict can be expressed by denying both parts (of the proposition). As if someone said: 'This thing is inanimate and animal', and we answered him saying: 'Either it is not inanimate or not animal'. In this case 'either' does not indicate a division (qisma) (of the possibilities into two)[2]; nor does it indicate that the thing is exclusively either not inanimate or not animal. What it indicates is that the thing is one of the parts or the other but in a different way. As if a person says: It is exclusively one of two things; either it is false to say that the thing is inanimate or it is false to say that it is animal. Thus, in this form the above proposition can be reduced to the real sense of conflict, for the statement 'Either it is false to say that the thing is inanimate or it is false to say that it is animal' expresses the real sense of conflict. What we did here was to put the word 'false' instead of 'it is not'; since a statement is false if the thing is not what the statement claims it is. As if he said: The thing is either not inanimate and in this case what you said will be false, or it is not animal in which case what you said will be false. In this case (3) we cannot express both complete and defective conflict, for, in this case also, both have one and the same sense. The parts in (3) can be both true though conflict is understood to indicate that the

parts (of the separative proposition) cannot be both true. The word
'either' does not [only] refer to a meaning common to the first and the
second cases. For the word is used to indicate not only the case of plain
(*sarīḥ*) conflict but also the fact that the second [i.e. the consequent] is if
the first is not. To indicate plain conflict, one may use the words which
form connective propositions, [such as 'if' and 'always: when'], or express
it in a predicative statement.

[*Other usages of 'either'*]

Though it is necessary for the word 'either' to indicate conflict, it may
indicate it in the sense in which a word can indicate part of its definition
or one of the suppositions on which the concept expressed by it rests.
Sometimes they use the word 'either' in another sense and say 'I met
either Zayd or ʿAmr', in which case the parts are not in conflict with each
other at all. For what the speaker implicitly said is this: I met either Zayd
alone or ʿAmr alone and I did not meet anyone else. Sometimes the word
'either' indicates that a thing is exclusively this or that, with the possibility
of being both without affirming or denying this (possibility) – as they say:
'A *sciens* either worships God or helps people'. This does not indicate
that he can only be one of them, but that he is exclusively one of them.
Thus, when we express the notions of complete and defective conflict we
use 'either' univocally, for, in reality, they do not have the same meaning.
But in complete and incomplete connection the (same) word [i.e. 'if'] indicates the same sense.

[*The antecedent and the consequent of the separative proposition are interchangeable, but not so in the connective*]

Further, whereas the parts in conflict are equivalent, this is not so in
the case of connection. For the two parts of a connective proposition are
distinguished and separated by attaching a different word to each part –
'if' is attached to the protasis to make it the antecedent *per se* and 'then'
to the apodosis to make it the consequent *per se*. The antecedent of a
connective proposition becomes the consequent and the consequent the
antecedent when we introduce a new thesis and abandon the first one or
when it is not the form of the proposition which we are considering but
particular subject-matters. But this [namely the subject-matter of the
proposition] is not what concerns us. Similarly we do not distinguish

between affirmative predicative propositions saying that some, which are convertible, express complete predication and others, which are not convertible, express defective predication, if the propositions in either case represent different considerations. But in (discussing) conflict it is appropriate to take this [i.e. the equivalence between its parts] into account, since the parts in conflict are equivalent. And it is for this reason that we attach to its parts words which have the same force.[3] It is only by convention, and not by nature, that a certain part happened to be an antecedent and another a consequent. Therefore, the fact that the parts (of a separative proposition) are equivalent needs to be taken into consideration. But in a connective proposition every part has a different word attached to it; and, as a connective proposition, its parts must not be equivalent.

[An analysis of (1)]

We must examine now what is said of the three divisions of the separative propositions. We will explain why only one of them is pure (basīt) and real. We say: The first division can take the words 'it is exclusively'; and it agrees with the meaning which these words express – as when you say 'It is exclusively either this thing is plant or it is inanimate'. While this is not so with the other two divisions. For you can neither say 'It is exclusively either the thing is plant or it is inanimate' nor can you say 'It is exclusively either this thing is not plant or not inanimate'. For in the first division what we say is that the thing is exclusively one of the two parts. This means that if it is not one of them, it will necessarily be the other, which is not true of the second division; or if it is one of the parts, it will not be the other, which is not true of the last division.[4] Someone may say that a proposition [of the first division] can be true though when we deny one of its parts we do not necessarily need to affirm the other. This happens when we assert a true statement which consists of more than two parts – as, for example, when you say 'This quantity is exclusively either equal to or greater or smaller than (another)'. When the mentioned quantity is not equal to (the other), it will not necessarily be greater than it. The answer to this is that when we deny (the possibility) of its being equal to (the other quantity), we affirm all the rest taken together. For if it is not equal to (the other quantity, the other possibility) must be that it is either greater or smaller than it. What comes after (the possibility) of being equal to (another quantity) is two (possibilities) stated in a separative proposition and not either one of them (taken independently). Therefore, what is to be excluded is the (possibility) that it is equal to some other quantity and one of the two others. What we are saying is this: A quantity should be exclusively one (of the above three possibilities); and if one of them is excluded, then it has to be one of the remaining parts which are to be taken together [as a separative proposition].[5]

[(2) and (3) are compared with each other]

We explained the difference between the first and the second divisions. The difference between the second and the third is the following: the two parts of the third division can be true of one and the same thing. Thus, you can truthfully assert that the thing is not plant and not inanimate. In the second division we cannot truthfully assert the two parts of one and the same thing, since they are in conflict with each other. There is something in common between the third and the first divisions, namely that in the third we can insert the words 'it is exclusively' after we assert the contradictory of any one of the parts – as when you say 'If it is plant, it must exclusively be not inanimate' or 'If it is not even, then it must exclusively be odd'. In the second division you cannot say 'If it is not plant, it must exclusively be inanimate'. The second and the first have the following in common: the two parts are in conflict with each other and both are affirmative (statements). And this is what in appearance the separative is to be like. The second and the third have the following in common: both do not take the words 'It is exclusively' since neither of them include all the possibilities. Also, both are neither pure nor real separative propositions, and for this reason it is appropriate to give them the name 'defective conflict'. The words 'it is exclusively', which indicate a division (of the possibilities into two) only fit the real separative statement. Both have the same force as (*fī quwwati*) the first, but they do not take the words 'it is exclusively'. Also, both contain an implicit statement which, when explicitly stated, turns the separative proposition into a [combination of] a separative and a connective proposition. Thus, we cannot call them pure separative propositions. For example, if a proposition of the third[6] division is fully expressed, it should be stated in the following way: This thing is either not plant or it is; if it is, then it should

5

10

15

[248]

not be inanimate. What we drop is the part which says 'It is (plant)' and in its stead we put its implicate, namely 'It is not inanimate'. (If this part is not dropped, then) it will be correct to mention any one of its implicates, which are infinite, and say for example, 'It is not a celestial sphere', 'It is not white' and 'It is not a king'; or say in the affirmative 'It breathes' or 'It has root and branch'. (If we drop it, then) it will not be correct to mention save a specific thing. However, it is customary for the sake of brevity to omit the (implicitly stated) implicance if the mind, though conscious of it, does not need to state it explicitly. But a real statement is one in which what is audible coincides with the order of the intelligible in thought. Thus, the above statement [i.e. 'Either this thing is not plant or not inanimate'] is distorted, it disregards (the rules) and it is abridged to an extent that its full meaning is not revealed in the sentence. The same is true of the second[7] division. For what the proposition of this division actually says is this: Either this thing is plant or it is not, and in the latter case it could be inanimate.

[A comparison between (1) on the one hand and (2) and (3) on the other]

We have shown you that both the second and the third divisions are in fact compounded of two propositions one of which is incorporated (*udghim*) in the other. Someone may say the same thing of the first division. But the difference between the first and the other two is the following: To say that a number is not odd is the same as saying that it is even and vice versa. But to say that something is plant is not the same as saying that it is not inanimate or having the property of an inanimate object, since these can be implied not only by the fact that the thing is plant but also by other (facts). Though it is possible to treat the real separative proposition as a combination of a separative and[8] a connective proposition, yet to express it as a complete statement, we do not actually represent it in the mind as two propositions. For the mind can confirm it without noticing that it can be so represented. But in the case of the other two divisions, the mind does not confirm the proposition unless it is represented in the form of two propositions – (one is connective and the other is separative). (In this context we must remind you that) there is a difference between a state which belongs necessarily to something and a state which may possibly belong to it. The third division is not used in conjunctive-(*iqtirānī*) conditional syllogisms, though it may be used in exceptive (*istithnā'ī*) syllogisms.[9] The real separative and the second division are used in both kinds of conditional syllogisms. For the two divisions have the following in common: when the contradictory of any part is posited, the other will necessarily be affirmed. The real separative proposition has a peculiar characteristic, namely when any one of its parts is posited, the contradictory of the other part must necessarily be affirmed.

10   You should know that what applies to the (separative proposition) which is compounded of one negative and another affirmative part applies also to the separative which is compounded of two negative parts. It is not impossible for the real separative to have two negative parts, or one negative and another affirmative part, if it is not only meant to indicate what the separative proposition with two negative parts indicates, but if it is also meant to express a division (of the possibilities into two). As if one says 'One of the following things is exclusively true: Either A is not B or C is not D'. In other words, it is exclusively either 'A is not B' is true

15   or 'C is not D' is true. If this is what it says, then the proposition with two negative parts can take the words 'it is exclusively'.

[250]   You should know that if we add a third part to the real separative proposition, it becomes unreal (ghayr ḥaqīqī), for the real separative cannot have more than two parts. For example, they say 'Either this number is even or odd or it is not a number'. This example has the ad-

5   vantage of showing that we use 'either' here in a sense different from that used in the real separative proposition.

[*There is no separative proposition in which the meanings of the antecedent and the consequent are not related*]

Let us see if we can talk of conflict between parts which are related by chance; as we did in the case of connection where we distinguished between a connection in the general sense and a connection which is regarded as an implication. In connective propositions, for example, it is true to say 'Always: when man exists, then void exists'. Is it also true to say in separative propositions 'Either man exists or void exists', where

10   the parts are not in conflict with each other but related by chance in the same sense in which the parts of the previous connective proposition are connected by chance? We say: This is not true of conflict at all. For the words 'it is exclusively' cannot be used in this sense nor do they agree with this (notion) of (things related by) chance. It is not true to say 'It is

exclusively either man exists or void exists', for none of the different meanings of the word 'either' is true here except metaphorically. We may refer to this metaphorical usage later on.[10] If man does not exist, it will neither be necessary that void exists nor that it may happen by chance that it exists. Also, if void exists, it will neither be necessary that man does not exist nor that it may happen by chance that he does not exist. Also, if void does not exist, we cannot truthfully assert with it that man does not exist whether we want the latter to be implied or not implied by the first. None of the above mentioned meanings of the word 'either' agree with this (notion of things related by chance). For man, who always or sometimes exists, and void, which is always non-existent, can neither exist together nor can they be in conflict with each other in the sense that the contradictory of the one is implied by the other. We must keep in mind that this is different from saying that it is necessary for a separative proposition to have equivalent parts (mukāfiʾa). For only when we express conflict in a real separative proposition can the parts, which are in conflict with each other, be equivalent. But this is not a serious matter if the proposition is not a real separative. We must say that the parts of connective propositions are not necessarily equivalent. There is another reason why it is possible to apply this notion (of things related by chance) to the connective rather than the separative proposition. For it is not unlikely that things which are connected together by chance may have common relations in respect of which some of them will imply the other though we are not conscious of these relations. This is not so in the case where things exclude each other [by chance]. For in this case the parts may be impossible in themselves, or there may be some other reasons which make them exclude each other. But there will never be one common cause which makes them exclude each other necessarily.

[Other forms of conditional propositions]

You should know that there are conditional propositions expressed in other literal forms than those we mentioned before. These are equivalent in force either to a connective or to a separative proposition. Of these propositions we mention, e.g., 'A is not B or (aw) C is D' or 'A will not be B unless (ḥattā) C is D', or 'A will not be B except (illā) when C is D'. These are necessarily conditional propositions and they are equivalent in force to the conditional propositions we mentioned before, for they include (*tataḍamman*) a relation between two judgments. They resemble the following connective proposition: 'If A is B, then C is D', and also the following separative proposition: 'Either C is D or A is not[11] B'. It is more appropriate to include them with separative propositions, for we can turn them into separative propositions without changing the quality of either

[252] one of their parts. Another one of such propositions is 'Sometimes[12] A is B and (*wa*) C is not D'. This, as you know, is a conditional proposition.[13] It resembles, in fact it is identical with, the following connective proposition: 'Sometimes: when A is B, then C is not D'. Further, the proposition 'A is B only if C is not D' (*'innamā yakūnu ... idhā*') is also a connective-conditional proposition. The words 'only if' indicate that the

5 consequent will be specified when we let it follow the antecedent. This is the same as saying 'Man is the creature-that-laughs". Both the above predicative and conditional propositions are indefinite. There may be other combinations similar to the above which can be reduced to connective or separative propositions in the same way in which the above propositions are reduced. To sum up, all these propositions are conditionals expressed in a modified literal form. Also, there may be predicative propositions which are expressed in a modified literal form.

NOTES

[1] The edited text reads *aw* not *wa*. The editor does not give any further readings; but in consulting the B.M. MS. we found that the text reads *wa*.

[2] This is case (1) which he calls 'real conflict'.

[3] Avicenna uses the words '*immā ... wa immā*', which can be literally translated as 'Either ... and either', to express the separative proposition.

[4] The text in fact says that the first case is not true of the last division; and that the second case is not true of the second division, which does not make sense.

[5] See 404, 5–12.

[6] The text reads 'the second'.

[7] The text reads 'the third'.

[8] Reading with the majority of MSS. *wa*.

[9] For an explanation of the conjunctive and the exceptive syllogisms see 389 and 390, 1–5, and the Introduction, pp. 18–20.

[10] There is no such reference in the book.

[11] Reading with F and J *lā yakūnu* instead of *yakūnu*.

[12] Reading *qad yakūnu* instead of *yakūnu*.

[13] Avicenna does not discuss what modern logicians call conjunctive propositions though, as his sentence shows, he includes them with conditional propositions.

ON THE KINDS OF COMBINATIONS IN PURE CONDITIONAL PROPOSITIONS[1] AND IN THE CONDITIONAL COMPOUNDED OF PREDICATIVE AND CONDITIONAL PROPOSITIONS

[The different forms the antecedent and the consequent of a conditional proposition take]

Every connective and separative proposition is either compounded of
5   two predicative[2] propositions; or of two connective propositions; or of
two separative propositions; or of a connective and a separative proposition; or of a predicative and a connective proposition; or of a predicative
and a separative proposition.

The example for the first [kind when the principal proposition is
connective] is: 'If the sun rises, then it is day'. When (the principal proposition) is separative, the example is 'Either this number is even or odd'. The
example for the second kind when the (principal) proposition is connective
10   is: 'If always: when it is day, then the sun has risen, then always: when it is
night, then the sun has set'. The example (for the second kind) when the
(principal proposition) is separative is: 'Either always: when the sun rises,
then it is day, or sometimes: when the sun rises, then it is not day'. The
example for the third kind when the (principal proposition) is connective
is: 'If the body is either at rest or in motion, then some substances are
either at rest or in motion'. The example (for the third kind) when the
15   (principal proposition) is separative is: 'Either this fever is either yellowish
or scarlet, or this fever is either phlegmish or melancholic'. This proposi-
4]   tion has nearly the same force as a single separative statement that contains all the parts of the above proposition. Except that in the above
proposition the second division follows the first in a particular order; but
when the above proposition is turned into a separative proposition in
which all the parts are once divided, the division will have no order. The
example for the fourth kind when, first of all, the (principal proposition)
5   is separative is: 'Either if the sun rises, then it is day, or either the sun rises
or it is day'. [The example] when the (principal proposition) and its antecedent are connective propositions is: 'If always: when the sun rises,
then it is day, then either it is day or the sun has not risen'. When the

consequent is a connective proposition, the example is: 'If either this
10 number is even or it is odd, then if it is even, then it is not odd'. The example
for the fifth kind when, first of all, the (principal proposition) is separative
is: 'Either always; when it is day, then the sun has risen, or it is not the
case that the sun is the cause of day'. The example (for the fifth kind)
when the (principal proposition) is connective and the antecedent is a
predicative proposition is: 'If the sun is the cause of day, then always:
when it is day, then the sun has risen'. When the consequent is a predicative
15 proposition, the example is: 'If always: when it is day, then the sun has
risen, then the sun is the cause of day'. The example for the sixth kind when
the (principal proposition) is separative is: 'Either this is either even or
odd, or it is not a number'. The example for the same kind when the
(principal proposition) is connective and the antecedent is a predicative
[*255*] proposition is: 'If this is a number, then either it is even or odd'. The
example for the same kind when the consequent is a predicative proposition is: 'If this is either even or odd, then it is a number'.

[*The separative can have more than two parts;*]

You should know that the separative proposition may have two parts
(*juz'ayn*) – as, for example, when we say 'This number is either even or
odd'. One or both of its parts may be negative. Further, it may have several
5 parts which are either potentially or actually finite – as when you say
'Either this number is perfect or over-perfect or defective'. It may have
potentially infinite parts – as when you say 'Either this number is two
or three or four … etc.'. It may contain negative and affirmative parts.

[*but the connective has only two*]

The connective, however, consists only of two parts: the antecedent
and the consequent. The antececent [of the connective proposition] can
10 be, either actually or potentially, more than one proposition which form
with the consequent one actual proposition – as when you say 'If this
man has chronic fever, hard cough, laboured breathing, proding pain,
and saw-pulse (*nabḍ minshārī*), he has pleurisy'. The (connective) proposition will be actually more than one proposition if the consequent consists
of many parts. For example, when you convert the above example you
15 will say 'If this man has pleurisy, then he has fever, hard cough, … etc.'.
This is not one proposition, but actually more than one. For the sentence

'He has fever' is a complete statement and so also is the sentence 'He has hard cough'.

Someone may say that though the consequent [of the connective proposition] may consist of many propositions, the connective must be considered as one proposition; for in order to consider the statement 'If it is sometimes A and not B, and sometimes B and not A, then neither B is a condition of A nor A is a condition of B', as complete, we need to

20   state both (parts of the consequent) together. The answer to this is the following: Though it is more significant to state them together, the state-

56]   ment will be regarded as complete if we accept one of them; for the consequent is not an [essential] definition of the antecedent. While if a [verbal] definition is stated as a predicative proposition with the definiens as predicate, there will be no reason why part of the definiens cannot be a predicate. However, one can reformulate the above proposition so that it will not give a complete statement except when both parts are stated together – as when one says 'If sometimes it is A and not B, and B and not

5   A, then neither one is a condition for the other'. However, the consequent (in the last example) is a single proposition.

[*The subject and/or the predicate of the parts of a conditional can be identical*]

You should know that in the connective or the separative proposition one or both parts of the antecedent and the consequent are often shared (*mushtarikati 'l-ajzā*)[3]. For example, you say 'If every A is B, then some A is B'; or when you say 'If A is B, then A is C', or when you say 'If A is B, then C is B'. Also, when you say 'Either A is B or A is not B'; or when you

10   say 'Either A is B or A is C' or 'Either A is B or C is B'.

[*The reduction of conditionals to predicative propositions*]

All connective and separative propositions, and in particular the connective in which the antecedent and consequent share one part can be reduced to predicative propositions – as when you say, for example, 'If a straight line falling on two straight lines makes the angles on the same side such and such, the two straight lines are parallel'. This is equivalent in force (*fī quwwati*) to the predicative proposition: 'Every two straight

15   lines on which another straight line falls in a certain way are parallel'. We shall prove this in the place where the proof belongs.[4] Also, connective

and separative propositions are sometimes equivalent in force. We shall soon come back to this point.[5]

['*If*' and '*Either*' etc. *can be put after or before the subject of the antecedent; and in the first case the proposition would be indeterminable*]

[257]   You should know that in connective and separative propositions (the words used) to indicate connection and separation, I mean the words which are responsible for the connection like 'if' and 'always: when' and the words which are responsible for the separation like 'either', come either after or before the subject.[6] Thus, we shall have two kinds of propositions

5   in each type. The example for the connective proposition in which the word that is responsible for the connection comes after the subject is: 'The sun always when it rises, then it is day'. This kind is very similar to a predicative proposition. For we can give one name to all that comes after the subject. For instance, the above example is the same as the following [predicative] proposition: 'The sun is something of which one can say that when it rises, it will be day'. All what we said of the sun can be called

10   '*Alpha*'. When you say 'The sun is *Alpha*', it will be the same as saying the (original) proposition. Thus, these propositions are indeterminable (*mutaraddida*) – they can be either conditional or predicative. The example for the connective proposition in which the word that is responsible for the connection comes before the subject is: 'If the sun rises, then it is day'. This is an actual connective proposition. Though it cannot (be reduced to) a predicative proposition, it may imply a predicative proposition. The two kinds of connective propositions mentioned above are everywhere

15   equipollent but as will be proved to you, the two corresponding separative[7] propositions are not. If the word which is responsible for the separation comes after the subject, then the antecedent and the consequent must have the same subject. For example, you say 'Every number is either even or odd'. This (kind of separative propositions) has the same force as a predicative proposition. It is the same as the proposition which says

[258]   'Every number is something which can be described as being one of the above things'. If you call what is said of numbers '*Gama*', you can correctly say 'Every number is *Gama*'. This proposition is indeterminable. It can be used either as a separative or as a predicative proposition. Its being indeterminable is not a case of far potentiality: it is rather a potentiality

5   which is almost an actuality. The example of the (kind) in which the word

which is responsible for the separation comes before the subject is: 'Either every number is even or every number is odd'. The difference between the two separative propositions is that the latter is false and the former is true. The latter becomes true if a third part is added to it. But the former does not take a third part. For it is true to say 'Either every number
10 is even or every number is odd or some numbers are even and some are odd'. But if the word which is responsible for the separation comes after the subject, then we cannot have a true statement consisting of the above three parts. Also, the latter separative proposition is not equivalent in force to the predicative which is formed of the former (separative proposition).

[*The view that the connective is an affirmative statement and the separative a negative one. His view on what affirmation and negation in conditional propositions are*]

You should know that literally speaking and according to widely-accepted opinion (*al-mashhūr*), the connective is similar to the affirmative and the separative to the negative proposition; for there is neither affirmation nor negation in conditional propositions. We first say: It is not correct
15 to say that if the antecedent and the consequent of a connective proposition are neither affirmed nor denied, then the (connective) proposition [itself] should not be affirmed or denied; as it is not correct to say that if the parts (of the connective proposition) are not considered true or false, the proposition itself will not be true or false. Just as in affirming a predicative proposition we affirm the statement of predication, so also with connective and separative propositions: in the former we affirm the connection and in the latter we affirm the separation. If someone says 'If the sun
59] rises, then it is day' he affirms the statement that the consequent follows the antecedent and that it [i.e. the consequent] is true with it. If someone denies this connection, i.e. he does not consider it true, and says 'Not: if the sun rises, then it is day', then what is negated will be the connection.
5 This negation is not, as some people thought, a separative proposition, though it implies a separative proposition. Also, we do not, as some people thought, negate the connective proposition by negating its consequent – as when we say 'If the sun rises, then it is not day'.[8] We can show that this proposition is not a negation of the connective if we put the words 'always: when' instead of 'if'. For if you said: 'Always: when the sun rises,

then it is cloudy' and someone denied what you said, then the contradictory of your statement will not be 'Always: when the sun rises, then it
is not cloudy' but 'Not always: when the sun rises, then it is cloudy'. Thus
what we do is to keep the antecedent and the consequent as they are and
10   negate the universal connection. The same is true of conflict. If someone
said: 'Either this thing is an articulate creature or a creature-that-laughs'
and his statement was false, he should be told: 'Not: either it is an articulate creature or a creature-that-laughs'. The last proposition is not (equivalent) to the connective or the separative proposition in which one part
is affirmed and the other is denied. In other words, the negation of the
above affirmation of the separative proposition is not 'Either Zayd is an
articulate creature or he is not a creature-that-laughs'. We can show that
15   this is not so in another example. If a person said: 'Either Zayd is a writer
or a jurist' and someone answered him saying: 'Not: either he is a writer
or a jurist', this will not mean that (Zayd) is either a writer or not a jurist.
For (Zayd) can be a writer without being a jurist; or a jurist without being
[260]   a writer; or a writer as well as a jurist; or neither a writer nor a jurist. All
these things show that the negation of a separative proposition may imply
the affirmation of the connective or the affirmation of the separative
proposition; and that the negation of the connective proposition may
imply the affirmation of the connective or the affirmation of the separative
proposition. And that when we say, 'If the sun rises, then it is not night'
this is not a negation of a connective proposition but a connective pro-
5   position with one of its parts being nagative. On the whole, the connective
would be considered an affirmative proposition not because its consequent or antecedent is affirmative; nor would it be considered a negative
proposition for a similar reason. When we affirm or negate a connective
proposition we affirm or negate the connection. A connective proposition
may have a negative consequent or a negative antecedent and consequent
and still be affirmative – as when you say 'If man is a writer, then he is not
illiterate'; and when you say 'if this is not animal, then he is not man'.
A negative proposition can have two affirmative parts as our previous
examples show.
10   Just as a predicative proposition is affirmative or negative not because
its parts are affirmative or negative but because the statement of predication is affirmed or negated, so also with the connective proposition – its
affirmation or negation does not depend on whether its parts are affirmed

or negated. All what we said (of the connective) is also true of the separative proposition.

[*The truth-conditions of the connective and the separative*]
    Further, the truth of a connective proposition does not depend on the truth of its parts. For a [connective:]-conditional proposition can be true though both its parts are false – as when you say 'If five is even, then it is not divisible into two equal integers'; and the separative proposition as a separative is true though only one of its parts may be true and the rest are false. A [true] connective proposition cannot have a true antecedent and a false consequent. But it may have a false antecedent and a true consequent as we described before.[9] For example we say 'If man is stone, then he is body'. Both parts can be false – as when we say 'If man is stone, then he is inanimate'. If both parts are true, then the affirmation of the connective proposition will not be false. It is true if both parts are true or if both parts are false, as it is clear from our previous examples. Sometimes the parts are neither true nor false in themselves but the proposition is true – as when we say 'If ʿAbd Allāh is writing, then he is moving his hand'. On the other hand, one part of the separative proposition can be true. If all the parts are true, then the proposition will be false – as when you say 'Either man is an articulate creature or a creature-that-laughs'.[10] Thus, on the whole, when dealing with connective and separative propositions what will be misleading is the prejudice that our aim must be to examine the state of the antecedent and consequent; and the inability to realize that in conditional propositions we only consider the relation between the (antecedent and the consequent) not the relation between the parts of the (antecedent and the consequent).

NOTES

[1] A pure conditional proposition is one which is either compounded of predicative or of conditional propositions, not both.
[2] The edited text reads *hamlī wa kullī* and the editor does not give any further readings. However, the B.M. MS. read *ḥamlī wa ḥamlī*.
[3] In this context *yashtarik*, share, may very likely be a translation of κοινωνέω which is used in Galen's *Inst. Log.*, VI. 3, to explain coterminous propositions. See note 1 to Book VI, Chapter One.
[4] See 376 ff.
[5] *See* 376 ff.

[6] Assuming that the antecedent and the consequent are predicative propositions which have one common subject.

[7] The edited text reads *al-muttaṣil* without giving any further readings. The B.M. MS., however, reads *al-munfaṣil*.

[8] Reading with D *falaysa al-nahāru* for *falaysa al-laylu*.

[9] 239–41.

[10] This is so only when the separative proposition expresses complete conflict. See pp. 222–23.

CHAPTER FOUR

ON EXPLAINING THE MEANING OF THE UNIVERSAL, THE PARTICULAR, THE INDEFINITE AND THE SINGULAR [CONNECTIVE-]CONDITIONAL PROPOSITION

[*A certain view on how to determine the quantity of a connective proposition. His view on this issue*]

Just as it is thought that connective propositions contradict or oppose each other in respect of their parts; so also with their being universal, particular, indefinite and singular; for these forms of connective propositions are thought to be what they are because of their parts. *They said:* Just as universal predicative premisses are those which have universal subjects and predicates; so also with universal connective premisses: they are universal because their antecedents and consequents are uni-, versal. Thus, the sentence 'If every A is B, then every H is Z' is, for these people, a universal conditional premiss. A more satisfactory examination of the above example would have led them to the right course. For a predicative proposition is considered universal because the judgment which says that something is predicated of another is universal, and not because its subject and predicate are universal. What corresponds to the statement of predication in conditional propositions is the statement that something is connected or is in conflict with another. Just as it is necessary in predicative propositions to inspect the judgment not the terms which are the constituent parts of the judgment; so also with connective propositions: what is to be inspected is the judgment not the constituent parts of the judgment.

[*When is a conditional considered universal or indefinite?*]

The connective-conditional proposition is universal if the connection is asserted under any condition (*ishtirāt*) and (at any time) we posit the thesis (which the proposition expresses). The separative proposition is universal if the same is said of things which are in conflict with each other. The proposition is indefinite if no such requirement is stated. If someone says: 'Always: when it is so, (then it is so)' the proposition will be a universal connective. If someone says: 'Always: either it is so or it is so', the proposition will be a universal separative. If someone says: 'If so (is so), then so is so' or 'When so (is so), then so is so' the proposition will be indefinite. However, in a peculiar way, the word 'if' seems to indicate a particular kind of indefiniteness. As though when we say 'If A is B, then H is Z'. what we are actually saying is that 'At any time in which A is B, whenever A is B, H is Z'. As if 'H is Z' follows 'A is B' itself with no reference to any of the conditions, which we will mention later on [1], that are required when the words 'Always: when' are used. The word 'when' does not seem to indicate this peculiar meaning, for it says that 'H is Z' will follow from 'A is B' even if this is true at one time only.

[When is the conditional regarded as singular?]

They also said: A singular premiss is the one which has a singular antecedent or consequent. This point of view also is not the one to be followed in this book. For propositions of this type [i.e. with singular antecedents or consequents] can take the words 'always: when'. For we say 'Always: when Zayd is writing, then he is moving his hand', in which case the condition is universal and not singular. Also when someone says 'Either Zayd is moving or he is at rest', since conflict here is true not in a particular case but always when Zayd moves.

[A criticism of the view that a universal connective is equal to a universal predicative]

[264]   The person who thought that the proposition 'Always: when A is B, then H is Z' is predicative because 'Always: when this is a man, then he is an animal' is equal to 'Every man is an animal' is mistaken for the following reasons. First because the above two propositions are not equal. For the statement 'Every man is an animal' is a universal affirmative proposition which does not refer to any person at all; while in saying 'this' the (conditional) proposition refers to a specific person, e.g., 'Zayd'. It would be more reasonable to say that what is equal to the above (conditional) proposition is the predicative proposition 'This man is an animal'. But there is nothing in the last proposition which corresponds to the quantifier 'always: when'. If we add 'always: when' to the predicative proposition, then we cannot refer to the person 'Zayd'. If we refer to 'Zayd', then we cannot use the [universal] quantifier. Therefore, the above connective and predicative propositions are not equal. Second, even if they were equal, the connective proposition must not be considered non-conditional.

For some propositions may belong to different types and can still imply each other. They can be equal in respect of what they signify (*dalāla*) though different in the way their subject-matters are treated (*i'tibār*). To treat 'animality' as something which belongs to 'man' is one thing and to say that the judgment 'He is an animal' is true whenever the judgment 'He is a man' is true is another. For these two are not the same. The latter has a more general meaning than the first. For many things can be truthfully stated in the latter way though they cannot be stated in a predicative proposition. One can find many examples in which the consequent is true with the antecedent though it is not predicated of it. Further, one can say that the following statement, which every one concedes to be a connective, namely 'If this is a man, then he is an animal', is equal to a predicative proposition. Why is the proposition ('Always: when this is a man, then he is an animal') considered to be equal to a predicative proposition and not the proposition ('If this is a man, then he is an animal'), knowing that if we turn the last two statements into predicative propositions nothing will be omitted from the latter, while in the former the quantifier will be omitted?

[*The universal affirmative connective proposition*]

Let us discuss now the universal affirmative among connective-conditional propositions. We say: In the statement 'Always: when C is B, then H is Z' the words 'always: when' are not only meant to generalize the occurrances of the statement, as if one said 'Every time C is B, then H is Z', but they are also meant to generalize the conditions which we may add to the sentence 'C is B' [2], which is to say that there will be no condition or state that we may add to (the antecedent) which does not make 'H is Z' true when it makes 'C is B' true. For the antecedent may refer to something which does not recur and is not repetitive; in other words, it may refer to something which has a stable existence and is not affected by anything at all. But, as you will soon know, it can be associated with certain conditions which will specify it. What remains to be done is to discuss and examine these conditions. [3]

[*Can a connective expressing chance connection be universally affirmed?*]

We say: Can one say 'Always: when man talks, then the donkey brays' as one can say 'If man talks, then the donkey brays', meaning that both the antecedent and the consequent correspond to reality without the consequent being implied by the antecedent? We say: The latter (connective proposition) is true. For it says that if the antecedent is true, the consequent will also be true. Here the truth of the consequent is a sufficient condition for the truth of the proposition. Thus, the truth of this proposition is evident. Someone may think that the truth of the proposition 'Every donkey brays' is not a sufficient condition for the truth of the proposition 'Always: when man talks, then the donkey brays'. For (he may think that) two (conditions) must be satisfied in order to consider (the universal connective) a true proposition: (a) It must be true that everything described as donkey should bray; and (b) the proposition must be true in respect of the quantifier (*al-sūr*). To say that at a certain time no donkey exists is not incompatible with the statement 'Every donkey brays'. It might be thought that at this specific time and under such state and condition, the proposition 'Always: when man talks⁴, then the donkey brays' is false. For at this specific time there are no donkeys to bray. But this is a false opinion. For the statement 'Every donkey brays' is true even if there are no donkeys at all. As you know, when we say 'Every donkey brays' we do not mean every existing donkey. For if we meant every existing donkey, then the statement 'Always: when every man talks, then every donkey which exists at this time brays' is evidently neither true as a statement expressing chance connection nor as one expressing implication; whether we meant the implication which is evident or the one which is not but can be shown to be evident.

[*Is 'Always: when every donkey talks, then every man brays' true in either one of the senses of following?*]

Someone may ask whether one can assert the following of the false consequent (in a universal connective proposition), in which case it will be true to say 'Always: when every donkey talks, then every man brays', on the basis that if we assume that the false antecedent is true the false consequent will be true with it. Some people thought that this following is valid. We say: This is not so. For the consequent is neither necessary in itself nor is it necessary for the person who admits the antecedent. For this following can either be by implication, in which case the false antecedent implies the false consequent, or by chance. We say: But the above following is not an implication for the consequent is not [formally] implied by the antecedent, whether the latter is considered true or false. Because from 'man talks' we can neither [formally] imply that the donkey brays nor that it does not bray. In fact ('The donkey brays') is in itself true. It [i.e. the following] is also not by chance, namely it is not the kind where this [i.e. the antecedent] is assumed to be true, and that [i.e. the consequent] is found to be true with it. For (the consequent) is not true at all and, therefore, it is not a case of true statements being connected by chance.[5] If the consequent is neither true with the antecedent nor is it implied by it, then it does not follow it in any sense at all. Of course if the thesis 'Every man talks' implies 'Every donkey brays', then the thesis 'Not every donkey brays' will imply the statement 'Not every man talks'. But 'Every man talks' does not imply 'Every donkey brays', for the first statement is true in itself and it is connected (by chance) with the second. Therefore, the false statement 'Not every donkey brays', does not imply the false statement 'Not every man talks'. In such cases we must judge the consequent in itself, and not as something which is implied, and therefore affected, by another thing.

[An objection and an answer related to the above issue]

Someone may say: Since the statement 'Every man talks' and 'Every donkey brays' are true and connected by chance, how can one assume that 'Every donkey does not bray' and at the same time find the statement 'Every man talks' to be true? For we said that it [i.e. 'Every man talks'] is true with 'Every donkey brays'. This will result in saying: though not every donkey brays, it is found that every donkey brays. This argument can be (reconstructed) in the form of two conditional premises leading to contradiction in the following way: 'Sometimes: when not every donkey brays, then every man talks'; and 'Always: when every man talks, then every donkey brays'; therefore, 'Sometimes: when not every donkey brays, then every donkey brays'. The conclusion is a contradiction. Since one of the conditional premises [i.e. the second] is true and the other [i.e. the first] is false, (the first) must be 'Never: when not every donkey brays, then every man talks'. The answer is that the above conclusion is not a contradiction. This can be shown by indicating that in saying 'sometimes' you do not assert that the thing exists, rather you assume that it does. When you say 'Sometimes: when not every donkey brays' your statement is not related to reality at all, it is to be understood as an as-

5   sumption. The consequent, like the major premiss of a (predicative) syllogism, is the part which must correspond with reality. If you bear this in mind, you will realize that the conclusion produced in the above argument is not a contradiction. For whenever you assume the false statement ('Not every donkey brays), you will find that the statement 'Every donkey brays' corresponds with reality. Thus, the conclusion in the above argument is not false because the statement 'Every donkey brays' is true in itself and whatever you assume or produce will constitute with it a chance connection. Therefore, the statement ('Every donkey brays') is not

10   [formally] implied by your assumption 'Not every donkey brays'. To sum up, the fact that the (consequent) corresponds with reality is not an evidence that the assumption is false. A contradiction occurs if both correspond with reality, i.e. if both 'Not every donkey brays' and 'Every donkey brays' are said to correspond with reality. But this is not what the conclusion of the above argument says. The conclusion says: The statement 'Every donkey brays' which corresponds with reality is connected by chance with the statement 'Not every donkey brays' which is assumed to be true. And these two [i.e. the assumption and the statement of fact]

15   neither contradict each other nor do they exclude each other. We must add that a contradiction may occur if our assumption 'Not every donkey brays' implies 'Every donkey brays'. This is not the case here, since the statement 'If every man talks, then every donkey brays' is not an implication: and, as you will soon know, the statement derived from it is also not an implication. But if it were an implication, then it would be true to

[269]   say that (the conclusion is a contradiction). A contradiction which is called an 'impossible' is produced if (the true statement) is implied by a false statement. But neither the argument is harmful nor our discourse will be impossible if (the antecedent) is assumed to be false and (the consequent), which is true in itself, is connected with it by chance. This is not the same as saying that (the consequent) is true because it is derived from (an antecedent) which is assumed to be true. If this procedure [namely to assume that the antecedent is false and connected by chance with a true consequent] were not possible, then we would not be able to con-

5   struct a proof *per impossible*. To construct a proof *per impossible* we first raise objections against (a discourse). Then we assume that its contradictory is true. We do not say: Since every false statement implies a false statement, the contradictory of the true statement, when assumed,

would make the other true statement [i.e. the consequent] false. If the procedure were not as we described, the result would be that any statement you deny will imply that any other true statement must be denied, as if there is no difference between what is implied by a certain thing and what has no relation with it at all.

But you must not be confused when you find that some people affirm (*awjabū*) the contradictory of the antededent whenever they except (*istathnū*)[6] the contradictory of the consequent. You should know that when you except you do not just make an assumption. An exception is rather an evidence to the existence and occurence (of something). And this can mean one of two things: (a) That the thing [excepted] is in itself true; which means that the contradictory of the consequent (which is in the above case excepted), can never be false, or (b) that it is true because the disputant acknowledges its truth, namely that he does not consider it impossible. In this case, what is derived is the same as what is implied by what we conceded to be false. Which is to say that what we derive is not true in itself. Also, the conclusion does not follow not because it is just a converse of some sort, but because it is admitted that the antecedent as such corresponds with reality. If our assertion is taken in the sense (a), then nothing will follow from asserting the contradictory of the consequent unless the following condition is satisfied: that there is a protasis and that something is implied (by it).

Let us go back to the main point. Does the conclusion follow necessarily because someone admitted the contradictory of the consequent, in which case the form of the derivation will be: If someone admits the contradictory of the consequent, then he must also admit the contradictory of the antecedent? We say: This is inconceivable because the person who admits the contradictory of the consequent does not derive the contradictory of the antecedent unless he accepts the conditional proposition and its protasis. But he cannot accept the conditional proposition and at the same time posits the contradictory of the consequent, for the conditional proposition which is accepted is not an implication; it only says that the second thing [i.e. the consequent] is true with the first [i.e. the antecedent] and that the consequent exists in itself, or assumed to exist, without being implied by the antecedent. Therefore, we cannot say that the acceptance of the contradictory of the consequent leads to a contradiction, since he did not say that 'The donkey does not bray' after he said that 'The donkey always brays'. If he did assume and accept that, then he will accept that 'Every man talks' and that 'Every donkey does not bray'.

[*A proposition expressing chance connection is true when the consequent is true*]

Let us see if the statement 'If every donkey talks, then every man talks' is true as a proposition which expresses chance connection. We say: It is true in this case; for the statement 'Every man talks' is true whether we assume that 'Every donkey talks' or that 'No donkey talks'. The statement 'Always: when the donkey talks, then every man talks' is true if the consequent is true in itself. But it is not true if the consequent is implied by the antecedent.

[*The antecedent of a connective proposition is not a statement-making sentence*]

You should know that though the literal form of the words '*in kāna*' and '*idhā kāna*'[7] refer to existence, the utterance itself must not suggest to you that something exists or does not exist. That the thing exists or does not exist is one of those things which you know from outside. What the above words indicate, wherever they are used, is something more general than saying that a thing exists or does not exist. They indicate, whenever used in a conditional proposition, that something is assumed, without any concern over whether this assumption corresponds with reality or not. Therefore, it is clear that we should not expect the antecedent as an antecedent to correspond with reality, for it is only an assumption. When this assumption is specified; it may either be true in itself; or true in relation to some other assumption; or suspended, namely that we ignore the question of its truth [or falsity] altogether. When we say that it is an assumption we do not mean that it is actually assumed or it will be assumed in the future. What it means is that if our assumption is correct, then what follows from it must be correct. If the impossible is assumed and made an antecedent, then there will be nothing in it but the fact that it is an impossible assumption. The consequent, however, must be stated as something which corresponds with reality and which occurs with the antecedent; for they say 'Then it is day' after saying 'If the sun rises'. This means that the judgment 'It is day' occurs with the assumption ('The sun rises') whether they are connected by chance or by

implication. But the antecedent is an antecedent not because it is something which corresponds with reality. It transcends both the state of
being merely an assumption, and reality in itself. An assumption remains
so whether it corresponds or does not correspond with reality. But when
15   the assumption is specified, it indicates something beyond that which a
pure assumption indicates. You should know that if the antecedent is an
assumption and it is not in itself impossible, then it must be connected
with the consequent either by chance or by implication. If it is false, it
will be followed either by a true or a false consequent. If it is followed
by a true consequent, then this following can be understood in two ways:
72]   (a) That both parts correspond with reality. This is always false and must
not be followed. (b) That the consequent is true in itself while the antecedent is false by assumption; which is always true. For it is true to say
'Always: when man does not talk', namely assuming that this is so, 'then
man talks'; and this [i.e. the consequent] is true in itself. In case the relation of following is an implication, then the consequent will often be
true. For the consequent in this case is not true in itself but derived
5   necessarily by the person who makes the assumption in which case he
will be committed to it. We mentioned this point before.[8] A false antecedent is followed by a false consequent only if the relation of following
is an implication. You should know that when we say 'Always: when
every man talks, then every donkey brays' we take the antecedent to be
an assumption, and the consequent to be a statement which corresponds
with reality. As if we said: Always: when we assume that man talks – an
10   assumption which can either be true in itself, namely that it corresponds
with reality, or it is true because someone assumed that it is so, or it is
a suspended judgment – then 'Every donkey brays' will be connected
with it by chance. If instead of 'Every donkey brays' we say 'Every man
laughs', we can still consider 'Every man laughs' as being followed by
'Every man talks'. In both cases, we say that the implicate follows from
the assumption.

[*A return to the discussion of universal affirmative connective propositions*]
    Let us discuss now what makes the connective proposition a universal
statement. We say again that the conditional proposition is universal
(a) if every time we posit the antecedent the consequent will follow it in
15   what it intends to say; and (b) if the consequent follows from the ante-

cedent and whatever states (we may add to the antecedent). I mean those states which can either be discourses derived necessarily from an assumed antecedent; or assumed discourses which are said of an antecedent and which follow it and can be with it. Either because they are predicates which can be predicated of the subject of the antecedent, if the antecedent is a predicative proposition; or, if the antecedent is not a predicative proposition, because they are linked to the antecedent as new premisses in which case these premisses must be consistent with the antecedent

[273]   and should not contradict it even if it is in itself an impossible; or because they are conceded as statements which turn the impossible antecedent into a necessary or a possible statement. In all these cases the antecedent may not only be true but it may also be a false statement which is posited as an assumption. For even when it is (false and posited as an assumption) there will be statements that can be derived necessarily from it and others that can be accidentally connected with it. There will also be statements that can be derived necessarily from it and others

5   which can be accidentally connected with it, if it is assumed to correspond with reality. Also, there will be certain statements that can be conceded with it by a dialectician if the conditional proposition is introduced in a dialectical dispute.

[*Would they be affected if impossible conditions are added to their antecedents?*]

Someone may ask whether the fact that the antecedents of conditional propositions can be accompanied by impossible conditions prevents the universal following of the consequent. Can one say, for example, that the statement 'Always: when so is a man then he is an animal' cannot be

10   universal because one is permitted to say 'Always: when this is a man who is neither a creature-that-senses nor a creature-that-moves, then he is an animal'? One can also say 'Always: when this is a pair which is not divided into two equal integers, then it is odd'. We cannot claim that the last two propositions are false on the basis that their antecedents are impossible. For the truth of the conditional proposition depends on the state of the implication not on the truth of its antecedent and consequent. Most of the conditional propositions used in science, where proofs

15   *per impossibile* are used, have impossible antecedents. For the fact that a conditional proposition has an impossible antecedent and consequent

does not make it false. The statement 'Always: when this is a pair which is not divided into two equal integers, then it is odd' is true in spite of the fact that its antecedent is impossible. Therefore, there are cases in which the consequent does not follow the antecedent because the antecedent is accompanied by some other statements which make this antecedent impossible, not impossible to assume but impossible when corresponded with reality. For example, it is not true that 'Always: when this is assumed to be a pair, then it is, by implication, even'. This is true only if nothing that contradicts this (implication) is assumed with the antecedent. If such a thing is assumed, then the above (implication) will be contradicted, though[9] this is impossible in existence. For the fact that something does not possibly correspond with reality, will not prevent us from assuming it. Thus, it is not the case that every time we assume that something is a pair it must follow that it is even. For there are certain assumptions which prevent this following. If, for example, the antecedent 'Always: when a pair is a number' is a statement which can possibly correspond with reality, then we will not be allowed to introduce impossible antecedents, for in this case it is essential for the conditional proposition not to have impossible antecedents. But an antecedent is introduced as an assumption and not as something which should correspond with reality. We say: We must remember that all this is true if the conditional proposition is an implication. But it will not be true if the conditional proposition has true parts (which are connected by chance). Therefore, the above argument against the possibility of constructing a universal conditional proposition would apply only if the [conditional] proposition is an implication; but not if it has true parts (which are connected by chance).

Someone may conclude that we will never find an affirmative universal proposition which expresses an implication. We say: We do. And that is when we add to the antecedent the condition that we are not allowed to add to the antecedent any statement which will make it imply a consequent that is not implied by the antecedent itself – as when you say 'Always: when this is a pair, in the sense a pair should be, then it is even' or 'Always: when this is a void, namely assuming that void exists the kind of existence which we assume; or that void necessarily exists the kind of existence which we assume; or that it possibly exists the kind of existence which we assume, and there is no condition added to it which

contradicts the concept of void, then void is a dimension'. Therefore, a
connective proposition cannot be universal at all unless an additional
5   condition of the above sort is added to it. All these problems arise when
the universal proposition is an implication, and not if it has true parts
(connected by chance). Universal propositions which express implication
are used in proofs *per impossible*; but they are not needed in direct proofs.
In case you use these propositions, and you don't know whether you can
treat them as universal propositions or not, make it a condition that you
will ignore any of the [impossible] conditions that you can add (to the
antecedent), and consider the proposition according to what is actually
10   stated in it. All you need is to notice what is stated in a statement like
'Always: when this is a man, then he is an animal', where no impossible
conditions are added to the antecedent, to consider it a universal proposition. If the antecedent corresponds with reality, we only add true
propositions to it; and if the antecedent is impossible, then we add to it
those propositions which do not contradict it or those which are validly
inferred from it whether they are true or false propositions.

[PARTICULAR CONNECTIVE PROPOSITIONS]

15   With the knowledge you acquired of the universal connective proposition, you will be able to know the particular connective. As we said in
our discussion of particular predicative propositions, a particular proposition is divided into two kinds:

[*The first kind of particular connective propositions*]
      This is the particular proposition which is derived from the universal,
namely that which is true whenever the universal proposition is true. If
something belongs to the whole, it will, in effect, belong to the part.
[*276*]   Thus, the universal and the particular, in the above sense of the particular
proposition, are together true. The same is true (of the relation) of following when it is expressed in a connective proposition. If it is true that
something follows every time we posit the antecedent, then it is true that
sometimes when the antecedent is posited, the thing must follow from
it. In this sense of the particular the universal connective will be true
together with the particular; and the particular proposition will be
derived from the universal.

[*The second kind of particular connective propositions*]

This is the kind of particular proposition which is not derived from
the universal, namely that it is true in itself apart from the universal. The
predicate in the second kind of particular (predicative) propositions is
necessarily affirmed of some (members) of the subject and negated of the
others. However, if the nature of the subject is abstracted in the mind, it
will be possible for the nature of the predicate to belong to it – as for
example when you say 'Some animals are men'. You know that some of
the things which are animals are necessarily men, and some are not. But
if 'animal' is treated as such without attending to any of its particulars,
then it will be possible for 'man' to belong to the nature of 'animal' without considering that [i.e. belonging] as necessary or impossible. The
predicate may also belong to the subject if both are existing objects – as
when you say 'Some people are creatures-that-write'. In connective-conditional propositions the kind of particular propositions which are not
derived from the universal is also divided into that in which the consequent follows necessarily from the antecedent, and that in which it can
possibly follow from it. For example, when someone says 'Sometimes:
when this thing is an animal, namely a rational animal, then he is a man',
this will be a necessary following. If the following is possible, then we
say 'Sometimes: if this is a man, then he is a creature-that-writes'. In the
first example there is no doubt that the consequent does not follow by
chance from the antecedent, rather it is implied by it.

One may think that the second kind can only express chance connection and it can never express implication. However, we can reformulate
it to make it express implication. Let us see whether it can be reduced to
the first kind when it is made to express implication. (First,) how do we
turn it into an implication? It is true to say 'Sometimes: if so is a man,
then he is necessarily a creature-that-writes' if this person expresses himself using inscriptions. For in this case he will necessarily be a creature-
that-writes or an artificer (*sāniᶜ*). Therefore, 'Sometimes: when this is a
man, then he is necessarily a creature-that-writes'. To the problem
whether it can be reduced to the first kind we say: In one sense it can be
reduced to it, though in another sense it cannot. It can be reduced to it
because some people are creatures-that-use-inscriptions and others are
not. A person who uses inscriptions is necessarily a creature-that-writes;
but the person who doesn't [10] is not necessarily a creature-that-writes.

10   In another sense it can neither be reduced to the first kind nor does it resemble it, for when we say 'this is a man', and we assume that he exists, this statement may imply at one time that he writes; but it may not imply it at another. And this is not the case in the first kind; for we cannot say 'If it is an animal, then sometimes it is a man and sometimes it is not'. The second kind can either express chance connection or necessary connection. Since it is a particular proposition, there will be no harm if we consider it true in case it expresses chance connection or implication. Exactly as we say that a particular proposition is true whether it is taken

15   to be a necessary or an absolute statement [11] (*muṭlaqa*); though implicative necessity is not the same as the modal necessity indicated in the connective proposition which you know.

[*Is it possible for the particular connective to have universal parts?*]

   There is only one problem here. In some particular connective propositions we say 'Sometimes: when every so is so, then every so is so'.

[278]   How can we say this knowing that 'every' includes all the particulars? How can the particular in this case be true without the universal being true? We say: This can be true if what we say of things is something possible, namely an accident which may change though it will not be impossible to assume that it does not change. Therefore, we can say 'Sometimes: if every C is B, then every H is Z', in case (a) every C is D,

5   namely, every C can possibly have D [12] as an accident, and (b) if 'Every C is D' can possibly be connected with it. For example, 'Sometimes: when every man moves his hand, then every man is a creature-that-writes', namely if every one of them does not move his hand except when he starts writing. And this is not impossible. Also when we say 'Sometimes: when every man is a creature-that-writes, then no man is a marksman or every man does not know how to shoot'. This is true if we assume

10   that every man is so weak that he can be devoted to nothing but writing. Thus, when we say 'Every man is a creature-that-writes' we have two cases in mind: (a) the case where we assume that every man is incapable of learning any other art, and (b) the case where we do not make such an assumption. In (a) the consequent implied is different from the consequent implied in (b). However, the particular proposition specifies the case, which is to say that it specifies the assumption. Therefore, the particular proposition which has a universal antecedent is true if the as-

5 sumption is specified, or else it will not be true. After we mentioned the
answer to the above objection, let us proceed to complete our comprehensive account of conditional propositions.

NOTES

[1] See 272 ff.
[2] Reading *jīm bāʾ* for *kullu jīm bāʾ*.
[3] See 272, 13–18 to 275, 1–14.
[4] Reading *nāṭiqan* for *ḥayawānan*.
[5] Reading *ʿalā sabīl al-muwāfaqa* instead of *ʿalā sabīl al-luzūm*.
[6] An exceptive premiss is the one in which we, say, affirm the antecedent of a conditional
proposition. In such inferences the conditional proposition would be the first premiss and
the exceptive premiss the second. The exceptive premiss is usually preceded by the word 'but'
which seems to be the reason for giving it such a confusing name. See p. 28, note 110.
[7] In Arabic the verb *kāna* (to be) is sometimes mentioned after *in* (if) and *idhā* (when).
[8] 239, 9–17 and 140, 1–16.
[9] Reading with D and E *waʾin* for *faʾin*.
[10] The edited text reads *lā biraqmi* without giving any further readings. The B.M. MS. reads
lā yuraqqim.
[11] An absolute statement is a non-modal statement.
[12] Reading *dāl* for *alif.*

ON THE UNIVERSAL NEGATIVE IN
[CONNECTIVE-]CONDITIONAL PROPOSITIONS

[*The universal negative connective proposition*]

   The rule which the universal negative [in connective propositions]
5 must follow is that there can be no single incident in which the consequent
follows from or is implied by the antecedent. Just as the unrestricted
connective-conditional proposition expresses chance connection, and
the restricted expresses implication; so also with the negative [connec-
tive-]conditional proposition: it either expresses the negation of chance
connection – as when we say 'Not: if this is a man, then void exists'; or
the negation of implication – as when we say 'Not: if this is a man, then
he is a creature-that-writes'. The difference between them is this: If someone says 'Not: if man talks, then the donkey brays' and he wants to ex-
10 press the negation of implication, his statement will be true. If he wants
to express the negation of chance connection, then the statement will be
false.

[*The two kinds of negation in connective propositions*]

   The universal negative can also mean one of two things: (a) That what
is to be negated is the implication. And the implication is negated when
the consequent is negated, since the implication is part of the consequent
as a consequent. (b) That what is to be negated is chance connection.
And chance connection is negated when the consequent is negated; since
the chance connection is part of the consequent as a consequent. In both
cases the negation of the consequent is in addition a negation of what is
part of it [namely the relation of following whether it is an implication
or a chance connection]. What is negated in (a) is the implication, and
what is negated in (b) is chance connection. However, in case the consequent is connected by chance with the antecedent, it [i.e. the conse-
15 quent] will be considered as no more than a proposition which is constructed to be true, which is the same as being a true proposition. While
if the consequent is implied by the antecedent, it will not only be a proposition but something more, namely an implied proposition; for impli-

0] cation is something added to the consequent. The same rule which applies to the particular affirmative [in connective propositions] applies also to the particular negative [in the same kind of propositions]. The example for the particular negative is 'Sometimes not: if A is B, then C is D' or 'Sometimes not[1]: if every A is B then every C is D'.

[(1) The universal negation of chance connection]

5   Let us examine the truth-conditions of the universal proposition in the two kinds of negation mentioned before. We say: It is easy to understand negation [in connective propositions] and to find an example for it if it is meant to refer to chance connection. For example when we say 'Never: when A is B, then H is Z'. What this proposition says is that 'H is Z' can never be true with 'A is B'; for ('H is Z') is not true in itself and, therefore, it will never be true with anything we assume, except when it is implied by it. If it is implied by it, then it may become true though it is false in itself – as when we say 'Never: when man brays, then void exists', or 'Never: when man does not bray, then void exists'. These (are examples of) the negation of chance connection in an unrestricted connective proposition. For one (of the parts) which we made to be a consequent

10   cannot be connected by chance with the other [i.e. the antecedent] because (the consequent) is false; nor is (the consequent) true by implication, because it is not implied by the antecedent. If this is what we mean by negation, then the consequent will not follow from the antecedent whether the consequent is (a) possibly true – as when we say 'Never: when Zayd is white, then he is black'; or (b) it is necessarily true – as when we say 'Never: when Zayd is not a body, then he is an animal' or

15   when we say 'Never: when Zayd is a body, then he is white'.

[(2) The universal negation of implication]

The other kind of negation is the negation of implication. For example, we say 'Never: when man exists, then void does not exist' or 'Never: when man exists, then the angles of the triangle are not equal to

31] four right angles'. For the above two consequents are not implied by the fact that man exists, though they are true in their negative forms and thus true with the true statement that man exists. Therefore, following in the above case is true if it expresses chance connection, while it is false if it expresses implication.

Let us see if this kind of negation can be absolutely true, namely that the consequent will never follow from the antecedent whatever particular states we may assume with the latter. One is inclined to think that this

5   is not so. For we can add certain conditions (to the antecedent) which will enable the consequent, whose following is denied, to follow from the antecedent – as when 'man' is said to be 'a creature-that-moves' so that it will be followed by 'void does not exist'. But the truth is that (a) the condition which is brought forward (to enable the antecedent to) imply the consequent might turn out to be an assertion that the consequent can never be implied by the antecedent and would keep the consequent as it is; or that (b) the condition we assumed would let the consequent be implied by the antecedent. If it is (the second case), where we except [i.e. assert] the conditions which will let the consequent be implied by the antecedent, then the negation of implication will be universal if it is asserted that all such conditions are to be excluded, and the assertion that

10   all such conditions are excluded is added to the universal [negation of the] connective proposition. If it is the first case, then the negative proposition is true; otherwise it is not true. For example, let the antecedent be 'C is D' and the consequent be 'H is Z'. Let be one condition or more than one condition which will make the antecedent imply the consequent. Let us assume that we have only one condition of this kind, and let this be 'E is T'. Thus, if 'C is D' and 'E is not T', then we cannot imply 'H is

15   Z'. Therefore, the proposition 'Always: when C is D and E is not T, then we cannot imply H is Z' is true. If we say 'Not: if C is D and E is not T^2, then it is necessary that H is Z', the proposition will be true as a

[282]   negation of implication. If this is not so, i.e. that (H is Z) is implied though E is not T, and that nothing hinders the consequent from being implied by whatever condition there is, then the proposition which expresses the negation of implication is false. As we said before, these conditions, namely those which make the antecedent imply the consequent, perform their task when they are, or [if it is one condition], when it is, assumed together with the antecedent. Since there are cases where a limited number of conditions can make an antecedent imply a certain consequent, it

5   will be possible for us to exclude them all. Therefore, it is possible to formulate a universal proposition in which the implication is negated. In these negative propositions the implication is part of the consequent. Thus when you say 'Never: if so is so, then so is so', you mean 'Never:

when so is so, then we imply that so is so'. You can treat the affirmative proposition in the same way.

[*Can a connective with a false antecedent and consequent be universally negated?*]

The objection that one can raise in connection with this (discussion) is whether it is possible to have a universal negation of a following in which the antecedent and the consequent can never correspond with reality. A person who admits that the propositions 'Never: when this were a number, then it would be a line', 'Never: if this were plant, then it would be animal' and 'Never: when the plant were a number, then it would be odd' are true, may think that they will become false when their antecedents become impossible. For if the number were made to be the extremity of the plane, then it would become a line. Thus we can explicitly say 'If this were a number and it were the extremity of the plane, then it would be a line', 'If this were a man and he neighed, then he would be a horse', and 'If this were a pair and it were not divisible into two equal integers, then it would be odd'. The fact that the antecedents of the above propositions are impossible does not mean that these conditional propositions must be false. For when you say 'If void existed, then it would be a dimension' and 'If a pair were not divisible into two equal integers, then it would be odd', you make true statements though their antecedents are impossible. Conditional propositions used in proofs *per impossible* are of this sort. Therefore, if the antecedent of a certain proposition is false, it does not follow that the proposition must be false. We discussed this problem in connection with universal affirmative propositions.[3] The answer given there will help you to find out the answer here. The particular negative among connective propositions can be easily understood. For you know about negation from our discussion of the universal negative (in connective propositions); and you know about the particular[4] from our discussion of the particular affirmative (in connective propositions).

[THE FOUR FORMS OF SEPARATIVE PROPOSITIONS]

As we have reached this point in our explanation of affirmation and negation in connective propositions, it is time to explain now the same forms in separative propositions.

[The universal affirmative separative proposition]

We say: A real separative proposition is universally affirmed if, as its appearance indicates, the conflict between its equivalent parts occurs every time the antecedent is posited.

[The universal negative separative proposition]

What in fact needs to be explained is the universal negation of separative propositions. Let us start with the most complicated cases – as when we say 'Never: either every A is B or every C is D'. We say: The above proposition is true in three states: (1) When both its parts, namely 'Every A is B' and 'Every C is D', are always true. For example, we say 'Never: either every man talks or every donkey brays'. (2) When both its parts are always false – as when we say 'Never: either every man brays or every donkey talks'. (3) When one of the parts is always true, and the other is an impossible ̩which is neither in conflict with nor does it oppose the other part – as when we say 'Never: either two is even or it is a quality', which is a necessarily true proposition; or when we say 'Never: either every man is an animal or void exists'. For the parts in this case are neither in conflict with each other nor does the one imply the contradictory of the other; though the contradictory of the impossible part can always be true with the other part itself. But [5] the true part is not implied by (the contradictory of the impossible) part, for if (the contradictory of the impossible) part were false, we would not necessarily negate the other part. (All what we said of (3)) is true if the word 'either' mentioned in such propositions is supposed to mean that the antecedent and the consequent are in conflict with each other, namely that positing one of them prevents us from asserting the other. But if 'either' is used in the sense in which it is used with unreal separative propositions, where a part is negated on the basis of what we know of it as such and not as a result of positing the antecedent, then the negative statements included in (3) will be false. However, separative propositions necessarily express conflict. If the parts are negative, the proposition cannot be included in anyone of the above three cases; for in this case it is possible that both parts are true. For example, the statement 'Never: either A is not B or C is not D' is not true; since it is not a negation of the false statements 'A is not B' and 'C is not D'. For both these parts of the above separative proposition can be true and, therefore, the (separative) proposition will not be false.

15

[284]

5

10

15

[285]

If this (separative) proposition is true when both its parts are true, then, contrary to the case in affirmative propositions, its contradictory is not necessarily true.

[*Can the separative have universal parts?*]

We have shown how these propositions are to be understood in case their opposites, namely the affirmative ones, are false; and we have (mentioned) the reasons for this. The problem that arises here is whether we can truthfully say 'Either every ... or every' or 'Either nothing ... or nothing'. Someone may object and say how can we say that two universal parts can be in conflict with each other? For how can it be true to say 'Either every A is B or every C is D' or 'Either A is not B or C is not D'? We say: This problem arises mainly in those (separative) propositions whose parts have one common subject. For how can we say 'Either every A is B or every A is C' without adding another part, namely 'or some ... and some'? We say: First what is evident and what is agreed upon is that no third part of the above kind is needed when the separation comes after the subject – as when you say 'Every number is either even or odd'. For in this case the universal (quantifier) covers both parts of the separative proposition. But does the problem arise in case the separation comes before the subject? Our answer is this: (1) We do not treat these propositions as true or false but as propositions. Therefore, if, among them, we find a false proposition, then there is no reason why we should not mention it with the rest. (2) It is enough for a proposition to be widely-accepted (*al-shuhra*) in order to include it with the rest, for we need not demand that the proposition should express real truth. What I mean is that we may accept it though it may not express a real thing. (3) Even if we demand that among true propositions we should only include those separative propositions which express real truth, we are not necessarily obliged to count only those which are intuitively true. For we can count those which are proved to be true, since these too are counted among true propositions. The example of a widely-accepted proposition of the above mentioned type is: 'It is widely-accepted and agreed on among those who think it is correct and are also convinced that there is only one actor, that either God or man is the origin of every movement'. When they except [i.e. assert] that 'God is not the origin of every movement', the conclusion will be 'Man is the origin of every movement'. They

will also consider the following proposition as widely-accepted: 'Either nothing is determined by God or nothing is done by man'. This proposition, I mean the one with two universal negative parts, may not be so much widely-accepted. But it will be a widely-accepted proposition to them if the parts become affirmative. For example, they say 'Every thing
15 is either determined by God or it is done by man, since there is only one actor'. We can be certain of the truth of the (separative) proposition in which one of the parts is the opposite of the other, if the subject of our enquiry is something necessary and essential for the species and not a general and perishing accident. For, in science and in case real truth is
[287] expressed, what the species require to be affirmed or negated, like fire and earth seeking by nature a particular place, includes all the particulars. To sum up: A separative proposition constructed of two opposing
5 parts – one expressing the thing and the other its opposite – is certainly true if (what is said of its subject) is not a general and perishing accident but something which is necessary (*lāzim*) or subordinate (*faḍl*) to the species. For example, we say 'Either every fire moves upwards or downwards', namely either the natural place of every fire is upwards or downwards. Though the intuitive division expressed in the above example may include a third division, namely 'or some fire is such and some fire is such', this inclusion of a third division cannot possibly be stated if the
10 division comes after the subject [i.e. 'fire']; for by its nature fire does not move except in one direction. Therefore, it will be satisfactory to mention only two divisions so that if we except [i.e. assert] one of them, we will deduce the contradictory of the other; and if we assert the contradictory of one of them, we will say: Therefore, it must be the other itself. If the divisions were three, we cannot necessarily affirm the second after excluding the first. In case the subject of our enquiry is unknown we must
15 add a third division. And in this case we cannot affirm the second division after asserting the contradictory of the other; not because it cannot in itself be true of the subject, but because we do not know if it is so. It is clear now that there are (separative) propositions compounded of three
[288] parts. Examples for these propositions can be found in the second exceptive syllogism with a separative premiss where we first except [i.e. assert] one of the divisions deducing a conclusion which has two divisions one of which is to be asserted in a second syllogism.[6]

[The particular affirmative separative proposition]

As to particular [separative] propositions one can raise objections
against them and say: How is it possible to say 'Sometimes: either so or
so', by which is meant that the statement is not universal and permanent,
except when conflict is incomplete? We say: The divisions can be, for
example, three if the proposition is supposed to give the absolute number
of divisions; while they can be two, or less than the inclusive number of
divisions, when we make a certain assumption or in particular cases. For
example, in the proposition 'Every quantity is either equal to or less or
more than (another quantity)', the divisions are three. If we assume or
except [i.e. assert] that it is not equal to (a certain quantity), then we get
a proposition which has two divisions, one of which is to be asserted.
Therefore, when such a condition is made, the quantity is to be either
more or less than the other. In this case conflict will be complete, because
the affirmation of one division leads to the exclusion of the other, and
the exclusion of the first leads to the affirmation of the second. Someone
may say that in view of this last case the statement 'Every quantity is
either equal to or more or less than (another quantity)' cannot always be
affirmed; for there are cases in which this proposition cannot be true.
We say: If you think that in these cases the proposition will be false, then
we will grant you this and say that it cannot always be affirmed, since it
is sometimes true and sometimes false. It seems from this that every
separative proposition which has originally more than two parts cannot
be universally affirmed, since it is possible to posit the contradictory of
one part. Nor is it always true to affirm the separation of only two of its
parts. Thus, in this case the separative proposition which has more than
two parts cannot be affirmed. Nor can we say that a separative proposition which has only two parts is always true. It is true when it has originally two parts. This criticism does not hold if the separative proposition, which follows after we made the first assertion, is true; for the truth
of the separative proposition does not depend on the truth of its parts.

There is still a problem concerning the particular proposition. For
someone can raise the following objection in connection with separative
propositions which are compounded of universal parts: How can a
proposition like 'Either every ... or every' be said to indicate specificity?
Let us first solve the problem in the case of the affirmative particular
proposition. We say: As we said in connection with connective prop-

ositions, this kind of particular propositions also specifies some state of affairs. For the full number of parts the proposition could have might be more than that which we have in any such particular proposition as the above [i.e. 'Sometimes: either every ... or every']. What we do in these particular propositions is to specify no more than two. For example, there are three kinds of relations between quantities: equality, more and less. But there are cases in which only two of them, not the three relations, are required. For sometimes a quantity can be either equal to or less than a certain quantity, since the last quantity is so large that no quantity in existence can be larger than it, like, for example, the diameter of the cosmos. Thus, if we say 'Sometimes every line is either equal to or less than any other line', the particular proposition will be true. But it will be false if we turn it into a universal proposition and say 'Always and in every case and consideration: either every line is equal to or less than another line'; except if you mention in name the quantity by which the others are measured and say 'Always: either every line is equal to or less than the diameter of the cosmos'. However, there are cases in which we, say, have more than two alternatives. If we make a universal statement, (we should state all the alternatives). If we refer to a specific case, then the parts must be two or less than the number of alternatives in the original proposition. If we say that this specific case is the one in which we assume that there is only one actor, then it will be true to say that the origin of action is either God or man. In this case there is no need to mention a third division, I mean, to say 'or some ... and some', for the proposition will be true without it. The same assumption mentioned [i.e. there is only one actor] makes it necessary that the particular should be true. By this I mean that it may be true to say 'Sometimes: either God or man is the origin of every action' if we make a specific assumption. If this assumption is true and necessary in itself, then the particular becomes universal and the statement will be true in itself not in respect of the specific case to which the proposition refers. It is not one and the same thing to say that a statement is an assumption and to say that it is true. An assumption may not correspond to reality, for it may express either a possible or an impossible case. A true proposition is that which corresponds to reality and not one which is posited or assumed to be true. Someone may say that the assumption 'There is only one actor' is impossible and, therefore, what it implies cannot be truthfully asserted.

We can, however, give a possible assumption. For example, one can assume that at one time, every thing which is a fire moves accidentally in one direction. In such a case you would be allowed to say 'Either every fire moves upwards or downwards or to a place in between these two'. But this will not always be true. It will be true in respect of the assumption which is possible in itself. For though it is possible that movement belongs to every fire, when fire reaches its natural place it will not move. Therefore, 'Sometimes: every fire is either so or so'. This means that there is only one case in which this statement is true. If you put instead of 'fire' 'a sparkle' or 'a cod of earth', the statement will no longer be universal.

[Modal conditional propositions]

After all this, you must know that if you want to treat modality in conditional propositions, it is more appropriate to treat modal connective propositions. You must know that just as a connective proposition is considered affirmative, negative, indefinite, true and false not in respect of its parts but in respect of the judgement which connects its parts, so also with modal connective propositions; for modality refers to the judgment which connects the parts of the proposition, and not to the connected parts.

You must know that just as in the case of belonging, something may belong to another in existence without the first being implied by the second; or it belongs to it and is implied by it but without this being necessarily so; or it necessarily belongs to it; so also with following. For example, in the case of belonging if we say 'Zayd is a writer', and the statement turned out to be true, it will be a statement about existence without there being any necessity in it. If we say 'The moon is eclipsed', this will be a statement about existence in which there is some kind of necessity, since the predicate is not always true of the subject. If we say: 'Zayd is a body' or 'The moon is a body', the predication will be a pure necessity. The same is true of connective propositions. For the fact that a proposition expresses implication, which is to say that we must assert the consequent, once the antecedent is posited, does not make it necessary. And obviously it is not necessary when it expresses chance connection. Nor can we say that it is not necessary if the proposition expresses chance connection, i.e. if it is not an implication. (The connective

proposition is considered necessary) if it always expresses an implication or a chance connection and if it will do so whatever you posit as its antecedent at any time. So that if this implication or chance connection
15 does not always hold, the proposition will not be considered necessary.[7] A universal affirmative proposition is necessary if the connection lasts as long as the assumption does and with every assumption whether it expresses implication or chance connection. An existential implication can be universal without being necessary if the implication exists every
[292] time we posit the antecedent but (the consequent) does not, or does not necessarily, last as long as the antecedent lasts; and this can only happen if the connective proposition expresses implication. For example, they say 'Always: when this is a man, then he breaths' or 'Always: when the sun rises, then it reaches the ecliptic'. For the sun reaches the ecliptic or it moves towards it long after it rises. If the connection does not express implication, then the objection will be whether a connective
5 proposition which expresses chance connection can be universal in case the consequent is not always connected with the antecedent. It seems that a proposition of this kind cannot be universal. For if something is not in any way implied by the posited antecedent nor is it always connected with it by chance but follows accidentally from it, then at some time it may not follow since it is not necessarily implied by the posited thesis. But in particular propositions this is permissible. The purely possible proposition is the one in which the consequent may or may not be connected by chance with the assumption, since the connection is
10 not necessary. If the connective proposition expresses universal implication, then it cannot be possible. Not because the possible consequent cannot be implied by anything, for it is possible that man can be a writer and that the fact that he is a writer can be implied when we add a certain condition as we have shown before, but because the condition cannot always accompany the posited antecedent. For some of the theses which we posit as antecedents are those to which we can add certain conditions that prevent this implication. If we posit an antecedent of this kind, the consequent will not be implied by the posited antecedent.
15 What you have already known of affirmation will help you to know the negation. As regards particular propositions, the case is more obvious.

NOTES

[1] Reading with D *qad lā yakūnu*.
[2] The edited text reads *wa laysa jīm ṭā'*, without giving any further readings. The B.M. MS. reads *wa laysa ḥā' ṭā'*.
[3] See 239, 8–17 and 240.
[4] Reading with F *juz'iyya* for *juz'iyya mūjaba*.
[5] Reading with G and J *walākin* for *walyakun*.
[6] See 401, 8–18 and 402.
[7] Reading *dā'iman lam* with D, E, G, and J.

BOOK VI

5

ON THE SYLLOGISMS COMPOUNDED OF CONNECTIVE-CONDITIONAL PROPOSITIONS ARRANGED IN THREE FIGURES

[*The three figures of the syllogisms compounded of connective premisses*]
The syllogisms compounded of connective propositions are syllogisms whose premisses share one of their parts (*tashtarikāni fī ḥadd*)[1]: the antecedent or the consequent. This combination takes the form of the three figures described in connection with predicative syllogisms. The middle part is either (a) the consequent of one of the premisses and the antecedent of the other, in which case the syllogism is called the first figure; or (b) the consequent of both, in which case the syllogism is called the second figure; or (c) the antecedent of both, in which case the syllogism is called the third figure. There is no syllogism from two particular or negative propositions, or from a negative minor premiss and a particular major premiss.

The first figure

96]   This figure is compounded of two connective propositions. The condition for its production is the same as the condition stated in connection with the first figure of the predicative syllogism. In representing these figures, 'A is B' or 'C is D' will indicate a predicative proposition which can take one of eight forms.[2]

[*Its moods*]
The first mood: This mood is compounded of two universal affirmative premisses

> always: when A is B, then C is D,
> and always: when C is D, then H is Z,   (1) AA/A
> therefore always: when A is B, then H is Z.

This is a perfect (*kāmil*) syllogism.

5   The second mood: This mood is compounded of two universal premisses of which the major premiss is negative

> always: when A is B, then C is D,

and never: when C is D, then H is Z,   (2) AE/E
therefore never: when A is B, then H is Z.

This is a perfect syllogism.

The third mood: This mood is compounded of two affirmative premisses of which the minor premiss is particular

sometimes: when A is B, then C is D,
and always: when C is D, then H is Z,   (3) IA/I
therefore sometimes: when A is B, then H is Z.

10   This is a perfect syllogism.

The fourth mood: The minor premiss of this mood is particular affirmative and the major is universal negative

sometimes: when A is B, then C is D,
and never: when C is D, then H is Z,   (4) IE/O
therefore, not always: when A is B, then H is Z.

This is a perfect syllogism.

[An objection against the first figure and an answer to it]

Certain objections can be raised against this figure. Someone may say
15   that this figure is unproductive. For we can derive from the following
true premisses 'Always: when two is odd, then it is a number', and 'Always: when two is a number, then it is even', the proposition 'Always:
[297]   when two is odd, then it is even' which is a contradictory statement. We
say: We derived the above conclusion because the minor premiss is in
itself false. However, as we said before³, for the person who accepts that
'Two is odd', and that 'Every odd is a number', the above conclusion
follows necessarily; not because it is true in itself but because he accepted
a false premiss. So the above conclusion follows necessarily from the
above premisses, and it is true if we take the premisses to be true. In this
5   case the proposition 'Always: when two is odd, then it is even' will be
true by implication. It is not one and the same thing to say that a certain
proposition is derived necessarily, and to say that it is true. The same
argument can be applied if this time the minor and not the major premiss
is false. If the minor, middle, and major parts are impossible, then in
[the derived conclusion] the major part, which is the consequent of the

conclusion, will be true by implication, but it does not correspond with reality. Let us treat the case in which the major part is connected with the middle by chance not by implication, and in which the middle part is connected with the minor part in the same way. We say: Even if we can derive a conclusion from these premisses, it is preferable not to call it a syllogism, since it does not inform us of anything which we do not already knew. If the middle part does not imply the major part and it is connected with it by chance, then we will be in a position to know before constructing the syllogism, that the major is connected with the minor or with anything which corresponds with reality or assumed to be so whether we have noticed the middle or not. If the case is one in which something is proved by another, then, in the mind, it is derived from it. The same thing can be said when the minor premiss is an implication whose antecedent is not impossible [and whose major premiss expresses chance connection].

Let us see whether, in case the antecedent mentioned above is impossible, we can derive, say from the premisses, 'Always: when two is odd, then it is a number' and 'Always: when two is a number, then white is a colour', the conclusion 'Always: when two is odd, then white is a colour'. We say: We do not know that white is a colour from knowing that two is odd. For even if the antecedent is 'Two is even', the consequent would still be 'White is a colour'. That white is a colour is, in this example, something which is known by itself. One may think that the syllogism constructed of a minor premiss expressing chance connection and a major premiss expressing implication is a syllogism which leads to a new information (mufīd). For, though we don't know whether there is a relation between the major and the minor parts, we know that the major part is connected with something which exists with the minor. Thus, we know now something which we did not know before, namely, that the major part exists with the minor. But this is an information reminiscent to a degree of what we already knew. For you know that both the middle and the major part correspond with reality, and that the major part is connected with the minor part and with any thing that corresponds with the world. Therefore the major part is known by itself and not through the syllogism. Thus, by introducing the minor part no information of any value is reached. All this is true if the major premiss is affirmative. What if (the major premiss) is (a) a negation of implication and (b) a negation of chance connection? In either case the other affirmative premiss [i.e. the minor] would express either chance connection on implication. If it expresses chance connection [and the major premiss is (a),] then nothing will follow from the middle part when it is connected by chance with the minor part, since (the major premiss) says that the major part is not implied by the middle part whatever possible state it is in. And in this case, the state of the middle is that it is connected by chance with the minor part. This is also obvious in case (the minor premiss) expresses implication. If the minor part[4] is an impossible, the middle part is possible, and the major premiss is a negation of implication, then the major part will never be implied by the minor part. Otherwise the universal negation would be false. I don't mean false in itself but by implication. For if we treat the parts in themselves, then the minor premiss will be false whether the middle is possible or true. This is something which you have known before. If both [the minor and the middle parts] are impossible and they are affirmative propositions, and it is false to affirm the connection between the major part and the middle, then the major part will never be implied by the minor. For if it is implied by it, then it will be necessary to assume the middle when the minor part is assumed with it. And as you know, the conclusion, which is a negation of implication, will be true. But if in all the above cases the major premiss is a negation of chance connection[5], the affirmative premiss is a chance connection, the middle part is without doubt possible, and the major part is impossible, then the (conclusion) which is a negation of chance connection will be true. It is also true when the minor premiss expresses implication and the minor part is possible. If the minor part is impossible, the middle is a true statement implied by the minor part, while [the major premiss] denies either the implication of an impossible by the middle part or their being connected by chance, then the conclusion will be a negation of chance connection; which is the same as being an implication whose antecedent is impossible and whose consequent is not.

The second figure

In this figure there is no production from two affirmative or particular premisses or when the major premiss is particular. This you would know with the slightest effort by applying the principles you have learned (in our discussion of the second figure in predicative syllogisms); for the parts of the conditional proposition play the same role as the terms in predicative propositions. If the two premisses are universal and the major is negative – as when you say 'Always: when H is Z, then C is D' and 'Never: when A is B, then C is D', then it will depend on whether (a) the two premisses express chance connection, or (b) they express implication, or (c) one of the premisses expresses chance connection and the other expresses implication. If both express chance connection, then they will tell us nothing new for the same reason we gave in the discussion of the first figure. You also know from what we said in the discussion of the first figure what follows when the affirmative premiss expresses chance connection and when it does not express chance connection. If the negative premiss [i.e. the major] is a negation of implication, which means that it expresses chance connection, and the affirmative premiss expresses chance connection then the syllogism will not be productive at all – as when we say

> always; when man talks, then the donkey brays,
> and never: when a pair is even, then we can imply that the
>   donkey brays,

therefore never always: when man talks, then a pair is even. If instead of 'a pair is even' we say 'man is an animal', then the following true conclusion will follow: 'Always: when man talks, then man is an animal'. If instead of 'man is an animal', you say 'man is plant', it will be true that 'Never: when man talks, then man is plant'. If the affirmative premiss is an implication, then the combination will be productive whether it is combined with a statement which is a negation of an implication or a negation of chance connetion; and the conclusion will be an affirmative proposition. The condition for its production is the same as that of the second figure in predicative syllogisms. As we said when we discussed predicative syllogisms, in order to be productive, the negative premiss must be one of the two convertible necessary propositions. We can prove it either by conversion or by *reductio ad absurdum*, or by introducing an assumption.[6] The following mood will be an example that clarifies what we said of this figure.

[*Its moods*]

The first mood: This mood is compounded of two universal premisses of which the major premiss is negative – as we say

> always: when A is B, then C is D,
> and never: when H is Z, then C is D,   (1) AE/E
> therefore never: when A is B, then H is Z.

This mood can be proved by converting the major premiss, and thus reducing is to the second (mood) of the first (figure). It can also be proved by *reductio ab absurdum* [as follows]: If the above conclusion is false, then its contradictory, namely, 'Sometimes: when A is B, then H is Z' will be true. If you add to it 'Never: when H is Z, then C is D', the conclusion will be 'Not always: when A is B, then C is D'.

The second mood: This mood is compounded of two universal premisses of which the minor premiss is negative

> never: when A is B, then C is D,
> and always: when H is Z, then C is D,   (2) EA/E
> therefore never: when A is B, then H is Z.

This mood can be proved by converting the minor premiss and the conclusion. It can also be proved by *reductio ad absurdum* by assuming the contradictory of the conclusion and adding it to the major premiss, from which follows the contradictory of the minor premiss. The cases here are the same as in the first mood.

The third mood: This mood is compounded of a minor premiss which is a particular affirmative proposition, and a major premiss which is a universal negative proposition.

> Sometimes: when A is B, then C is D,
> and never: when H is Z, then C is D,   (3) IE/O
> therefore not always: when A is B then H is Z.

It can be proved by converting the major premiss or by *reductio ad absurdum*.

The fourth mood: This mood is compounded of a particular negative minor premiss and a universal affirmative major premiss

> not always: when A is B, then C is D,

and always: when H is Z, then C is D, (4) OA/O
therefore not always: when A is B, then H is Z.

This mood can be proved by *reductio ad absurdum*. It can also be proved by introducing an assumption in the following way: We specify the case and the time in which 'A is B' and 'Never C is D'. Let this case or time be whenever 'E is T'. In this case we can correctly say

never: when E is T, then C is D,
and always: when H is Z, then C is D,
therefore never: when E is T, then H is Z.

If we add to the above conclusion (the proposition) 'Sometimes: if A is B, then E is T' both will yield the following conclusion:

Not always: when A is B, then H is Z.

Someone may say: It will be better if the above negative propositions have impossible antecedents, since in this case they will not be convertible. We say: If the antecedent in the affirmative premiss is not impossible, then its consequent, which is the middle part (of the syllogism), will not be impossible. If this antecedent is impossible and it is in conjunction with the middle part, while the other, viz. the antecedent of the minor premiss, is not, which means that they can never be true together, then the conclusion will be true.

The third figure

If you make the same kind of investigations you did before, you will find out that the use of affirmative propositions which are connected by chance is unlimited. The only thing we say after that is that the condition (for production) in this figure is the same as that of the third figure in predicative syllogisms. It has six moods like the third figure of predicative syllogisms.

[*Its moods*]

The first mood: This mood is compounded of two universal affirmative propositions

always: when C is D, then H is Z,
and always: when C is D, then A is B, (1) AA/I
therefore sometimes: when H is Z, then A is B.

We prove this mood by converting the minor premiss and thus reduce it to the first figure. Or we can prove it in the following way: Let (the conclusion) be 'Never: if H is Z, then A is B'. If we add to it 'Always: when C is D, then A is B', both will yield the following conclusion: 'Never: if H is Z, then A is B'. This is a contradiction.

15   The second mood: This mood is compounded of two universal premisses with a negative major premiss

> Always: when C is D, then H is Z,
> and never: when C is D, then A is B,   (2) AE/O
> therefore not always: when H is Z, then A is B.

[303]   We can prove it by converting the minor premiss. We can also prove it by *reductio ad absurdum* by adding the contradictory of the conclusion to the major premiss, from which you produce the contradictory of the minor premiss.

The third mood: This mood is compounded of two affirmative premisses with a particular minor premiss

> sometimes: when C is D, then H is Z,
> and always: when C is D, then A is B,   (3) IA/I
> therefore sometimes: when H is Z, then A is B.

5   We can prove this mood by converting the minor premiss, or by *reductio ad absurdum* in which case we produce the contradictory of the minor premiss.

The fourth mood: This mood is compounded of two affirmative premisses and the major premiss is particular

> always: when C is D, then H is Z,
> and sometimes: when C is D, then A is B,   (4) AI/I
> [therefore sometimes: when H is Z, then A is B.]

The premisses produce a particular affirmative conclusion. It can be proved by converting the major premiss and the conclusion, or by *reductio ad absurdum*.

The fifth mood: This mood is compounded of a universal affirmative minor premiss and a particular negative major premiss

10   always: when C is D, then H is Z,

and not always: when C is D, then A is B,   (5) AO/O
therefore not always: when H is Z, then A is B.

This mood can be proved only by *reductio ad absurdum*, or by introducing
an assumption in the following way: Let the case in which 'C is D' and
'A is not B' be 'E is T'. Therefore 'Never: if E is T, then A is B'. We, therefore, say

always: when C is D, then H is Z,
and sometimes: when C is D, then E is T,
therefore if H is Z, then E is T.

Add to the above conclusion

never: when E is T, then A is B,

therefore not always: when H is Z, then A is B.
The sixth mood: this mood is compounded of a particular affirmative
minor premiss and a universal negative major premiss – as when you say

sometimes: when C is D, then H is Z,
and never: when C is D, then A is B,   (6) IE/O
therefore not always: when H is Z, then A is B.

This mood can be proved by converting the minor premiss, or by *reductio
ad absurdum*.

In case the premisses are modal propositions, the syllogisms will be
treated in the same way as we treated predicative syllogisms. Notice that
the major connective premiss can either be unrestricted or an implication.

NOTES

[1] Like ὅρος the original meaning of *ḥadd* is 'limit'. It is defined in Aristotle's *Pr. An.* I, 24b11
as that into which the premiss is resolved. The context there is the treatment of categorical
(Avicenna's predicative) syllogisms. ὅρος and *ḥadd* in that context mean simply a 'term'.
Avicenna here is clearly using it to refer to a proposition, for that is what a conditional
premiss is resolved into. To avoid confusion, we translate it here as 'part' (*juz'*), a word which
he used before in the same sense indicated (*al-Qiyās*, 232 and 255). As to *mushtarak*, it seems
to be a translation of ἀμφότερος which is used in the same sense in Galen's *Institutio
Logica*, VII, 6.

[2] Universal affirmative, universal negative, particular affirmative, particular negative, absolute, necessary, possible and impossible.

[3] See 239, 9–17 and 240.

[4] Reading *al-aṣghar* with D and J.

[5] This is case (b) mentioned above.

[6] This method of proof is used below (301, 13–17 ff).

ON THE SYLLOGISMS COMPOUNDED OF
CONNECTIVE AND SEPARATIVE PROPOSITIONS

[*When the minor is connective and the major a real separative;*]

Let us start with the syllogisms in which the minor premiss is a connective proposition. What the premisses share together is either their antecedents or their consequents or the antecedent of one of them and the consequent of the other. Further, in every one of the divisions either the separative is real or the other [namely the connective] is a restricted proposition.[1]

[*and the middle part is the consequent of the minor and the antecedent of the major*]

The combinations in which the minor premiss is a connective proposition, the major is a real separative and the sharing (*al-sharika*) occurs in the consequent of the connective proposition:

(a) The moods which are compounded of two affirmative premisses. For example, when the premisses are universal

> always: when H is Z, viz. without making any further conditions, then C is D,
> and always: either C is D or A is B,
> therefore always: when H is Z, then A is not B.
>
> (a) AA/A

It can be proved by reducing the separative proposition to 'Always: when C is D, then A is not B'.

[(*b*) *IA/I*]

(b) The mood constructed of two affirmative premisses, of which the minor premiss is particular, will give the same conclusion as the former except that the conclusion in this case is a particular proposition.

[(*c*) *AI/–*]

(c) There will be no production if the separative premiss is a particular proposition. The examples in words for the last construction are[2]:

(1)   Always: when Zayd is walking, then he is moving in a place,
             and sometimes: either Zayd is moving in a place or he is
15   not walking.
(2)   Always: when this is a musk, viz. without any further con-
             ditions, then it is black,
[306]   and sometimes: either a thing is black or it is sweet-smelling.

In (1) the conclusion is a universal affirmative proposition and in (2) it is
a universal negative proposition.

(d) Their moods when the connective premiss is a convertible negative
proposition:

Never: when H is Z, then C is D,
and always: either C is D or A is B,   (d) EA/E
5   therefore never: either H is Z or A is B.

Another conclusion we infer 'Always: when H is Z, then A is B', and also
'Never: if H is Z, then A is not B'. The (second) conclusion is necessarily
implied because we can look at it as being produced necessarily from the
two conditional premisses in the following way:

Always: when H is Z, then C is not D,
and always: when C is not D, then A is B,
therefore, always: when H is Z, without any further condition, then A is B.

Another conclusion we can infer 'Never: either H is Z or A is B'. I.e. this
mood can also have a conclusion which is the negation of a separative
statement.

[(*e*) *It is productive when either one of the premisses is particular*]
10   (e) It will also be productive if the connective or the separative premiss is
particular, since the connective is convertible. And the converted premiss
implies 'Always: when C is D, then H is not Z'. If we add to the latter
'Sometimes: when C is D, then A is not B', we produce 'Sometimes:
when H is not Z, then A is not B'; which implies that 'Not always: either
H is Z or A is B'.

[(*f*) *No production when the separative is negative*]
(f) The moods when the separative proposition alone is negative are

5   not productive at all. The following are examples in words of those (inconclusive moods);

(1)   Always: when this is even, then it a number,
       and never: either it is a number or a multiplicity which is divisible into two equal integers.

(2) (The same example with the consequent of the major premiss changed into) 'or a multiplicity which is not divisible into two equal integers'. Sometimes we get a universal affirmative conclusion and sometimes a universal negative.

[(g) *No production from two negative or two particular premisses*]
(g) The sterillity of the moods constructed of particular premisses is more obvious. There is no production from two negative or particular premisses.

[*When the minor is connective and the major is unreal separative; and the middle part is the consequent of the first and the antecedent of the second*]
7]   The combinations in which the minor premisses are connective propositions, the major are unreal separative propositions, and the sharing occurs in the consequent of the connective proposition: First let the separative premisses contain a negative and an affirmative part, and let the sharing occur in the affirmative part. No attention is to be paid to that part of the connective premiss in which no sharing takes place, since it does not affect what we produce at all.
5   (a) The moods when the combinations consist of two affirmative propositions. Let them be universal.

       Always: when H is Z, without any further conditions,
             then C is D,   (a) AA/–
       and always: either C is D or A is not B.

This mood is unproductive. The following is an example of this mood

       always: when so is a man, then he is an animal,
       and always: either he is an animal or he is a creature-that-flies.
Or again

       either he is an animal or he is not rational.

[*Sterile moods*]

(b) From this it is clear what will happen when the connective is particular.

10   (c) When the separative is particular, it will also be unproductive. For example

> always: when he is a creature that walks, then he is a creature-
> that-has-a-will
> and sometimes; either he is a creature-that-has-a-will or he
> is not a creature-that-moves.

or

> sometimes: either he is a creature-that-has-a-will or he is not
> a creature-that-moves, i.e. a creature whose will
> is not to move.

Different results are obtained in the above examples.

(d) The moods when the connective is negative, whether it is restricted

15   or unrestricted. When the combinations are of two universal premisses:

> Never: when H is Z, then C is D – whether it ex-
> presses a restricted or an unrestricted
> following.   (d) EA/E
> and always: either C is D or A is B,
> therefore never: when H is Z, then A is B.

[*308*]   Or, therefore, 'Never: either H is not Z or A is B'. The above syllogism can be reduced to a syllogism which is compounded of connective propositions in the following way:

> Always: when H is Z – in the same sense as in the previous
> negative premiss – then C is not D, or H is Z does
> not imply C is D,
> and always: when C is not D, then A is not B,
> therefore always: when H is Z, then A is not B.

From the above syllogism we can infer 'Never: when H is Z, then A is B' and 'Not: either H is Z or A is not B'.

[(e) *The connective is particular*]

5   (e) The same happens if the connective premiss is a particular proposition.

[(*f*) *The separative is particular*]

(f) If the separative is particular, the conclusion will be the same as in the similar syllogism in which the separative proposition is unreal.

[(*g*) *No production when the separative is negative*]

(g) The moods when the separative proposition is negative are all unproductive. Here are examples in words which represent these moods:

> Always: when this is an accident, then absolutely and unconditionally, it must have a bearer,
> and never: either it has a bearer or it is not a substance

or [3]

10
> never: either it has a bearer or not every quantity is finite, i.e. if no false condition is given to qualify it.

From these examples contradictory results are obtained.

[(*h*) *No production when the premisses are particular*]

(h) When the premisses are particular it is more obvious that they will be sterile.

[*The same figure but the middle is negative*]

Suppose that the sharing occurs in the negative part.

[(*a*) *When the premisses are affirmative and one of them is universal it will be sterile;*]

(a) The moods when the combination is of two affirmative premisses.

> Always: when H is Z, then C is not D,
> and either C is not D or A is B.

This is unproductive. The following is an example in words which represents this mood:

Always: when this is a man, then he is not an accident,
                      and either he is not a stone or he is a body.

Or instead of the last premiss you may say 'Either he is not a stone or he is
a body'.

[(*b*) *and when one of them is particular it will be sterile*]
    (b) You can find yourself the examples for those syllogisms in which
one of the premisses is particular.

[(*c*) *When the separative is negative it is sterile*]
[*309*]   (c) The moods when the separative proposition is negative are unproductive. We shall give one example of this mood:

                      Always: when this is an accident, then it is not a substance,
                      and never: either this is not a substance or it in an object

or

                      never: either this is not[4] a substance or the quantity
                      is actually infinite.

[*When the parts of the separative are negative*]
5   From what we said before you can easily find out what happens in case
the separative premiss in the combination has negative parts; for these
follow the same rule as the syllogisms in which the middle part is negative
and the other parts are affirmative.

[*When the separative is real and the middle part is the antecedent of both
premisses*]
    Let us now examine the moods which are similar to the above except
.that the sharing occurs in the antecedent of the connective premiss. Let
us start with those in which the separative is real.
10   (a) The moods when the two premisses are universal affirmative propositions.

                      Always: when H is Z, then C is D,
                      and always: either H is Z or A is B,   (a) AA/I
                      therefore sometimes: when C is D, then A is not B.

For it is not always the case that either C is not D or A is B. We prove this mood in the following way: We turn the separative into 'Always: when H is Z, then A is not B', and in the same way, as we did in the third figure, we add it to the other premiss. The conclusion will be the same as in the third figure. A universal conclusion can also be derived if the connective premiss is converted by contraposition in the same way as before. Thus, it becomes 'Never: when C is not D, then H is Z'. We add it to 'Always: when A is not B, then H is Z' which is inferred from the connective premiss in the above syllogism. It will produce 'Never: when C is not D, then A is not B'; from which we infer 'Never: either C is D or A is not B'.

[(b) *When either one of the premisses is particular*]

Either the connective or the separative can be particular. In this case the conclusion will be 'Sometimes: when C is D, then A is not B'. We prove it by converting the connective proposition, in which case it will be reduced to those combinations in which the sharing occurs in the consequent of the connective proposition, as we did in the previous case.

(c) The moods when the connective premiss is a convertible negative proposition.

> Never: when H is Z, then C is D,
> and always: either H is Z or A is B,   (c) EA/E
> therefore never: when C is D, then A is not B.

Another conclusion we infer 'Always: when C is D, then A is B', and 'Never: either C is D or A is B'. We prove it by converting the connective premiss into a universal proposition, in which case it will be reduced to one in which the sharing is in the consequent.

(d) When the connective proposition is particular, we prove the mood by turning the connective proposition into an affirmative proposition, and then we convert it.

> Sometimes: when C is not D, then H is Z,
> and always: when H is Z, then A is not B,   (d) IA/I
> therefore sometimes: when C is not D, then A is not B.

Another conclusion we infer 'Not always: when C is not D, then A is B'.

[(e) *When the separative is particular*]

(e) When the saparative is particular, we prove it by turning the negation of the connective into an affirmative proposition. It becomes 'Always: when H is Z, then C is not D'. Also, we turn the separative into a connective proposition. It becomes 'Sometimes: when H is Z, then A is not B'. The conclusion is 'Sometimes: when C is not D, then A is not B'. From this we infer 'Not always: when C is not D, then A is B'.

[311]   (f) The moods when the separative proposition is negative.

> Always: when H is Z, then C is D,
> and never: either H is Z or C is D.   (f) AE/–

This mood is unproductive. For when you say 'Always: when this is even, then it is divided into two equal integers' and 'Never: it is either even or a number' it would be correct to say 'Always: when this is divisible into two 5   equal integers, then it is a number'. But if you put 'void' instead of 'number' the negative conclusion would be the correct one. The same happens if the premiss is a particular proposition.

[*When the separative is unreal and the middle part in the same position and it is affirmative*]

The same combinations when the separative is unreal. Let the sharing be in the affirmative part.

(a) The moods when the premises are affirmative.

> Always: when H is Z, then C is D,
10 and always: either H is Z or A is not B,   (a) AA/I

In one way the conclusion would be 'Sometimes: if C is D, then A is B'. From this we infer 'Not always: either C is D or A is B'. We prove it in the following way:

> Always: when A is B, then H is Z,
> and always: when H is Z, then C is D,
> therefore always: when A is B, then C is D,

and then convert the conclusion.

You can also derive a universal proposition in the same way we mentioned before.

[(b) *The separative is particular*]

(b) The same thing happens if the separative is a particular proposition.

15   (c) The moods when the connective is negative.

> Never: when H is Z, then C is D,
> and always: either H is Z or A is not B,   (c) EA/E
> therefore never: when C is D, then A is B.

Another conclusion we infer 'Always: when C is D, then A is not B';
and also 'Not: either C is D or A is not B'. We prove it by converting the
connective proposition.

[(d) *The connective is particular*]

(d) When the connective premiss is a particular proposition, we do the
same thing which we did in the corresponding syllogism.

[(e) *No production when the separative is negative*]

(e) The moods when the separative premiss is negative are unproductive. An example in words of this mood:

> Always: when Zayd is sinking, then he is in the water,
> and not: either Zayd is sinking or he does not fly

or

5   not: either Zayd is sinking or void does not exist.

[*Now the middle part is negative*]

The same combinations when the sharing is in the negative part. Let
us start (a) with the moods which have two affirmative premisses:

> Always: when H is not Z, then C is D,
> and always: either H is not Z or A is B,   (a) AA/I
> therefore sometimes: when C is D, then A is not B.

Another conclusion we infer 'Not always: either C is D or A is not B'.

[(b) *One of the premisses is particular*]

10   (b) The same happens when one of the premisses is particular. We
prove it by conversion in the following way:

Always: when A is not B, then H is not Z,
and always: when H is not Z, then C is D.

The conclusion will be a universal proposition which is to be converted into 'Sometimes: when C is D, then A is not B'. You can derive the unversal by yourself in the same way you learned before.

(c) The moods when the connective is negative.

Never: when H is not Z, then C is D⁵,
and always: either H is not Z or A is B,   (c) EA/E
therefore never: when C is not D, then A is B.

15

Another conclusion we infer 'Always: when C is D, then A is B'; from which we infer 'Never: either C is D or A is B'. It can be proved by converting the connective premiss as it is into a universal proposition.

[(*d*) *One of the premisses is particular*]

(d) The same happens if one of the premisses is a particular proposition. You can treat it in the same way you treated the corresponding syllogism.

[(*e*) *No production when the separative is negative*]

[313]

(e) The moods when the separative premiss is negative are unproductive. If you want examples in words for these moods, take the examples given in the corresponding mood where the separative is real. But instead of 'sinking' put 'not sinking'.

[(*f*) *The separative with both parts negative*]

(f) The moods in which the separative propositions have two negative parts follow the same rule as the previous ones and it is not difficult for you to find them by yourself.

[*When the connective is the major premiss and the middle part is the antecedent of both*]

5

Let us now concentrate on examining the same combinations when the connective is the major premiss. Let us start with those in which the sharing occurs in the antecedent [of the connective], and the separative premiss is real.

(a) The moods when the premisses are affirmative.

Always: either H is Z or C is D,
and always: when C is D[6], then A is B,   (a) AA/A
therefore always: when H is not Z, then A is B.

Another conclusion we infer 'Either H is Z or A is B'. We prove this
mood by turning the separative into 'Always: when H is Z, then C is D'
and when we add it to 'Always: when C is D, then A is B' we produce
'Always: when H is not Z, then A is B'.

[(b) *The separative is particular*]
   (b) You will know what happens when the separative is a particular
proposition by comparing it with the above case.

[(c) *The connective is particular*]
   (c) If the connective is a particular proposition, then you should turn
the separative premiss into a connective proposition. It will become
'Always: when C is D, then H is not Z', which is to be added to the other
premiss. The syllogism will have the same form as the third figure, and the
conclusion will be 'Sometimes: when H is not Z, then A is B'.
   (d) The moods when the separative premiss is a negative proposition.

Never: either H is Z or C is D,
and always: when C is D, then A is B.   (d) EA/—

This mood is unproductive. The following is an example in words to
represent this mood:

Never: either this thing is a void or it is even,
and always: when it is even, then it can be divided into two
equal integers.

Put instead of 'void', 'the multiple of an even number'.[7]
   (e) The moods when the connective premiss is negative.

Always: either H is Z or C is D,
and never: when C is D, then A is B.   (e) AE/E

Convert the separative into a connective proposition. It becomes 'Always:
when H is not Z, then C is D', after which we produce 'Never: when
H is not Z, then A is B': and also 'Not: either H is Z or A is B'.

[(ƒ) *The connective is particular negative*]

(f) If the connective premiss is a particular proposition, do the same thing as you did in the corresponding mood when the connective was an affirmative proposition.

[*When the separative is unreal and the middle is in the same position*]

The same combinations when the separative premiss is unreal and the sharing is in the affirmative part:

(a) The moods when the two premisses are affirmative propositions.

10

> Always: either H is not Z or C is D,
> and always: when C is D, then A is B,   (a) AA/A
> therefore always: when H is Z, then A is B.

Another conclusion we infer 'Never: either H is Z or A is B'. For the separative becomes a connective proposition, namely 'Always: when H is Z, then C is D'.

[(b) *The separative is particular*]

(b) The same happens when the separative is particular.

[(c) *No production when the connective is particular*]

(c) The mood will not be productive if the connective is particular. The following is an example in words to represent this mood:

> Always: either this is not even or it is a number,
> and sometimes: if it is a number, then it is the multiple of an
> even number.

15   And instead of the latter you can say: 'If it is a number, then it is the multiple of an odd number' [to obtain a different result].

[(d) *No production when the separative is negative*]

(d) The moods when the separative is negative are unproductive. An example in words:

> Never: either this does not talk or he is a man,
> and always: when he is a man, he is an animal.

Put 'void' instead of 'does not talk' [and you obtain different results].

5]   (e) The moods when the connective is negative.

> Always: either H is not Z or C is D,
> and never: when C is D, then A is B,   (e) AE/E
> therefore never: when H is Z, then A is B.

Another conclusion we infer 'Never: either H is not Z or A is B'. For the separative becomes 'Always: when H is Z, then C is D'.

[(*f*) *The separative is particular*]

5   (f) The same happens when the separative premiss is a particular proposition.

[(*g*) *No production when the connective is particular*]

    (g) The mood will be unproductive if the connective is a particular proposition. The example in words that represents this mood will be the same as the example given when the mood was constructed of two affirmative premisses, except that the particular affirmative becomes a particular negative.

[*When the middle is negative and it is the consequent of the first and the antecedent of the second*]

    The same combination when the sharing occurs in the negative part:

    (a) The moods when the premisses are affirmative propositions.

> Always: either H is Z or C is not D,
> and always: when C is not D, then A is B,   (a) AA/A
> therefore always: when H is not Z, then A is B.

10   Another conclusion we infer 'Never: either H is not Z or A is B'. For the separative becomes 'Always: when H is not Z, then C is not D'.

[(*b*) *The separative is particular*]

    (b) The same happens when the separative is particular.

[(*c*) *No production when the connective is particular*]

    (c) The mood will be unproductive if the connective is a particular proposition. The example in words that represents this mood is:

always: either the subject which we describe is a number or
it is not even,
and sometimes: when this is not even, then it is white

or

sometimes: when this is not even, then it is odd

[and you obtain different results].

[(*d*) *No production when the separative is negative*]

15   (d) The moods when the separative premiss is negative are unproductive. The example in words is:

never: either man is not a body or he is not a creature-that-
moves,
and always: when he is a creature-that-moves, then he is a
body.

Put 'void' instead of 'not a body' [and you obtain different results].

[*316*]   (e) The moods when the connective premiss is negative.

Always: either H is Z or C is not D,
and never: when C is not D, then A is B.   (e) AE/E

The separative becomes 'Always: when H is not Z, then C is not D' and 'Never: when H is not Z, then A is B' will be the conclusion; or we can infer 'Not: either H is not Z or A is B'.

[(*f*) *The separative is particular negative*]

(f) The case when the separative premiss is a particular proposition is evident.

[(*g*) *No production when the connective is particular negative*]

5   (g) The mood will be unproductive if the connective premiss is particular. The examples which represent this mood in words are

(1)   never: either this is a void or it is not even,
and not: if[8] it is not even, then it is odd.

And

(2)   never: either it is divisible into two equal integers or it is
not even,
and not: every thing which is not even then it is odd.

[1 and 2 will give different results.]

[*When the separative is real and the middle is the consequent of both premisses*]

The combinations when the connective is the major premiss and the
sharing is in the consequent of the connective premiss. Let us start with
those in which the separative premiss is real.

(a) The moods when the premisses are affirmative propositions:

Always: either H is Z or C is D,
and always: when A is B, then C is D.   (a) AA/E

From the separative premiss we infer 'Never: when H is Z, then C is D',
and [added to the above connective] we produce 'Never: when H is Z,
then A is B'; or 'Not: either H is not Z or A is B.[9]

[*(b) The separative is particular*]
  (b) The case is obvious [10] when the separative premiss is particular.

[*(c) The connective is particular*]
  (c) If the connective is a particular proposition, then it will become
the minor premiss; and we produce 'Sometimes not: if A is B, then H is Z'.
From this we infer 'Sometimes: if A is B, then H is not Z'[11] which can be
converted into 'Sometimes: if H is not Z, then A is B'. Therefore, 'Not:
either H is not Z or A is B'.

[*(d) No production when the separative is negative*]
  (d) The moods when the separative premiss is negative are unproductive. The examples in words are:

(1)   Never: either this is moving or it is a substance,
and always: when it rests, it is a substance.

And

(2)   'Always: when it is moving, it is a substance'.

[from 1 and 2 we obtain different results.]
 (e) The moods when the connective premiss is negative.

Always: either H is Z or C is D,
and never: if A is B, then C is D.   (e) AE/E

For the separative premiss can be converted into a connective, and it becomes 'Always: when H is not Z, then C is D'. Therefore, 'Never: if H is not Z, then A is B', or 'Never: either H is Z or A is B'.

[(ƒ) *The separative is particular negative*]
 (f) The same happens when the separative premiss is particular.

[(g) *The connective is particular negative*]
 (g) If the connective is particular we add to it 'Always: when H is not Z, then C is D'. Therefore, 'Not always: when A is B, then H is not Z'. From this we infer 'Sometimes: if A is B, then H is Z' which is converted into 'Sometimes: if H is Z, then A is B' from which we infer 'Not always: either H is Z or A is B'.

[*When the separative is unreal and the middle is the consequent of both premisses and it is affirmative*]
 The same combinations when the separative premiss is unreal and the sharing occurs in the affirmative part:
 (a) The moods when the two premisses are affirmative propositions.

Always: either H is not Z or C is D,
and always: when A is B, then C is D.   (a) AA/E

For the separative becomes 'Always: when H is Z, then C is not D', after which we infer 'Never: when H is Z, then C is D'. The rest are to be treated in the same way as you know.
 (b) The moods when the separative premiss is negative.

Never: either H is not Z or C is D,
and always: when C is D, then A is B.   (b) EA/−

This is unproductive. The examples in words are the same as the examples given in the corresponding mood except that you should put in the separative premiss 'it is not at rest' instead of 'moving'.

(c) The moods when the connective premiss is negative.
Always: either H is not Z or C is D,
and never: when A is B, then C is D.   (c) AE/E

For the separative becomes 'Always: when H is Z, then C is D', which
in turn becomes 'Never: when H is Z, then C is not D', after which we
produce 'Never: when H is Z, then A is B'.

[(d) *The separative is particular*]
(d) The case when the particular is the separative is evident.

[(e) *The connective is particular*]
(e) If it [i.e. the particular] is the connective proposition, then it should
be treated in the same way as in the corresponding mood.

From this you can find out what happens when, in all the combinations mentioned above, the sharing occurs in the negative part, and when
the two premisses are negative.

NOTES

¹ The editor of the text added *wa* after that which is not needed.
² Reading *lidhālik* with the majority of MSS.
³ Reading with F *aw*.
⁴ Reading *lā yakūnu* with G.
⁵ The edited text reads *jīm hā'* without giving any further readings. The B.M. MS. reads
jīm dāl.
⁶ The edited text, which does not give any further readings, reads *jīm hā'*. The B.M. MS reads
jīm dāl.
⁷ By that he means to say that you would get different conclusions in different examples.
⁸ Reading *idhā* for *ḥukman*.
⁹ Reading with D *alif bā'*.
¹⁰ The B.M. MS. reads *ẓāhir*. The edited text, which does not give any further readings,
reads *ẓāhira*.
¹¹ Reading with C, D, F, G, I and J *falaysa hā' zāy*.

ON THE SYLLOGISMS COMPOUNDED OF
SEPARATIVE PROPOSITIONS

[*Syllogisms from two separative premisses and the conditions for their production*]

We say: There is never a syllogism from two real separative premisses. For the statement 'It is exclusively either A is B or C is D' is true only if it has no third part. What is meant by saying 'It is exclusively either A is B or C is D' is the following: 'A is B, and if not, then it is necessary that C is D'. If it is not the case that 'C is D', then the statement will be false. Except, as we said before [1], when you turn it into a particular proposition; for in this case it should not take a third part. We shall prove that there is no syllogism from two affirmative premisses one of which is a particular premiss.

If the premiss 'Either A is B or C is D' is true in one case only, namely, when it does not take a third part, then if we add to it a new premiss, say 'Either C is D or H is Z' in which one part of the first premiss is repeated – the middle part, then 'H is Z' must be 'A is B'. Therefore, the two propositions are one and the conclusion is incorrect. For the conclusion will be 'Either A is B or H is Z', namely 'Either A is B or A is B'; if 'H is Z' is not the same as 'A is B', then there must be a third part, which means that both separative propositions are false. If the premisses were affirmative propositions which express incomplete conflict, then it will be possible to combine them in a syllogism though it will not give any information. It is also possible to combine separative propositions in a syllogism if the premisses are other than those mentioned before.

[*II/–*]

Let us first see if we can make a combination of two affirmative premisses one of which is a particular premiss, and both have two affirmative parts – as when we say 'Sometimes: either C is D or H is Z' and 'Either C is D or H is Z or A is B'. The last premiss is made of three parts in order that the particular be actually a particular and not a universal. We say: It is more likely that this is not a syllogism, for the minor premiss is actually contained in the major. Also, the conclusion produced from the premises is 'Sometimes: either H is Z or A is B', and this conclusion is not an unknown judgment which we came to know through the syllogism, though it follows from the syllogism. We are allowed to use a syllogism if it leads us from that which we know better to the unknown.

Let us leave this now and attend to those combinations which are more akin to the doctrines of syllogism. We shall not treat them in their real order or in the order of excellence; we will rather follow the order which is more appropriate to teaching and understanding.

[*There are no figures in this kind of syllogism*]

Moreover, we will not divide these syllogisms into figures since, as you know, we do not distinguish between an antecedent and a consequent in separative premisses or conclusions.[2] Also, we will not distinguish between minor and major premisses in any one of the conjunctions (*iqtirānāt*). Instead we will only have a simple (*sādhaj*) conjunction. Let us start with those combinations in which the real separative premisses are affirmative. We shall mix them either with unreal separative premisses, whether these premisses are affirmative or negative; or with the negations of the real premisses; since there will be no syllogism from the first premisses alone.

[*The mood where both premisses are affirmative one of which has a negative part*]

The mood compounded of two affirmative premisses one of which has a negative part:

> Always: either H is Z or C is D,
> and either: C is D or A is not B.

We say: This mood is productive. We prove it by turning the two premisses (respectively) into:

> always: when H is Z, then C is not D,
> and always: when C is not D, then A is not B,
> therefore always: when H is Z, then A is not B.

Another conclusion we infer 'Either H is not Z or A is not B'.

[There is no production if the premiss with the negative part is negative]

If the premiss in which one part is negative becomes negative, then there will be no production; because when the universal separative premiss, which is an affirmative proposition, is true, we produce the universal negation of the above separative premiss; and we produce the same conclusion when the above premiss is not true. Therefore, it does not produce one specific conclusion. An example of the first case will be

either: two is even or it is odd,
and never: either it is even or it is not odd.

It would be correct here to conclude 'Not always: either two is an odd number or it is not odd' also 'Either two is odd or it is not odd' is true.
The example for the second case will be

either: two is even or it is odd,
and never: either two is even or it is not a void.

From which we conclude 'Never: either two is odd or it is not void'.

[There is no production if one of the premisses is particular; or when the negative premiss has affirmative parts]

The mood will evidently be unproductive if one of the premisses is a particular proposition. The same is true if the negative premiss has two affirmative parts. For example

either two is not even or it is a number,
and never: either two is a number or it is divisible into two equal integers.

From these propositions we can obtain 'Either two is even or it is divisible into two equal integers'. But if we say

either two is even or it is a number,
and never either two is a number or it is void,

it will be correct to say 'Never: either two is not a number or it is void'.
The mood will obviously be unproductive if in this kind of combination one premiss is particular.

[No production if one premiss is a real separative]

It is clear from what we said before that there is no syllogism if one of the premisses is a real separative proposition, except if the other premiss is an unreal affirmative proposition of which the part that is not shared with the other premiss is negative.

[When both premisses are unreal separative and the middle part is affirmative, the conclusion is not affirmative]
The combinations in which the two premisses are unreal separative propositions that share the affirmative part do not produce an affirmative separative conclusion at all. Take the following examples:

> Either two is not even or it is a number,
> and either two is a number or it is not odd,

from which follows that 'Not always: either two is not even or it is not odd'.
And then we say

> either two is even or it is a number,
> and either two is a number or it is not divisible into two equal integers,

from which follows that 'Not: either two is even or it is not divisible into two equal integers'.

[When the premisses are particular, the conclusion would be a connective proposition]
The same is true of particular premisses. But these produce a proposition which is not separative as follows:

> Either H is not Z or C is D,
> and either C is D or A is not B,

from which follows that 'If C is not D, then H is not Z'; also, 'If C is not D, then A is not B'. Thus, 'Sometimes: if H is not Z, then C is not D'. From the last proposition it follows that 'Not always: when H is not Z, then C is not D'. Therefore, 'Not: either H is Z or C is D'. This is a negative conclusion whose quality is different from that of the premisses. The same can be said if one of the premisses is negative.

[*When the premisses are unreal and the middle is negative*]
The combinations in which the two premisses are unreal separative propositions sharing a negative part:

[*When the premisses are affirmative*]
If the premisses are affirmative propositions, they will be productive. For example:

15
               Either H is Z or C is not D,
               and either C is not D or A is B.

[*324*]
It produces the same conclusion as in the previous case and that is: 'Therefore not always: either H is Z or A is B'. We prove it in the following way: the separative premisses become connective propositions combined, as in the third figure, thus

               always: when C is D, then H is Z,
               and always: when C is D, then A is B,
               therefore sometimes: if H is Z, then A is B.

5
From the conclusion we infer 'Not always: either H is Z or A is B'.

[*When one premiss is particular*]
The same happens if one of the premisses is particular.

[*When one premiss is negative there will be no production*]
If one of them is negative, it will be unproductive. We will give only one example of this.

               Either two is even or it is not the multiple of an even number,
          and never: either two is not the multiple of an even number
                   or it is odd.

The conclusion that one would derive above is the opposite of the conclusion which we would derive when we put 'quality' instead of 'odd'.

[*No production when both premisses are particular or when one of them has two negative parts. If between them they have three negative parts they produce when the middle is negative*]
If the premisses are particular propositions, it will be more evident that they are unproductive.

It is also impossible to find a middle part between a premiss which has two negative parts and a premiss in which the two parts are affirmative, and between a premiss with two negative parts and a premiss with only one affirmative part; except if they share the negative part.

The combinations of two separative premisses, one of which has two negative parts and the other has one negative part, follow the same rules as those combinations which have their premisses sharing the negative part.

[*Other combinations*]

The combinations of two separative premisses which have negative parts follow the same rules as those combinations which have separative premisses sharing the negative part.

NOTES

[1] See 288.
[2] 245, 9–17 and 246, 1–5.

ON THE SYLLOGISMS COMPOUNDED OF
PREDICATIVE AND CONDITIONAL PROPOSITIONS[1]

[*Syllogisms from a conditional and a predicative premiss:*]
5   In these syllogisms the predicative proposition is either the major or the minor premiss. Also, the predicative premiss shares [either its subject or its predicate] with [part of] the consequent or the antecedent (of the conditional premiss).

[(*i*) *the predicative is the major premiss and the middle term occurs in the consequent of the conditional and the predicative*]
    Let us start first with those syllogisms in which the predicative proposition is the major premiss and in which part of the predicative premiss is shared with [part of] the consequent (of the conditional premiss). The part which the consequent (of the conditional premiss) and the predicative premiss share will necessarily take anyone of the forms of the three figures. We are determined to enumerate the productive moods with the help of the knowledge we acquired from our previous investigations. We shall not lengthen the book by mentioning the unproductive moods,
10   since we have already found the terms (from which examples of such moods can be constructed).

[*The first figure and the conditions for its production*]
    [First] the moods when the combination takes the form of the first figure. In this case, the condition for production is that the predicative premiss and the consequent (of the conditional premiss) take the form of the first figure of predicative syllogisms. If the connective premiss is affirmative, the conclusion will follow necessarily from the premisses, as it is the case in predicative syllogisms. The difference between the two is that in the case of the predicative syllogism the conclusion follows un-
15   conditionally while here it follows if something is posited. The conclusion will be a conditional premiss whose consequent is the conclusion that follows from combining the consequent (of the conditional premiss)
[*326*]   and the predicative premiss, as if[2] both constitute a separate syllogism.

If the connective premiss is negative, then we cannot produce the conclusion directly, but after converting the negative premiss into an affirmative proposition.

[(a) *When the connective is universal affirmative*]
   (a) The moods when the connective premiss is affirmative.
   The first mood:

> Always: when H is Z, then every C is D,
> and every D is A,
> therefore always: when H is Z, then every C is A.   AA/A

5   One should not object to these moods and those similar to them saying
that since it is possible for the predicative premiss to be true in itself, and
since it might become false as a result of positing a particular antecedent,
therefore, no such syllogisms can be constructed – as when we say, e.g.
'Always: when void exists, it will be a dimension which exists by itself',
and 'Every dimension does not exist by itself' or 'Nothing which exists
by itself is a dimension'. For here the predicative premiss, which is true,
is equivalent to the contradictory of the consequent (of the conditional
premiss). There are two answers to this objection. The first is to say that
we must only enumerate those conjunctions in which the premisses are
10   not contradictory. The second is to say that whatever follows necessarily
from the two premisses must be true. For if 'void' exists, then 'dimension'
must be different from the dimension which follows necessarily from the
two contradictory propositions.
   The second mood:

> Always: when H is Z, then every C is D,
> and nothing of D is A,   AE/E
> therefore always: when H is Z, then nothing of C is A.

The third mood:

> Always: when H is Z, then some C is D,
> and every D is A,   IA/I
> therefore always: when H is Z, then some C is A.

The fourth mood:

> Always: when H is Z, then some C is D,   IE/O

and nothing of D is A,

15   therefore always: when H is Z, then not every C is A.

[(*b*) *When the connective is particular affirmative*]
(b) There are four other moods when the connective is particular.

[(*c*) *When the connective is universal negative*]
[*327*]   (c) The moods when the connective is negative. In this case the condition for production is to have a negative consequent and a universal
predicative premiss; or else there will be no production. For example,

never: when H is Z, then not every C is D,
and every D is A,   OA/O
therefore never: when H is Z, then not every C is A.

We prove it in the following way: From the connective premiss we infer
'Always: when H is Z, then every C is D'. Add to it the previous predica-
5   tive premiss 'Every D is A', therefore, 'Always: when H is Z, then every
C is A'. From this conclusion we infer 'Never: if H is Z, then not every
C is A'.

You can find out the remaining moods from the above case. These are:

Never: when H is Z, then nothing of C is D,
and every D is A,   EA/E
therefore never: when H is Z, then nothing of C is A.
And

never: when H is Z, then nothing of C is D,
and nothing of D is A,   EE/A
therefore never: when H is Z, then every C is A.

[(*d*) *When the connective is particular negative*]
10   (d) There are four other moods in which the connective premisses are
particular negative.

[*The second figure*]
[Second] the combinations which take the form of the second figure.

[(*a*) *When the connective is universal affirmative*]
(a) The moods when the connective is affirmative. The same condi-

tions which apply to predicative premisses in order that they become productive apply also to the consequent (of the conditional premiss) and the predicative premiss.

The first mood:

> Always: when H is Z, then every C is D,
> and nothing of A is D[3],   AE/E
> therefore always: when H is Z, then nothing of C is A.

We prove it by converting the predicative premiss. We can also prove it in the following way: 'Always: when H is Z, then C is D is true' and 'Nothing of A is D' is true. Also, 'Always: when C is D is true and nothing of A is D is true, then nothing of C is A is true'. Therefore 'Always: when H is Z, then nothing of C is A is true'.

The second mood:

> Always: when H is Z, then nothing of C is D,   EA/E
> and every A is D,

The conclusion will be the same as in the first mood. We prove it by converting the consequent (of the conditional premiss).

The third mood:

> Always: when H is Z, then some C is D,
> and nothing of A is D,   IE/O
> therefore always: when H is Z, then not every C is A.[4]

We prove it by converting the predicative premiss.

The fourth mood:

> Always: when H is Z, then not every C is D,   OA/O
> and every A is D.

The conclusion is the same as in the third mood. We prove it in the following way: 'Always: when H is Z, then it will be true that not every C is D' and it is true that 'Not every A is D'. Also, 'Always: when it is true that not every C is D and every A is D, then it is true that not every C is A'. Therefore, 'Always: when H is Z, then not every C is A'.

[(b) *When the connective is particular affirmative*]

(b) There are four other moods when the connective premiss is particular.

[(c) When the connective is universal negative]

10   (c) The moods when the connective premiss is negative. The condition for production is that the predicative premiss and the consequent[5] of the conditional premiss must have the same quality and the predicative premiss should be universal.

The first mood:

> Never: when H is Z, then not every C is D,
> and nothing of A is D,   OE/I
> therefore never: when H is Z, then some C is A.

Since from the conditional premiss follows 'Always: when H is Z, then every C is D'; from which follows 'Always: when H is Z, then nothing

15   of C is A'; therefore, 'Never: when H is Z, then some C is A'.

The second mood:

> Never: when H is Z, then some C is D
> and every A is D   EA/I

The conclusion here is the same as in the first mood.

[329]   The third mood:

> Never: when H is Z, then nothing of C is D,
> and nothing of A is D,   EE/A
> therefore never: when H is Z, then every C is A.

The fourth mood:

> Never: when H is Z, then every C is D,
> and every A is D,   AA/A
> therefore never: when H is Z, then every C is A.

[The third figure]

5   [Third] the combinations which take the form of the third figure.

[(a) When the connective is universal affirmative]

(a) The moods when the connective premiss is an affirmative proposition.

The first mood:

> Always: when H is Z, then every C is D,
> and every C is A,   AA/I
> therefore always: when H is Z, then some D is A.

We prove it by converting the consequent of the conditional premiss.
  The second mood:

> Always: when H is Z, then every C is D,
> and nothing of C is A,   AE/O
> therefore always: when H is Z, then not every D is A.

We prove it by converting the consequent of the conditional premiss.
  The third mood:

> Always: when H is Z, then some C is D,
> and every C is A.   IA/I

The conclusion here is the same as in the first mood. We prove it by
converting the consequent of the conditional premiss.
  The fourth mood:

> Always: when H is Z, then every C is D,
> and some C is A.   AI/I

The conclusion here is the same as in the first mood. We prove it in the
following way: 'Always: when H is Z, then it should be true that every
C is D' and it is true that 'Some C is A'. Also, 'Always: when every C is
D and some C is A, then some D is A'. Therefore, 'Always: when H is Z,
then some D is A'.
  The fifth mood:

> Always: when H is Z, then every C is D,
> and not every C is A,   AO/O
> therefore always: when H is Z, then not every D is A.

We prove it in the same way as we proved the fourth mood.
  The sixth mood:

> Always: when H is Z, then some C is D,
> and nothing of C is A.   IE/O

The conclusion here is the same as in the fifth mood. We prove it by
converting the consequent (of the conditional premiss).

[(b) When the connective is particular affirmative]
(b) There are six other moods when the connective premiss is particular.

[(c) When the connective is universal negative]
(c) The moods when the connective premiss is a negative proposition. The conditions for production are: (1) that the consequent should be negative, and (2) that either the consequent (of the conditional premiss) or the predicative premiss should necessarily by universal.
    The first mood:

    Never: when A is B, then nothing of C is D,
    and every C is H,   EA/E
    therefore never: when A is B, then nothing of D is H.

We prove it by converting the connective premiss into an affirmative proposition and by converting its consequent. From what follows, we infer the conclusion of the above mood.
    The second mood:

    Never: when A is B, then not every C is D,
    and nothing of C is H,   OE/O
    therefore never: when A is B, then not[6] every D is H.

We prove it by turning (*radd*) the connective into an affirmative proposition and by converting its consequent.
    The third mood:

    Never: when A is B, then nothing of C is D,
    and every C is H,   EA/E
    therefore never: when A is B, then nothing of D is H.

We prove it by turning the connective premiss into an affirmative proposition and by converting its consequent.

[*331*]   The fourth mood:

    Never: when A is B, then not every C is D,
    and some C is H,   OI/E
    therefore never: when A is B, then nothing of D is H.

We prove it by converting the connective premiss into an affirmative proposition, in which case its consequent will become affirmative. Then, detach the implicant of the result.

The fifth mood:

> Never: when A is B, then not every C is D,
> and not every C is H,   OO/A
> therefore never: when A is B, then every D is H.

We prove it by converting the connective premiss into an affirmative proposition. Then, detach the implicant of the result.

The sixth mood:

> Never: when A is B, then not every C is D,   OE/O
> and nothing of C is H.

The conclusion will be the same as in the second mood. We prove it by converting the connective premiss into an affirmative proposition. Then, detach the implicant of the result.

[(d) When the connective is particular negative]

(d) There are six moods when the connective premiss is a particular proposition.

[(ii) When the connective is the major premiss]

We will count now the types of conjunctions which these premisses take in case the connective is the major premiss.

[The first figure]

Let us first start with those which take the form of the first figure.

[(a) When the connective is universal affirmative]

(a) The moods when the connective premiss is an affirmative proposition. The condition for their production is that the predicative premiss and the consequent (of the conditional premiss) should be related in the same way as in the conjunctions of the first figure of predicative syllogisms. The conclusion will be a connective proposition whose consequent is produced by two predicative propositions as if they were not part of (a conditional syllogism).

The first mood:

Every C is B,
and always: when H is Z, then every B is A,   AA/A
15   therefore always: when H is Z, then every C is A.

The second mood:

Every C is B,
and always: when H is Z, then nothing of B is A,   AE/E
therefore always: when H is Z, then nothing of C is A.

[332]   The third mood:

Some C is B,
and always: when H is Z, then every B is A,   IA/I
therefore always: when H is Z, then some C is A.

The fourth mood:

Some C is B,
and always: when H is Z, then nothing of B is A,   IE/E
therefore always: when H is Z, then nothing of C is A.

[(b) *When the connective is particular affirmative*]
5   (b) There are four moods when the connective is a particular proposition.

[(c) *When it is universal negative*]
(c) The moods when the connective premiss is negative. The condition
for production is to have a particular consequent.[7]
The first mood:

Every C is B,
and never: when H is Z, then not every B is A,   AO/O
therefore never: when H is Z, then not every C is A.

We prove it by converting the connective premiss into an affirmative
proposition. Then, detach the implicant of the result.
10   The second mood:

Every C is B,
and never: when H is Z, then some B is A,   AI/I
therefore never: when H is Z, then some C is A.

The third mood:

> Some C is B,
> and never: when H is Z, then not every B is A,   IO/O
> therefore never: when H is Z, then not every C is A.

We prove it in the same previous way.
The fourth mood:

> Some C is B,
> and never: if H is Z, then some B[8] is A,   II/I
> therefore never: if H is Z, then some C is A.

We prove it in the same previous way.

[(d) When it is particular negative]
   (d) There are four other moods when the connective premiss is a particular proposition.

[The second figure]
   [Second] the combinations which take the form of the second figure.

[(a) When the connective is universal affirmative]
   (a) The moods when the connective premiss is an affirmative proposition. The conditions that determine the production from the predicative and the consequent (of the conditional premiss) are the same as in predicative syllogisms.
   The first mood:

> Every C is B[9],
> and always: when H is Z, then nothing of A is B,   AE/E
> therefore always: when H is Z, then nothing of C is A.

We prove it by converting the consequent (of the conditional premiss).
The second mood:

> Nothing of C is B,
> and always: when H is Z, then every A is B,   EA/E

The conclusion will be like the one in the previous mood. We prove it by converting the predicative premiss, the consequent (of the conditional premiss) and the conclusion.

The third mood:

> Some C is B,
> and always: when H is Z, then nothing of A is B,   IE/O
> therefore always: when H is Z, then not every C is A.

10

We prove it by converting the consequent (of the conditional premiss).
The fourth mood:

> Every C is B,
> and always: when H is Z, then not every A is B,   AO/O

The conclusion is the same as the conclusion in the third mood. We prove it in the following way: 'Always: when H is Z, then it is true that not every A is B' and it is true that 'Every C is B'. And always when both the above sentences are true, then 'Not every C is A'. Therefore, 'Always: when H is Z, then not every C is A'.

[(*b*) *When the connective is particular affirmative*]
15   (b) There are other moods when the connective premiss is particular.

[(*c*) *When it is universal negative*]
(c) The moods when the connective premiss is negative. The condition for its production is that the consequent (of the conditional premiss) should be particular, and it must have the same quality as the predicative premiss.

[*334*]   The first mood:

> Every C is B,
> and never: when H is Z, then some A is B,   AI/I
> therefore never: when H is Z, then some C is A.

The second mood:

> Nothing of C is B,
> and never: when H is Z, then not every A is B.   EO/I

The conclusion will be as in the previous case.
5   The third mood:

Some C is B,
and never: when H is Z, then some A is B,   II/A
therefore never: when H is Z, then every C is A.

The fourth mood:

Not every C is B,
and never: when H is Z, then not every A is B.   OO/A

The conclusion will be like that of the third mood.

All these moods are proved by converting the negative [connective] premiss into an affirmative proposition and then detach the implicant of the result.

[(d) When it is particular negative]
(d) There are six moods when the connective premiss is particular.

[The third figure]
[Third] the combinations which take the form of the third figure.

[(a) When the premisses are universal affirmative]
(a) The moods when the two premisses are affirmative propositions. The first mood:

Every C is B,
and always: when H is Z, then every C is A,   AA/I
therefore always: when H is Z, then some B is A.

We prove it by converting the predicative premiss.
The second mood:

Every C is B,
and always: when H is Z, then nothing of C is A,   AE/O
therefore always: when H is Z, then not every B is A.

We prove it by converting the predicative premiss.
The third mood:

Some C is B,
and always: when H is Z, then every C is A,   IA/I
therefore always: when H is Z, then some B is A.

We prove it by converting the predicative premiss.

The fourth mood:

> Every C is B,
> and always: when H is Z, then some C is A.   AI/I

The conclusion will be like that of the third mood. We prove this mood by converting the consequent (of the conditional premiss).

The fifth mood:

> Every C is B,
> and always: when H is Z, then not every C is A,   AO/O
> therefore always: when H is Z, then not every B is A.

We prove it in the following way: 'Always: when H is Z, then not every C is A' and 'every C is B'. Also, 'If not every C is A and every C is B, then not every B is A'. Therefore, 'Always: when H is D, then not every B is A'.

The sixth mood:

> Some C is B,
> and always: when H is Z, then nothing of C is A.   IE/O

The conclusion will be like that of the fifth mood. We prove this mood by converting the predicative premiss.

[(b) *When the connective is universal negative*]

(b) The moods when the connective premiss is negative.

The first mood:

> Every C is B,
> and never: when H is Z, then not every C is A,   AO/E
> therefore never: when H is Z, then nothing of B is A.

The second mood:

> Every C is B,
> and never: when H is Z, then some C is A,   AI/A
> therefore never: when H is Z, then every B is A.

The third mood:

Every C is B,
and never: when H is Z, then nothing of C is A, AE/E
therefore never: when H is Z, then nothing of B is A.

The fourth mood:

Some C is B,
and never: when H is Z, then not every C is A, IO/E
therefore never: when H is Z, then nothing of B is A.

The fifth mood:

Every C is B,
and never: when H is Z, then every C is A, AA/A
therefore never: when H is Z, then every B is A.

The sixth mood:

Some C is B,
and never: when H is Z, then some C is A, II/A
therefore never: when H is Z, then every B is A.

All these moods are proved by turning the connective premiss into an affirmative proposition, and, then, detach the implicant of the result; or by conversion except in one mood.

[(c) *When the connective is particular negative*]

There are also six moods in which the connective premisses are particular propositions.

NOTES

[1] Omitting with F and H *fī 'l-shakl al-awwal wa'l-ḥamliyya makān al-kubrā fī'l-ashkāl 'l-thalātha.*
[2] Reading with G and J *law* for *walaw.*
[3] Reading *alif dāl* for *dāl alif.*
[4] Reading *jīm alif* for *jīm dāl.*
[5] The B.M. MS. reads *wa'l-tālī.* The edited text reads *wa'l-thānī* without giving any further readings.
[6] Reading with G *falākullu* instead of *fakullu.*
[7] The B.M. MS. reads *al-tālī.* The edited text reads *al-thānī* without giving any further readings.
[8] Reading *bā'* for *jīm.*
[9] The B.M. MS. reads *bā'.* The edited text reads *dāl.*

ON THE THREE FIGURES OF THE SYLLOGISMS COMPOUNDED OF A PREDICATIVE AND A CONDITIONAL PROPOSITION WHERE THE PREDICATIVE SHARES [EITHER ITS SUBJECT OR ITS PREDICATE] WITH [THE SUBJECT OR THE PREDICATE] OF THE ANTECEDENT (OF THE CONDITIONAL PROPOSITION)

[*(iii) When the middle term occurs in the antecedent of the conditional and the predicative*]

5   Let us start with the syllogisms in which the predicative proposition is the minor premiss.

[*The first figure*]

[First] the combinations which have the form of the first figure. The condition for production is to have a true or not impossible antecedent. What is peculiar to this figure is this: If the predicative premiss is a universal affirmative proposition, the conclusion will be a particular proposition whose antecedent is a universal statement. The conclusion will be universal if the antecedent is particular. If the predicative premiss and the antecedent (of the conditional premiss) are particular, the antecedent of the conclusion will be universal. When the predicative premiss 10   is negative and the antecedent (of the conditional premiss) is particular, (the syllogism) will be valid if the antecedent of the conclusion is universal affirmative. There will be no production if the conditional premiss and its antecedent are particular propositions.

[*When the connective is universal affirmative*]

The first mood: The condition for its production is that the antecedent must not be impossible.

> Every C is B,
> and always: when every B is A, then H is Z,   AA/A
> therefore sometimes: when every C is A, then H is Z.

If this were not the conclusion then it would be 'Never: when every C is

is A, then H is Z', and 'Always: when B is A, then H is Z'; therefore
'Never: when every C is A, then every C is A'. But 'Every C is B', therefore,
'If every B is A, then every C is A'. This is a contradiction. The same
objection raised against the mood which is similar to it could be raised
here. The answer given there is the same as here.

The second mood:

> Every C is B,
> and always: when nothing of B is A, then H is Z,   AE/E
> therefore sometimes: when nothing of C is A, then H is Z.

If this were not the conclusion, then it would be 'Never: when nothing
of C is A, then H is Z'; add to it 'Always: when nothing of B is A, then
H is Z'; therefore 'Not always: when nothing of B is A, then nothing of
C is A'. But 'Every C is B'. This is a contradiction.

The third mood:

> Every C is B,
> and always: when some B is A, then H is Z,   AI/I or A
> therefore always: when every, or some, C is A,
>   then H is Z,

since C is some of B, therefore, 'If C is A, then some B is A'.

The fourth mood:

> Every C is B,
> and always: when not every B is A, then H is Z,   AO/O or E
> therefore always[1]: when not every C is A, or
>   nothing of C is A, then H is Z.

Since C is some of B.

[*When the connective is universal negative*]

The fifth mood:

> Every C is B,
> and never: when every B is A, then H is Z,   AA/A
> therefore sometimes not: when every C is A, then H is Z.

If this were not the conclusion, then it would be 'Always: when C is A,
then H is Z', add to it 'Never: when every B is A, then H is Z'. We produce 'Never: when every B is A, then every C is A'. This is a contradiction. We also prove it by turning the negative connective premiss into

an affirmative proposition, and then turn the conclusion into a negative proposition.

[339]   The sixth mood:

> Every C is B,
> and never: when some B is A, then H is Z,   AI/I or A
> therefore never: when every, or some, C is A,
>   then H is Z.

Since C is some of B.

The seventh and eighth mood:

> Every C is B,   AE/E
> and never: when nothing of, or not every, B is A,
>   then H is Z,
> therefore never: when nothing of, or not every, C is A, AO/O
>   then H is Z.

Since C is some of B.

[*When the connective is particular affirmative*]

5   The ninth mood:

> Every C is B,
> and sometimes: when every B is A, then H is Z,   AA/A
> therefore sometimes: when every C is A, then H is Z.

If this were not the conclusion, then it would be 'Never: [when every C is A, then H is Z.]' But we said that 'Sometimes: when B is A', then 'Sometimes: when every B is A, then not every C is A'. This is a contradiction.
The tenth mood:

> Every C is B,
> and sometimes: when nothing of B is A, then H is Z,   AE/E
> therefore sometimes: when nothing of C is A, then H is Z.

If this were not the conclusion, then it would be 'Never: [when nothing of C is A, then H is Z'] add to it 'Sometimes: when nothing of B is A,
10   then H is Z'. Therefore, 'Sometimes: when nothing of B is A, then it is not the case that nothing of C is A'. This is a contradiction.

[*When the connective is particular negative*]
          The eleventh mood:

Every C is B,
and not always: when every B is A, then H is Z,   AA/A
therefore not always: when every C is A, then H is Z.

We prove it by *reductio ad absurdum* and by turning (the negative premiss)
into an affirmative proposition.

The twelfth mood:

Every C is B,
and not always: when nothing of B is A, then H is Z, AE/E
therefore not always: when nothing of C is A, then H is Z.

We prove it by *reductio ad absurdum* and by turning (the negative premiss)
into an affirmative proposition.

[*When the connective is universal affirmative*]

The thirteenth mood:

Some C is B,
and always: when some B is A, then H is Z,   II/A
therefore always: when [every] C is A, then H is Z.

For if every C is A and it is true that some C is B, then some B is A.

The fourteenth mood:

Some C is B,
and always: when not every B is A, then H is Z,   IO/E
therefore always: when nothing of C is A, [then H is Z.]

For if [some] C is B and nothing of C is A, then not every B is A.

[*When the connective is universal negative*]

The fifteenth mood:

Some C is B,
and never: when some B is A, then H is Z,   II/A
therefore never: when every C is A, then H is Z.

We prove it in the same way we proved the previous mood.

The sixteenth mood:

Some C is B,
and never: when not every B is A, then H is Z,   AO/E
therefore never: when nothing of C is A, then H is Z.

[*The second figure*]

[Second] the same kind of combinations when they take the form of the second figure. They are unproductive when the antecedent (of the conditional premiss) is a universal affirmative proposition. It is productive when the antecedent is a particular affirmative proposition. If the antecedent is particular, the predicative premiss must agree with it in quality. If it is universal, it must not agree with it in quality, though the antecedent must correspond with reality. If the antecedent is universal, the conclusion will be particular. If it is particular, the conclusion will be universal. If the predicative premiss is universal, the conclusion will be universal, while its antecedent can be either universal or particular. If it is particular, the antecedent of the conclusion should be universal; and it is necessary that the antecedent of the connective premiss must be a universal negative proposition.

[*When the connective is universal affirmative*]
The first mood:

> Every C is B,
> and always: when nothing of A is B, then H is Z,   AE/E
> therefore sometimes: when nothing of C is A, then H is Z.

If this were not the conclusion, then it would be 'Never: [when C is A, then H is Z]. But we said 'Always: when nothing of A is B, then H is Z'. Therefore, 'Never: when nothing of A is B, then nothing of C is A'. But if 'Nothing of A is B' and it is true that 'Every C is B', then 'Nothing of C is A'. This is a contradiction. We can also prove it by converting the antecedent in case it is a universal negative proposition.

[*When the connective is universal negative*]
The second mood:

> Every C is B,
> and never: when nothing of A is B, then H is Z,   AE/E
> therefore not always: when nothing of C is A,
>   then H is Z,

We prove it by *reductio ad absurdum* as we did in the previous mood; or by converting the antecedent (of the conditional premiss); or by turning the negative premiss into an affirmative proposition.

[*When the connective is universal affirmative*]
  The third mood:

> Nothing of C is B,
> and always: when every A is B, then H is Z,   EA/E
> therefore sometimes: when nothing of C is A,
>   then H is Z.

If this were not the conclusion, then it would be 'Never: if nothing of C is A, then H is Z', and 'Always: when every A is B, then H is Z'; therefore 'Never: when every A is B, then nothing of C is A'. But 'If every A is B', and it is true that 'nothing of C is B', then it is true that 'nothing of C is A'. This is a contradiction.

[*When the connective is universal negative*]
  The fourth mood:

> Nothing of C is B,
> and never: when every A is B, then H is Z,   EA/E
> therefore sometimes not: when nothing of C is A,
>   then H is Z.

We prove it in the way described before.

[*The connective is universal affirmative*]
  The fifth mood:

> Every C is B,
> and always: when some A is B, then H is Z,   AI/A or I
> therefore always: when every C is A, or some
>   C is A, then H is Z.

Since some A is B.

[*The connective is universal affirmative*]
  The sixth mood:

> Nothing of C is B,
> and always: when every A is B², or some A is B³,
>   then H is Z.   EA/E
> [therefore always: when nothing of C is A, or some   EI/O
>   C is not A, then H is Z]

Since some A is B.

10   The seventh mood:

> Nothing of C is B,
> and always: when not every A is B, then H is Z,   EO/A or I
> therefore always: when every C is A, or some
> C is A, then H is Z.

Since not every A is B.

[*The connective is universal affirmative*]
    The eighth mood:

> Some C is B,
> and always: when nothing of A is B, then H is Z,   IE/O
> therefore sometimes: if not every C is A⁴, then
> H is Z.

The ninth mood:

15

> Some C is B,
> and never: when nothing of A is B, then H is Z,   IE/O
> therefore not always: when not every C is A,
> then H is Z.

We prove it by *reductio ad absurdum* and other means.⁵

[*When the connective is universal affirmative*]
[*343*]   The tenth mood:

> Not every C is B,
> and always: when [every] A is B, then H is Z,   OA/O
> therefore sometimes: when not every C is A,
> then H is Z.

If this were not the conclusion, then it would be 'Never: [when every C is A, then H is Z]'. But we said that 'Always: when every A is B, then H is Z'. Therefore, 'Never: when every A is B, then every C is not A'. But both are true; therefore, the negation (of the conclusion) is false.

[*The connective is universal negative*]
5   The eleventh mood:

> Not every C is B,
> and never: when every A is B, then H is Z,   OA/O
> therefore not always: when not every C is A,
>   then H is Z.

For if every A is B, then not every C is A and not H is Z. We can prove it by turning the negative premiss into an affirmative proposition.

[*When the connective is universal affirmative*]
   The twelfth mood:

> Some C is B,
> and always: when some A is B, then H is Z,   II/A
> therefore always: when every C is A, then H is Z.

Since some A is B.

[*When the connective is universal negative*]
0   The thirteenth mood:

> Not every C is B,
> and never: when not every A is B, then H is Z,   OO/A
> therefore never: when every C is A, then H is Z.

Since not every A is B.

When the connective premiss is particular negative or universal negative. Let us prove one of its moods:

> Every C is B,
> and not always: when nothing of A is B,   AE/E
>   then H is Z,
> therefore not always: when nothing of C is A,
>   then H is Z.

If this were not the conclusion, then it would be 'Always: [when nothing of C is A, then H is Z'.] When we add to it the premiss 'Not always: When
15 nothing of A is B, then H is Z', it will produce 'Not always: when nothing of A is B, then nothing of C is A'. But 'every C is B'; therefore, 'Always: when nothing of A is B, then nothing of C is A'.
4]   Let us prove another mood:

> Every C is B,
> and sometimes: when nothing of A is B,
>   then H is Z,   AE/E
> therefore sometimes: when nothing of C is A,
>   then H is Z.

It can be prove by *reductio ad absurdum.*

[*The third figure*]

[Third] the same combinations when they take the form of the third figure. These are the most perfect among the combinations. They are unproductive when the predicative premiss is negative. The conclusion will always have a universal antecedent.

[*When the connective is universal affirmative*]

5   The first mood:

> Every C is B,
> and always: when every C is A, then H is Z,   AA/A
> therefore always: when every B is A, then H is Z.

Since every C is A.

The second mood:

> Every C is B,
> and always: when nothing of C is A, then H is Z,
> therefore always: when nothing of B is A,   AE/E
>   then H is Z.

Since nothing of C is A.

The third mood:

> Every C is B,
> and always: when some C is A, then H is Z,   AI/A
10   therefore always: when every B is A, then H is Z.

Since some C is A.

The fourth mood:

> Every C is B,
> and always: when not every C is A, then H is Z,
> therefore always: when nothing of B is A,   AO/E
>   then H is Z.

Since not every C is A.

[*When the connective is universal negative*]
 The fifth mood:

> Every C is B,
> and never: when every C is A, then H is Z, AA/A
> therefore never: when every B is A, then H is Z.

Since every C is A.

The sixth mood:

> Every C is B,
> and never: when nothing of C is A, then H is Z, AE/E
> therefore never: when nothing of B is A,
> then H is Z.

Since nothing of C is A.
 The seventh mood:

> Every C is B,
> and never: when some C is A, then H is Z, AI/A
> therefore never: when every B is A, then H is Z.

Since some C is A.

The eighth mood:

> Every C is B,
> and never: when not every C is A, then H is Z, AO/E
> therefore never: when nothing of B is A,
> then H is Z.

Since not every C is A.

[*The connective is particular affirmative*]
 The ninth mood:

> Every C is B,
> and sometimes: when every C is A, then H is Z, AA/A
> therefore sometimes: when every C is A, then H is Z.

Since every C is A.

The tenth, elevent, twelfth, thirteenth, fourteenth, fifteenth and sixteenth moods have particular connective premisses. They all produce
particular conclusions with universal antecedents. You should know them
by yourself.

[*When the connective is universal affirmative*]
The seventeenth mood:

> Some C is B,
> and always: when some C is A, then H is Z,   II/A
> therefore always: when every B is A, then H is Z.

Since some C is A.

10   The eighteenth mood:

> Some C is B,
> and always: when not every C is A, then H is Z,
> therefore always: when nothing of B is A,   IO/E
>   then H is Z.

Since not every C is A.

[*When the connective is universal negative*]
The nineteenth mood:

> Some C is B,
> and never: when some C is A, then H is Z,   II/A
> therefore never: when every B is A[6], then H is Z.

The twentieth mood:

> Some C is B,
> and never: when not every[7] C is A, then H is Z,   IO/E
> *15*   therefore never: when nothing of B is A[8],
>   then H is Z.

[*346*]   In the twenty-first, twenty-second, twenty-third and twenty-fourth moods both the predicative and the connective premisses are particular. The antecedents and the consequents remain the same.

[(*iv*) *When the predicative is the major premiss*]
The same type of syllogisms when the predicative is the major premiss.

[*The first figure*]
[First] the combinations of these syllogisms which take the form of the first figure. They are unproductive except when the antecedent of the

conditional premiss is negative and the predicative premiss is universal.

[*The connective is universal affirmative*]
    The first mood:

> Always: when nothing of C is B, then H is Z,
> and every B is A,   EA/E
> therefore always: when nothing of C is A, then H is Z.

Since nothing of C is B.
    The second mood:

> Always: when nothing of C is B, then H is Z,
> and nothing of B is A,   EE/A
> therefore always: when every C is A, then H is Z.

Since nothing of C is B.
    The third mood:

> Always: when not every C is B, then H is Z,
> and every B is A,   OA/O or E
> therefore always: when not every, or nothing of,
>   C is A, then H is Z.

Since not every C is B.
    The fourth mood:

> Always: when not every C is B, then H is Z,
> and nothing of B is A,   OE/A or I
> therefore always: when every, or some C is A,
>   then H is Z,

Since not every C is B.
    The fifth, sixth, seventh and eighth moods have negative connective premisses. The conclusions here are the negations of the conclusions in the previous moods. The proofs are the same as in the previous moods.
    There are other eight moods when the connective premiss is particular affirmative or particular negative.

[*The second figure*]
    [Second] the combinations of these syllogisms which take the form of

the second figure. These are unproductive except if the predicative premiss is universal and the antecedent has the same quality as the predicative premiss.

[*When the connective is universal affirmative*]
   The first mood:

> Always: when every C is B, then H is Z,
> and every A is B,   AA/A
> therefore always: when every C is A, then H is Z,

5

Since every C is B.
   The second mood:

> Always: when nothing of C is B, then H is Z,
> and nothing of A is B,   EE/A
> therefore always: when every C is A, then H is Z,

Since nothing of C is B.
   The third mood:

> Always: when some C is B, then H is Z,   IA/A
> and every A is B.

The conclusion will be like in the first mood.
   The fourth mood:

> Always: when not every C is B, then H is Z,   OE/A
> and nothing of A is B.

10

The conclusion will be like in the second mood.
   There are other five moods in which the connective is negative, and other eight moods when the connective is particular negative or particular affirmative.

[*The third figure*]
   [Third] the combinations of these syllogisms which take the form of the third figure.

[*When the connective is universal affirmative*]
   The first mood:

Always: when nothing of C is B, then H is Z,
and every C is A,
therefore always: when nothing of B is A, then H is Z. EA/E

Since nothing of C is B.

The second mood:

Always: when nothing of C is B, then H is Z,
and nothing of C is A,   EE/A
therefore always: when every B is A, then H is Z.

Since nothing of C is B.
The third mood:

Always: when not every C is B, then H is Z,
and every C is A,   OA/E
therefore always: when nothing of B is A, then H is Z.

Since not every C is B.
The fourth mood:

Always: when not every C is B, then H is Z,
and nothing of C is A,   OE/A
therefore always: when every B is A, then H is Z.

Since not every C is B.

There are four other moods in which the connective premiss is universal
negative.

There are also another eight moods in which the connective premiss is
(a) either particular or universal, and (b) either negative or affirmative.

NOTES

[1] Reading *fakullamā* with E and J.
[2] Reading with E *alif bāʾ* for *jīm alif*.
[3] The text reads *jīm alif*.
[4] Reading *jīm alif*, with D, E and J, for *jīm dāl*.
[5] Reading with F and J *wa ghayr* for *huwa ghayr*.
[6] Reading *bāʾ alif* for *jīm alif*.
[7] Reading with D, E, F and J *lā kul* instead of *lāshayʾa min kul*.
[8] Reading with D and E *bāʾ alif* for *jīm alif*.

ON THE THREE FIGURES OF
THE DIVIDED SYLLOGISM[1]

[*The difference between the divided syllogism and induction*]
   Some of these syllogisms [i.e. the divided syllogisms] are compounded
of a separative premiss and several predicative premisses in the same way
5   as in induction. Except that, in induction, the predication is not real
(*ḥaqīqī*) but likely (*tashbīhī*). Also in induction, it is not necessary that
the divisions should be complete, for, as we shall explain to you[2], there
can be an induction from incomplete divisions. I call 'divided syllogism'
(*qiyās muqassam*) that in which the divisions are complete, and the predication, whose subject is the subject of the separative proposition, is real.
In this syllogism the parts of the separative premiss share one of their
parts. Also, the predicative propositions share together one of their parts.
10   This takes the form of the first, second and third figures.

[*A separative and several predicative premisses which share their predicates.
The first figure*]
   [First] the combinations which take the form of the first figure. In these
combinations the parts of the separative premiss must share the same
subject. All the predicative premisses share one predicate, though their
[350]   subjects are different. Moreover, the separative premiss must be an
affirmative proposition which has affirmative parts, the predicative
premisses must be universal and have the same quality, while the conclusion is to be a predicative proposition.
   The first mood:

> Every B is either C or H or Z,
> and every C and H and Z is A,
> therefore every B is A.

5   The second mood:

> Every B is either C or H or Z,
> and nothing of C and H and Z is A,
> therefore nothing of B is A.

The third mood:

> Some B is either C or H or Z,
> and every C and H and Z is A,
> therefore some B is A.

The fourth mood:

> Some B is either C or H or Z,
> and nothing of C and H and Z is A,
> therefore not every B is A.

If the separative premiss is a particular proposition no predicative conclusion will follow.

[*The second figure*]

[Second] the combinations which take the form of the second figure. The condition for production is to have an affirmative separative premiss.

The first mood:

> Every B is either C or H or Z,
> and nothing of A is C, H or Z,
> therefore nothing of B is A.

The second mood:

> Nothing of B is C or H or Z,
> and always either A is C, H or Z,
> [therefore nothing of B is A].

The third mood:

> Some B is either C or H or Z,
> and nothing of A is C, H or Z,
> [therefore some B is not A].

If the separative proposition is particular, no predicative conclusion will follow.

Also, no conclusion will follow if the separative proposition is the major premiss, the major premiss is not a particular proposition, and the relation between the parts is kept the same.

[*The third figure*]

[Third] when the syllogism takes the form of the third figure, the condition for production will be the following: The separative premiss must be universal and the part which the premisses share is universal. I mean that one of the predicative premisses and one of the parts of the separative premiss must be universal.[3]

10   The first mood:

> Always: either C is B or D is B,
> and every C and every D is H,
> therefore some B is H.

Since either one of C or D is some B.

The syllogisms will be unproductive when the separative premiss is negative. For example,

> never: either man is an animal or horse is an animal,
> and every man and every horse is a body.

Again,

15

> never: either man is a soul or the horse is a soul,
> and every man and every horse is a body.

The same conclusion will follow when the separative proposition is the major premiss.

If one of the predicative premisses is a particular proposition, the
[352]   syllogism will be productive. But in this case both parts of the separative premiss should be universal. For example,

> either every C is A or[4] every D is A[5]
> and every C is H[6] and some D is H.

The syllogism is productive if one of the two parts of the separative premiss is particular, or if in the separative premiss a universal part is shared with the predicative premisses. Otherwise it will be unproductive.

An example of the unproductive syllogism is:

5

> always: either every C is B or some D is B,
> and every C is H and some D is H.

The statement 'Every C is B' might not be true at all. Thus, we would be left with a conjunction of two particular propositions, from which follows a conditional conclusion, namely, 'If nothing of D is B, then some B is H'; since 'Every C is B'. The same is true when you convert the order.

If the conditional premiss is a particular proposition, then as you know, the conclusion will not be a universal proposition.

[*A separative premiss and several predicatives not sharing their predicates*]
The combinations in which there is a separative premiss and predicative premisses which do not share the same predicate.

[*The first figure*]
When these are arranged in the form of the first figure, the condition for production is to have an affirmative minor premiss and universal major premisses. For example,

> every D is either C or B,
> and every C is H and every B is Z,
> therefore every D is exclusively either H or Z.

The conclusion does not say that both parts cannot be (true) together, but that D is exclusively either H or Z.
Also,

> Every D is either C or B,
> and nothing of C is H and nothing of B is Z,
> therefore every D is exclusively either not H or not Z.

The other moods can be deduced in the same way.
If the predicative propositions are minor premisses, you say

> every C is H and every D is Z,
> and either every H is A or every Z is A,
> therefore either C is A, viz. when every H is A, or every Z is A.

If among the parts of the separative premiss one is a particular proposition, the syllogism will be unproductive.

If the separative premiss is a negative proposition, the conclusion will be a negative separative proposition. The condition for production is the same as before.

If the parts of the separative premiss are negative, it will be unproductive.

[*The second figure*]

In this figure the predicative premisses must be convertible negative
propositions. They are reduced (*tarji*') to the first figure, and what applies
to the first figure applies to the second.

[*The third figure*]

You can prove this figure, when you know what is inferred from converting the minor premisses; or by introducing an assumption.

[*One separative and one predicative premiss*]

The combinations in which the minor premiss is predicative and the
major is a separative proposition.

[*The first figure*]

The arrangement which the first figure takes:

> Every C is B,
> and always: every B is either H or Z,
> therefore every C is either H or Z.

Somebody may question (the validity) of this figure saying that we
would deduce from 'Every odd is a number' and 'Every number is either
odd or even' the nonsensical conclusion 'Every odd is either odd or even'.
The answer is that this syllogism is productive, but it produces an uninformative conclusion. And to say that a proposition is uninformative is
not the same as saying that it is false. For example if someone deduces
'Every rational is rational' from the premisses 'Every rational is a man'
and 'every man is rational', this will not mean that the mood is unproductive. What led us to this particular result is the premisses which
one chooses according to his own needs, and not the combination. Further, there is no doubt that every odd is either odd or even. For if it is
neither one of them, while at the same time it is considered to be a number,
then it must be other than these two; and this is impossible. If it is both,
then this must mean that both the odd and the even are said of one and
the same thing; and this is all the more impossible. The same is true if the
major and the minor are particular, and if the major is universal negative
or an affirmative with negative parts.

[The second and third figures]

The arrangement which takes the form of the second figure is unproductive. The arrangement taking the form of the third one produces what you know to result from converting the predicative premiss.

You should know that in all the syllogisms compounded of a predicative and a connective premiss, or a predicative and a separative premiss, we can substitute a connective premiss for the predicative if the new premiss shares with the other connective premiss either its antecedent or its consequent. The conclusion, which is in this case a connective and not a predicative proposition, is the same as the one reached when one of the premisses was predicative. You should know that all the conjunctions whose parts have one shared part, imply the conjunctions in which one of the premisses is the same as any one of the premisses in the first, and the other premisses equivalent in force to the second premiss of the first conjunction. However, in this case the shared part will be particular instead of being universal, or an affirmative instead of negative, or the contrary. Further, they will imply those conjunctions whose premisses are inferred from the premisses of the first conjunction. You must try it with every one of the (previous) conjunctions so that you can find out new conjunctions other than those we mentioned, but which are equivalent in force to them.

[Two separative premisses]

We come to the types of syllogisms in which the conditional premisses share one incomplete part. For instance, two separative propositions may have one incomplete part.

[The first figure]

When arranged in the form of the first figure the separative premisses might be affirmative. In this case it would be

> always: either C is D or H is D⁷,
> and every D is either B or A,
> therefore either C is D or H is B or H is A,

or else one of the premisses would be affirmative and the other negative,

> always: either C is D or H is Z,
> and never: either Z is A or Z is B,
> therefore either C is D or not H is B or H is A.

When one of the premisses is particular the conclusion will be particular.

[*The second figure*]

5   When it takes the form of the second figure it will have the following form:

> Always: either C is D or C is H,
> and never: either D or H,
> therefore C is never A.

The conclusion in this case is a predicative proposition.

The second mood is compounded of a negative minor premiss and an affirmative major premiss.

There are two other moods with a particular minor premiss. These have the same force as the predicative syllogisms.

[*The connective is the minor and the separative is the major premiss*]

10   (The divided syllogism) can have a minor connective and a major separative which share with each other either the predicate of the conse-quent[8] and the subject of the separative premiss or the predicate of both.

[*The first figure*]

The moods which take the form of the first figure.
The first mood:

> Always: when C is B, then H is Z,
> and every Z is either D or A,
> therefore always: when C is B, then every H is either D or A.

The second mood:

> Always: when C is B, then H is Z,
> and never Z is either D or A,
15   > therefore always: when C is B, then never Z is either D or A.

There are other two moods when the connective premiss is particular.

[*The second figure*]

[*356*]   The moods which take the form of the second figure.

(1)   Always: when C is B, then H is Z or D,

and nothing of A is Z^9 or D,
therefore always[10]: When C is B, then H is not A.

(2) Always: when C is B, then H is not Z or D,
and every A is Z or D,
therefore always: when C is B, then H is not A.

There are another two moods in which the particular premiss is an affirmative proposition. There are also four moods with negative connective premisses. These can be reduced to the previous ones, and their conclusions are the same as those which follow from the previous moods.

This concludes the summarized discourse on conditional propositions and syllogisms which we included in (this book).

In our native country we came to know a long annotated book on this subject which we have not seen since we left our country and travelled around to look for a means of living. However, it might still be there. After we obtained this part of knowledge nearly 18 years ago we came across[11] a book on conditional (propositions and syllogisms) attributed to the most excellent among later (scholars). It seems to be wrongly imputed to him. It is neither clear nor reliable. It neither gives an extensive survey of the subject nor does it achieve its purpose. It gives a mistaken exposition of conditional propositions, of a large number of syllogisms which accompany them, of the reasons for productivity and sterility, and of the number of moods in the figures. The student should not pay any attention to it – it is distracting and misleading. For the author did not know what makes conditional propositions affirmative, negative, universal, particular, and indefinite; nor did he know how conditional propositions oppose or contradict each other. He also did not know how one conditional proposition can be the subaltern of the other. For he thought that all these things are determined by the parts of the connective proposition. Also, he only treated one kind of conversion in conditional propositions. Further, he did not know of all the (conditional) conjunctions. Rather he confined himself to those conjunctions which are compounded of connective and separative premisses failing to give their full number. On the other hand he gave unnecessary additional conjunctions of connective and separative premisses because he treated certain things which follow one rule as though they follow different rules. He could have given the general rule which all of them follow. It is sufficient to classify these conjunctions according to the difference in quantity and quality of the antecedents and the consequents, for this classification is determined by one rule. Further, he thought of many sterile moods as being productive especially those he enumerated[12] first in the book. He thought that many of these sterile moods are evidently productive, namely, that they need no proof, because they are perfect syllogisms. He also thought of many productive moods as being sterile. Moreover, the proofs of many productive moods, which were in need of proof, were incorrect;

10   for he followed the wrong method. He thought that the antecedent and the consequent of the separative proposition must be distinguished from each other, and as a result of this he gave identical combinations of these propositions but in different figures, for in one figure he puts the middle part at the beginning and in the other at the end. He thought of many conjunctions in which the middle part is not definite as being simple (*basīt*) syllogisms though they are compound (*murakkab*), for in simple syllogisms the conclusion follows necessarily from a definite middle part.

15   All these and other similar considerations in the book are false.

NOTES

[1] In the absence of short vowels it is difficult to tell whether the syllogism described in the following pages is to be called the divided *al-muqassam* or the dividing *al-muqassim* syllogism. However, we preferred the first since A, F and H read *al-munqasim*.

[2] See 561–67.

[3] Omitting *thumma yakūnu al-juz'ī in kāna fi'l-ākhar mushārikan iyyāh.*

[4] Reading with F *wa immā an yakūn.*

[5] Reading *dāl alif* for *dāl bā'.*

[6] Reading *jīm hā'* for *jīm alif.*

[7] Reading *dāl* instead of *zāy.*

[8] Reading with D *al-tālī.*

[9] Reading *zāy* with E, G and J.

[10] Reading *fakullamā* with the majority of MSS.

[11] Reading *waqa'a* with J for *wa waqa'a.*

[12] The B.M. MS. reads *ya'udduhu.* The edited text reads *ba'dahu* without giving any further readings.

BOOK VII

5 ON EQUIPOLLENCE AND OPPOSITION BETWEEN
CONNECTIVE-CONDITIONAL PROPOSITIONS

[*Immediate inference in conditional prepositions*]

What we did until now is to give a general classification of conditional propositions. We did not classify separative propositions according to whether they are compounded of predicative or mixed, namely predicative and conditional, propositions; or of two or more than two parts. Also, we did not classify connective propositions according to their quality, quantity and modality; or according to whether their antecedents or consequents are one of the eight following things: definite, indefinite, dyadic, triadic, absolute, and specific (*munawwaᶜa*) which is to say that they are either necessary or possible or impossible; or according to any similar considerations. Further we did not construct the one from the other giving every kind a specific name. For all this work is worthy of the person who finds the time to occupy himself with what is not necessary. Working out and enumerating these kinds of propositions is, to the person who has the slightest intelligence and who is ready to do it, one of the easiest and simplest works.

However, what is worthy of us is to treat the inferential relations between conditional propositions. We say: What you learned of the affirmative, the negative, the universal, and the particular, will help you to know the contradictory, the contrary, the subcontrary and the subaltern. There is no need to start again teaching you all this. For, in these cases, what applies to predicative propositions applies also to conditional propositions. The person who thinks that (these relations) are determined by the antecedent or the consequent is mistaken. If it were true that the premises which have contradictory consequents contradict each other, then the following two premises would be considered contradictory: 'Always: when Zayd walks, he sees ᶜAmr', and 'Always: when Zayd walks, he does not see ᶜAmr'. But they are not, though in some places the latter follows from the contradictory of the first. The case is more evident when the antecedents are contradictory.

Let us explain the different cases of equipollence (*al-talāzum*). Let us start enumerating the kinds of propositions which belong to the same genus. Let us take those propositions which have quantified parts, for this is more relevant to our purpose. We shall explain how some of these propositions can be inferred from the others. We shall consider only necessary propositions. For absolute and possible propositions you have to wait, if you cannot apply to them the same rules applied in the parallel predicative inferences, for the book called *al-Lawāhiq*.[1] If you make the effort, you will be able to do it yourself. But first you must understand what is significant in every kind and when it is true.

Let us start with connective propositions. We shall give examples of the simple (connective propositions), namely those compounded of two predicative propositions:

(1) When it is compounded of two universal affirmative propositions: Always: when every A is B, then every C is D.

(2) When it is compounded of two affirmative propositions with a universal antecedent: Always: when every A is B, then some C is D.

(3) When it is compounded of two affirmative propositions with a universal consequent: Always: when some A is B, then every C is D.

(4) When it is compounded of two particular affirmative propositions: Always: when some A is B, then some C is D.

(5) When it is compounded of two universal negative propositions: Always: when nothing of A is B, then nothing of C is D.

(6) When it is compounded of two negative propositions with a universal antecedent: Always: when nothing of A is B, then not every C is D.

(7) When it is compounded of two negative propositions with a universal consequent: Always: when not every A is B, then nothing of C is B.

(8) When it is compounded of two particular negative propositions: Always: when not every A is B, then not every C is D.

(9) When it is compounded of two universal propositions with an affirmative antecedent and a negative consequent: Always: when every A is B, then nothing of C is D.

(10) When the antecedent is universal affirmative and the consequent is particular negative: Always: when every A is B, then not every C is D.

(11) When the antecedent is particular affirmative and the consequent is universal negative: Always: when some A is B, then nothing of C is D.

(12) When the antecedent is particular affirmative and the consequent

is particular negative: Always: when some A is B, then not every C is D.

(13) When it is compounded of two universal propositions with a negative antecedent and an affirmative consequent: Always: when nothing of A is B, then every C is D.

(14) When the antecedent is universal negative and the consequent is particular affirmative: Always: when nothing of A is B, then some C is D.

(15) When the antecedent is a particular negative and the consequent is particular affirmative: Always: when nothing of A is B, then some C is D.

(16) When the antecedent is particular negative and the consequent is universal affirmative: Always: when not every A is B, then every C is D.

(17) When the antecedent is particular negative and the consequent is particular affirmative: Always: when not every A is B, then some C is D.

The universal negative propositions:

(1) When it is compounded of two universal affirmative propositions: Never: when every A is B, then every C is D.

(2) When it is compounded of two affirmative propositions and the antecedent is universal: Never: when every A is B, then some C is D.

(3) When it is compounded of two affirmative propositions with a universal consequent: Never: when some A is B, then every C is D.

(4) When it is compounded of two particular affirmative propositions: Never: when some A is B, then some C is D.

(5) When it is compounded of two universal negative propositions: Never: when nothing of A is B, then nothing of C is D.

(6) When it is compounded of two negative propositions with a universal antecedent: Never: when nothing of A is B, then not every C is D.

(7) When it is compounded of two negative propositions with a universal consequent: Never: when not every A is B, then nothing of C is D.

(8) When it is compounded of two particular negative propositions: Never: when not every A is B, then not every C is D.

(9) When it is compounded of two universal propositions with an affirmative antecedent and a negative consequent: Never: when every A is B, then nothing of C is D.

(10) When the antecedent is universal affirmative and the consequent is particular negative: Never: when every A is B, then not every C is D.

(11) When the antecedent is particular affirmative and the consequent is universal negative: Never: when some A is B, then nothing of C is D.

(12) When it is compounded of two universal propositions with a negative antecedent and an affirmative consequent: Never: when nothing of A is B, then every C is D.

(13) When the antecedent is universal negative and the consequent is particular affirmative: Never: when nothing of A is B, then some C is D.

(14) When the antecedent is particular negative and the consequent is universal affirmative: Never: when not every A is B, then every C is D.

(15) When the antecedent is particular negative and the consequent is particular affirmative: Never: when not every A is B, then some C is D.

(16) When the antecedent is particular affirmative and the consequent is particular negative: Never: when some A is B, then not every C is D.

[Universal connective propositions]

A universal affirmative proposition can be inferred from every one of the 16 universal negative propositions. And the two forms are reduceable the one to the other (yarjiʿu baʿduhā ilā baʿd). The method of reduction (al-rujūʿ) is to preserve the quantity of the proposition, change the quality, keep the antecedent as it is, and let it be followed by the contradictory of the consequent. All these types (of connective propositions) are either unrestricted connectives, or implications. In the last case, we will put the word 'implies' in the proposition. The sentence 'Never: when every A is B, then every C is D', if taken in the general sense, will have the same force as the sentence 'Always: when all A is B, then not every C is D'. If it is taken as an implication, it would have the same force (fī quwwati) as the sentence 'Always: when every A is B, then every C is D should not be implied'. You can apply this law to all the other cases. In the same way the sentence 'Never: when some A is B, then every C is D' has the same force as the sentence 'Always: when some A is B, then not every C is D'. Also, the sentence 'Never: when some A is B, then some C is D' has the same force as the sentence 'Always: when some A is B, then nothing of C is D'. Moreover, the sentence 'Never: when some A is B, then every C is D' has the same force as the sentence 'Always: when some A is B, then not every C is D'. And so on. We will give the proof of one of these cases. We shall leave it to you to apply it to the other cases. We say: When the sentence 'Never: when every A is B, then every C is D' is true, the sentence 'Always: when every A is B, then every C is not D' must also be true. If not, then its contradictory 'Not always: when every A is B, then not every

C is D' would be true. This would mean that the negative consequent cannot be implied by all the theses which are posited as antecedents. Therefore, there is at least one posited thesis which does not imply the above consequent, in which case the contradictory of the consequent is true with the above antecedent. Therefore, 'Every A is B' and 'Every C is D'. But we said that 'Never: when every A is B, then every C is D'. This is a contradiction. If it is a negation of implication, then from the sentence 'Never: when every A is B, then every C is D is implied' we infer 'Always: when every A is B, then every C is D is not implied'. If not, then the sentence 'Not always: when every A is B, then every C is D' is not implied' would be true. Therefore, there is one incident in which 'Every C is D' is implied by the posited thesis 'Every A is B'; which is impossible.

To prove that this negative proposition is implied by the affirmative, you must consider both the case of unrestricted connection and the case of implication. For if the sentence 'Always: when every A is B, then every C is D' is true, and it is not true that 'Never: when every A is B, then not every C is D', then the contradictory of the latter, namely 'If every A is B, then not every C is D' is true. Therefore, it is possible to posit 'Every A is B' without having 'Every C is D' as a consequent, for the consequent is 'Every C is not D'. But we said that 'Always: when every A is B'. Thus one must posit as a consequent 'Every C is D'. This is a contradiction, since we assumed that this is either true with it or implied by it. Therefore, the universal connective propositions which agree in quantity, differ in quality, and have contradictory consequents are equipollent (*mutalāzima*). But in those propositions whose negation is true because they indicate that the antecedent when posited makes the consequent false, the contradictories (of the consequents) should be implied by the antecedents. They will be true whether implication is part of the consequent or not. But if (the negative propositions) are of the kind in which negation does not turn the consequent into a false proposition, but prevents it from being implied, regardless of whether it is true or false, and where the implication is to be part of the consequent, then we bring the contradictory of the consequent and make it a consequent which is implied by the antecedent. When the consequent is affirmative, the connective proposition which is inferred from it will be 'Always: when H is Z, then C is D is not implied by it'. If the consequent is negative, it will be: 'Always: when H is Z, then not every C is D is not implied by it'. Which means that 'C is D' can be assumed with it.

Therefore, the best way to put it is to say 'Always: when H is Z, then the assumption C is D is true with it'. It will be true as an assumption and not because it corresponds with reality.[2] From this it can also be shown that it is wrong to think that connective propositions which have contradictory consequents are contradictory, for if we have two universal affirmative propositions whose consequents contradict each other, they can be considered as two contrary propositions. They can both be false but they do not contradict each other, since one of these affirmative propositions is equivalent in force to a universal negative proposition which is contrary to the other proposition. The particular affirmative propositions:

(1) When compounded of two universal affirmative propositions: Sometimes: when every A is B, then every C is D.

(2) When compounded of two affirmative propositions with a particular consequent: Sometimes: when every A is B, then some C is D.

(3) When compounded of two affirmative propositions with a particular antecedent: Sometimes: when some A is B, then every C is D.

(4) When compounded of two particular affirmative propositions: Sometimes: when some A is B, then some C is D.

(5) When compounded of two universal negative propositions: Sometimes: when nothing of A is B, then nothing of C is D.

(6) When compounded of two negative propositions with a particular consequent: Sometimes: when nothing of A is B, then not every C is D.

(7) When compounded of two negative propositions with a particular antecedent: Sometimes: when not every A is B, then nothing of C is D.

(8) When compounded of two particular negative propositions: Sometimes: when not every A is B, then not every C is D.

(9) When compounded of two universal propositions with an affirmative antecedent and a negative consequent: Sometimes: when every A is B, then nothing of C is D.

(10) When the antecedent is particular affirmative and the consequent is universal negative: Sometimes: when some A is B, then nothing of C is D.

(11) When the antecedent is universal affirmative and the consequent is particular negative: Sometimes: when every A is B, then not every C is D.

(12) When the antecedent is particular affirmative and the consequent

is particular negative: Sometimes: when some A is B, then not every C is D.

(13) When compounded of two universal propositions with a negative antecedent and an affirmative consequent: Sometimes: when nothing of A is B, then every C is D.

(14) When the antecedent is particular negative and the consequent is universal affirmative: Sometimes: when not every A is B, then every C is D.

(15) When the antecedent is universal negative and the consequent is particular affirmative: Sometimes: when nothing of A is B, then some C is D.

(16) When the antecedent is particular negative and the consequent is particular affirmative: Sometimes: when not every A is B, then some C is D.

The particular negative propositions:

(1)   Not always: when every ..., when every ....
(2)   Not always: when some ..., then every ....
(3)   Not always: when every ..., then some ....
(4)   Not always: when some ..., then some ....
(5)   Not always: when nothing of ..., then nothing of ....
(6)   Not always: when not every ..., then nothing of ....
(7)   Not always: when nothing of ..., then not every ....
(8)   Not always: when not every ..., then not every ....
(9)   Not always: when every ..., then nothing ....
(10) Not always: when every ..., then not every ....
(11) Not always: when some ..., then nothing of ....
(12) Not always: when some ..., then not every ....
(13) Not always: when nothing of ..., then every ....
(14) Not always: when nothing of ..., then some ....
(16) Not always: when not every ..., then every ....
(17) Not always: when not every ..., then some ....

[*Particular connective propositions*]

We say: What is true of the equipollence between universal propositions is true of the equipollence between particular propositions. From
the sentence 'Not always: when every ..., then every ...', we infer 'Some-

times: when every ..., then not every ...'. Or else we would infer its contradictory, namely 'Never: when every ..., then not every ...'. From the latter we infer 'Always: when every ..., then every ...'. But we said 'Not always: when every ..., then every ...'. This is a contradiction. In the same way we prove the rest. A similar proof can be used to prove that from the above affirmative we infer a negative proposition. If a negative conclusion were not inferred, then it would be correct to infer its contradictory, namely 'Always: when every ..., then every ...'. From this we infer 'Never: when every ..., then not every ...'. But we said that 'Sometimes: if every ..., then not every ...'. This is a contradiction. You must consider the two cases when the connective proposition is unrestricted and when it is an implication.

What we said above also shows the falsity of the opinion that the connective propositions which have contradictory consequents are contradictory; for the last two particular propositions can be true together. But the negative proposition is equivalent in force to an affirmative whose consequent contradicts the consequent of the affirmative proposition. Also, the affirmative is equivalent in force to a negative whose consequent contradicts the consequent of the negative proposition. Thus, we have two affirmative and negative propositions with contradictory consequents which are true. You learned before that when the universal proposition is true, the subaltern which is a particular proposition and its implicant must be true; and if the particular is false, the universal and its implicant must be false. But neither case is convertible. You must note that an additional requirement is needed when the connective is an implication.

NOTES

[1] This book was, in Avicenna's words, planned to be a detailed supplement to *al-Shifā'*. But, from what we know of his extant works, it seems that Avicenna did not write it. Cf. *al-Shifā', al-Madkhal*, eds. C. Anawati and others, Cairo, 1952, p. 10. See also *Manṭiq al-Mashriqiyyīn*, Cairo, 1910, p. 4.

[2] Reading with H *fī'l-fard faqaṭ lā fī'l-wujūd*.

CHAPTER TWO

ON THE OPPOSITION BETWEEN SEPARATIVE-
AND CONNECTIVE-CONDITIONAL PROPOSITIONS
AND THE STATE OF THEIR EQUIPOLLENCE

5   Let us enumerate now the different types of separative propositions.

The particular affirmative propositions:

(1)   Always: either every A is B, or every C is D.
(2)   Always: either some ..., or every ....
(3)   Always: either every ..., or some ....
(4)   Always: either some ..., or some ....
(5)   Always: either nothing of ..., or nothing of ....
(6)   Always: either not every ..., or nothing ....
(7)   Always: either nothing of ..., or not every ....
(8)   Always: either not every ..., or not every ....
(9)   Always: either every ..., or nothing of ....
(10) Always: either some ..., or nothing of ....
(11) Always: either not every ..., or every ....
(12) Always: either some ..., or not every ....
(13) Always: either nothing of ..., or every ....
(14) Always: either not every ..., or every ....
(15) Always: either nothing of ..., or some ....
(16) Always: either not every ..., or some ....

The universal negative propositions:

(1)   Never: either every ..., or every ....
(2)   Never: either some ..., or every ....
(3)   Never: either every ..., or some ....
(4)   Never: either: some ..., or some ....
(5)   Never: either nothing of ..., or nothing of ....
(6)   Never: either not every ..., or nothing of ....
(7)   Never: either nothing of ..., or not every ....
(8)   Either not every ..., or not every ....
(9)   Never: either every ..., or nothing of ....
(10) Never: either some ..., or nothing of ....

10   (11) Never: either every ..., or not every ....
       (12) Never: either some ..., or not every ....
       (13) Never: either nothing of ..., or every ....
       (14) Never: either not every ..., or every ....
       (15) Never: either nothing of ..., or some ....
       (16) Never: either not every ..., or some ....

The particular affirmative propositions:

       (1)   Sometimes: either every ..., or every ....
15   (2)   Sometimes: either every ..., or some ....
[375] (3)   Sometimes: either some ..., or every ....
       (4)   Sometimes: either some ..., or some ....
       (5)   Sometimes: either nothing of ..., or nothing of ....
       (6)   Sometimes: either nothing of ..., or every ....
       (7)   Sometimes: either not every ..., or nothing of ....
5   (8)   Sometimes: either not every ..., or not every ....
       (9)   Sometimes: either every ..., or nothing of ....
       (10) Sometimes: either every ..., or not every ....
       (11) Sometimes: either some ..., or nothing of ....
       (12) Sometimes: either some ..., or not every ....
       (13) Sometimes: either nothing of ..., or every ....
       (14) Sometimes: either nothing of ..., or some ....
10   (15) Sometimes: either not every ..., or every ....
       (16) Sometimes: either not every ..., or some ....

The particular negative propositions:

       (1)   Not always: either every ..., or every ....
       (2)   Not always: either every ..., or some ....
       (3)   Not always: either some ..., or every ....
       (4)   Not always: either some ..., or some ....
       (5)   Not always: either nothing of ..., or nothing of ....
       (6)   Not always: either nothing of ..., or not every ....
[376] (7)   Not always: either not every ..., or nothing of ....
       (8)   Not always: either not every ..., or not every ....
       (9)   Not always: either every ..., or nothing of ....
       (10) Not always: either every ..., or not every ....

(11) Not always: either some ..., or nothing of ....
(12) Not always: either some ..., or not every ....
(13) Not always: either nothing of ..., or every ....
(14) Not always: either nothing of ..., or some ....
5   (15) Not always: either not every ..., or every ....
(16) Not always: either not every ..., or some ....

[*Inferences from separatives to connectives and vice versa*]

After enumerating these propositions, let us discuss first whether connective and separative propositions are equipollent.[1] We say: From real separative propositions, which are affirmative and have affirmative parts, we infer the connective propositions whose antecedents are the contradictories of any part of the separative, and whose consequents are the consequents of the separative. There is one condition here, namely that the propositions must have the same quality and quantity. For example, from
10 the sentence 'Always: either every A is B or every C is D' we infer 'Always: when not every A is B, then every C is D' and 'Always: when not every C is D, then every A is B'. We will prove one of these inferences since the case is the same in both.

We say: From the above separative proposition we infer not just a connective proposition but a connective in which the antecedent implies the consequent. If this is true of implication then it should be true of the unrestricted connective proposition which is a general case of the former.
15 For what is true of the special case is true of the general. We say: If we do not infer 'Always: when not every A is B, then every C is D is implied' then we infer its contradictory, that is 'Not always: when not every A is
'7] B, then every C is D is implied'. From the last connective proposition we infer 'Sometimes; when not every A is B, then every C is D is not implied'. This makes it possible that both 'Every A is B' and 'Every C is D' may not be true. But the affirmative separative proposition prevents the denial of both parts together, for when we posit one of them, we necessarily deny the other. And this connective proposition makes it possible that both
5 parts can be denied. This is a contradiction. We can also infer from ['Always: either every A is B, or every C is D'] any (connective) which agrees with it in quantity and quality, and in which the consequent is the contradictory of any of its parts and the antecedent is the same as the other part; like, for example, the sentence 'Always: when every A is B,

then not every C is D'. If we do not infer the above sentence, we should
infer 'Not always: when every A is B, then not every C is D'. But from
the last sentence follows 'Sometimes: if every A is B, then every C is D'
which permits the possibility of both parts being true; while the separative
does not permit this. This is a contradiction. What is said above explains
the case of the affirmative propositions whose parts are affirmative. We
proved the universal propositions among them, and in the same way we
can prove the particular. However, the converse (ʿaks) of the above case,
namely the case in which the separative propositions will be true when the
above connective propositions are true, is not necessary; for if it were
necessary, then every one of these connective propositions will be convertible if the parts of the proposition which express real conflict are convertible.

The consequent in the affirmative connective proposition could be
implied by sentences other than the antecedent. For example, 'Always:
when man moves or does not move, in both cases, it follows necessarily
that he is a body'. To prove this we say: Let the separative [which we
assume it is inferred from the connective] have the same antecedent as
the connective. For example, we infer 'Either every A is B or every C is
D' from 'Always: when every A is B, then not every C is D'. We say:
We do not infer 'Either every A is B or every C is D' from the above
connective proposition. For if we do, then we will also infer the following
connective proposition, 'Always: when not every C is D, then every A
is B', [viz. the converse of the above connective proposition], but this
conversion is not universally true. Moreover, it would be necessary to
infer its converse if the inferred proposition contradict the antecedent of
the proposition from which it is inferred. But we do not necessarily infer
its converse.

When one or both parts [of the separative proposition] are negative,
we can infer those connective propositions in which the antecedent contradicts the antecedent of the separative, and in which the consequent
agrees with the consequent of the separative. But we cannot infer a
connective proposition whose antecedent agrees with the antecedent of
the separative, and whose consequent contradicts the consequent of the
separative, as it is the case with those propositions which have affirmative
parts. For example, from the sentence 'Always: either nothing of A is B
or nothing of C is D' we infer 'Always: when some A is B, then nothing

of C is D' and 'Always: when some C is D, then nothing of A is B'. To prove it we say: If this (inference) is not valid, then we would infer 'Not always: when some C is D, then nothing of A is B'. From this we infer 'Sometimes: when some C is D, then some A is B'. But the separative does not permit at all the case in which both parts (of the last connective proposition) are true. This is a contradiction. We said before that we cannot infer a connective proposition whose antecedent agrees with the antecedent of the proposition from which it is inferred; for when we say 'Always: when it is not a plant' we can neither imply that it is inanimate nor that it is not inanimate. Also the implication here can be converted. For we can imply the contradictory of the antecedent when we posit the contradictory of the consequent. But the above conversion leads only to what we said. You know that the above connection is not just a simple connection but an implication. Notice that the affirmed separative must not have both its parts true as in the previous case, the implication must be part of the consequent, and the proof here is the same as before.

We say: It could be argued that the above connective can be inferred from the above separative proposition, for if it is true that 'Always: when some A is B, then nothing of C is D' then we can infer 'Either nothing of A is B or nothing of C is D'. If at a certain time and in a particular state this were not valid, then we could specify this time and state; which is to say that there is a case in which A is B and C is D. Thus, it would not be true to say that when A is B, nothing of C is D nor is it true to say that wen C is D, nothing of A is B. But we assumed that when A is B, then nothing of C is D. This is a contradiction. A contradiction like this did not follow in the previous case because in the previous case we cannot infer from the fact that the negation of the separative proposition is true, that both its parts are true; since the above separative can be true though both its parts are false. However, in this case the negation of the separative proposition is true only when it is possible that both its parts are true. Further, in this case it is not necessary that the parts of the connective remain as they are after the connective proposition is converted. But it is necessary that the contradictory of its consequent should be implied by the contradictory of the antecedent. In the same way described above you can examine the case where one of the premisses is affirmative and the other is particular. Once you find the law, you can test it in every one of the cases.

[Inferences involving separative propositions]

We will discuss now equipollence among separative propositions themselves. We say: From the affirmative separative which has affirmative
parts we infer those separative propositions which agree with it in quantity, differ in quality, and has an antecedent which contradicts its antecedent. For example, when the separative propositions are universal, we
infer from 'Always: either every A is B or every C is D' that 'Never: either
not every A is B or every C is D', and 'Never: either not every C is D or
every A is B'. Let us prove the first one, for the second follows the same
rule. We say: If [the disputant] considers the statement 'Never: either every A is not B or every C is D' false, then its contradictory, namely 'Sometimes: either not every A is B or every C is D' will be true. From the last
proposition we infer 'Sometimes: when every A is B, then every C is D',
in which case both parts can possibly be true. But the separative does not
allow this. However, it is not the case that when 'Never: either not every A
is B or every C is D' is true, 'Always: either every A is B or every C is D' will
be true; for a separative proposition can have an impossible part though
this part is not in conflict with the other – as when you say 'Never: either
not every man is an animal or void exists or does not exist'. For from this
proposition we cannot infer 'Either man exists or void exists, or does not
exist'. But it can be true that 'Not: either the thing is not an animal or it is
white', without necessarily inferring that 'The thing is either an animal
or it is white'. The same applies to [separative] particular propositions.
For example, from 'Sometimes: either every A is B or every C is D' we
infer 'Not always: either not every A is B or every C is D'. If this were not
true, its contradictory 'Always: either not every A is B or every C is D'
will be true; from which we infer 'Never: either every A is B or every C
is D'. But we said 'Sometimes: either every A is B or every C is D'. This
is a contradiction. But we cannot infer 'Sometimes: either every A is B
or every C is D' from 'Not always: either every A is B or every C is D',
for the same reasons we gave before. These are the inferential relations
between separative propositions.

*[Back to the subject of immediate inference from separative to connective
propositions and vice versa]*

We say: Every connective proposition can be inferred from an affirmative separative proposition, since the negation of the separative

[380]

5

10

15

[381]

5

10

which we infer from the separative proposition itself, is inferred from the connective proposition. For example, the statement 'Never: either some A is B or nothing of C is D' can be inferred from the statement 'Always: either nothing of A is B or nothing of C is D'. From this we infer the following connective proposition 'Always: when some A is B, then nothing of C is D'. We prove it in the following way: From the above connective proposition we infer the statement 'Never: either some A is B or nothing of C is D'. If not, we infer its contradictory, namely 'Sometimes: either some A is B or nothing of C is D'. From this we infer the following connective proposition 'Sometimes: if nothing of A is B, then nothing of C is D', and from this we infer 'Not always: when some A is B, then nothing of C is D'. But we said 'Always: when some A is B, then nothing of C is D'. This is a contradiction.

From this account you notice that from the affirmation of every connective proposition we infer the negation of that separative proposition which agrees with the connective in quantity, quality and the antecedent. The kind of proof we shall give below will show you this. But you cannot infer the negation of the separative from the affirmation of the connective, for though it is true to say 'Never: either some people are writers or some pairs are even', we do not infer from it that 'Always: when some people are writers, then none of the pairs are even'. We infer these negative propositions from the negations of the connective propositions, which can, in turn, be inferred from the negations of the affirmative propositions in which the antecedent contradicts the antecedent of the affirmative propositions. From the last one we infer the negation of the separative propositions. They can also be inferred from the separative propositions which oppose the negation of the separative propositions we inferred. Therefore, from every negation of a connective proposition we infer the universal negation of the separative proposition which has an antecedent that contradicts the antecedent of the negation of the connective. For when we say 'Never: when every A is B, then every C is D', we infer 'Never: either not every A is B or every C is D'. If not, then we infer 'Sometimes: either not every A is B or every C is D'. From this we infer 'Sometimes: when every A is B, then every C is D'. This is a contradiction.

Let us see if we can infer 'Never: if every A is B, then every C is D' from 'Never: either not every A is B or every C is D'. Let us posit that 'Never: either not every A is B or every C is D'. Let us take an example in words:

'Never: either man is not animal or void does not exist'. This as you know
is true. But it does not imply the connective-conditional which expresses

5   implication, namely 'Never: if man is an animal, then void does not exist'.
But if the connective proposition expresses the general sense of connection, then it seems that we can infer it; for if this were true and the statement 'Never: when every A is B, then every C is D' were not true, its contradictory 'Sometimes: when every A is B, then every C is D' would be
true. If 'Every A is B' and 'Every C is D' are both true at a certain time and
under a certain condition, then when this condition is given, we can assert

10   that 'If not every A is B, then not every C is D'. But we said 'Never So'.
This is a contradiction. You have known that from affirmative separative
propositions we infer the following connective propositions: an affirmative which has an antecedent that contradicts the antecedent of the
separative proposition, while agreeing with it in quantity and quality.
Also the negative, which is equivalent in force to that affirmative, differs in
quality, agrees with the affirmative in the antecedent and has a consequent
that contradicts its consequent. It differs from the separative in quality [2]

15   and in having an antecedent and a consequent that contradict the antecedent and the consequent of the separative, though it agrees with it in
quantity. These inferences are not convertible. Therefore the connective

[384]   propositions are not equivalent (tukāfi') to the separative propositions.
But the negation of separative propositions are inferred from these affirmative propositions, and from what is inferred from the affirmative. We
infer the affirmation of these separative propositions that agree with the
affirmation of (the connective) in quantity and contradict their antecedents; and the affirmation of the connective propositions which agree with
it in (a) quantity, (b) the antecedent and (c) the consequent; and the negation of the connective propositions which agree with it in (a) quantity, (b)

5   quality and (c) the antecedent, but whose consequent contradicts the
consequent of the connective.

You know now the states of equipollence in [conditional propositions].
From what you learned of the particular, universal, the affirmative and
the negative conditional propositions, you can know the contradictory,
contrary, subcontrary [3] and the subaltern. There is no need to enumerate
them, and therefore extend our discussions. Also, you can consider the

10   way their antecedents or consequents are related in every one of the above
relations. But there is no use in this. The useful thing to do is to consider

these relations in respect of the connection or the separation which a proposition expresses. Also, when you know the actual contradictory, what is inferred from it, and its converse, if it has a converse as in connective propositions, then you would know the potential contradictory, the potential contrary, the potential subcontrary and the potential subaltern. For these relations are either actual or potential. For example, when we say 'Always when so, then so' what actually contradicts it is 'Not always when so, then so', and what potentially contradicts it is 'Sometimes if so, then so'. There is not much benefit in discussing these inferences, especially the relation of contradiction, when the premises are absolute or necessary. We better postpone these discussions to *al-Lawāhiq*, for the apparent meaning of what we said is enough to lead to a useful result.

NOTES

[1] The equipollence between separative propositions will be discussed in 379, 17–18 and 380, 1–10.

[2] Reading *al-kayf* for *al-kamm.*

[3] Reading *wa mā tahta al-mutadāddāt* for *wa mā tammat al-mutadāddāt.*

ON THE CONVERSION OF THE
CONNECTIVE PROPOSITION

In the subject of conversion we shall only deal with the conversion of the connective proposition. We say: There are two kinds of conversion in the connective proposition. The one is the *conversion simpliciter*, and the other is the *conversion per contrapositionem*. In the *conversion simpliciter* you turn the antecedent into a consequent, and the consequent into an antecedent, while keeping the quality as it is. In this case truth will be transmitted. In the *conversion per contrapositionem* you put the contradictory of both the antecedent and the consequent.

Let us start with the *conversion simpliciter*. We say: From stating that 'Never: when every A is B, then every C is D', it will evidently follow that 'Never: when every C is D, then every A is B'. If this were not so, then let at one time 'Every C is D' be together with 'Every A is B'. Therefore sometimes 'Every A is B' and 'Every C is D' can be together. But we said that this can never be the case. However, this creates a problem in some cases – as when we say 'Never: if man exists, then void exists'. For it is not true to say 'Never: if void exists then man exists' if the statement is meant to indicate that when the antecedent is assumed, the consequent will not be connected with it by chance. But if it meant to indicate the negation of implication, then the above conversion will not be valid. But we say: In case the consequent is impossible the proposition ['Never: if every A is B, then every C is D'] cannot be converted into a negation of chance connection, but into a negation if implication, and in this case the above mentioned proof of conversion will not hold; since we cannot assume its affirmation nor can we specify it in existence. Also, the negation, and the affirmation of chance connection is more general than the affirmation of implication.

5

10

15

[*386*]

5

BOOK VIII

5

ON THE DEFINITION OF
THE EXCEPTIVE SYLLOGISM

[*The difference between exceptive and conjunctive syllogisms*]

After we discussed both kinds of conjunctive syllogisms, the predicative and the conditional, it is necessary to turn now to exceptive syllogisms. We say: The difference between the exceptive and the conjunctive syllogism is that the premisses in the exceptive syllogism actually contain either the *quaesitum* or its contradictory; while the premisses of the conjunctive syllogism contain them potentially – as when we say

10
>   every man is an animal,
>   and every animal is a body,
>   therefore, every man is a body.

In this conjunctive syllogism neither the *quaesitum* nor its contradictory are actually stated in the premisses. But when we say

>   If man is an animal, then he is a body,
>   but man is an animal,
>   therefore man is a body;

or when we say

>   If man is not a body, then he is not an animal,
>   but man is an animal,
>   therefore man is a body;

we find that in the first syllogism the *quaesitum*, which is affirmative, is
15 actually stated as the consequent [of the conditional premiss]; and in the
•90] second its contradictory is actually stated as the antecedent[1] [of the conditional premiss].

We say: Every exceptive syllogism is compounded of a conditional and an exceptive premiss, and the latter premiss must be any part of the conditional premiss or its contradictory, the conclusion must be the other part or its contradictory, and the conditional premiss is either a connective or a separative proposition. Let us start with those which have a

5   connective-conditional premiss. We say: What we except [i.e. assert] can either be in the side of the antecedent or in the side of the consequent.

[*When the connective expresses complete implication; (i) we assert the antecedent deducing the consequent*]

In the first indemonstrable (*mashhūr*) mood of this syllogism the exceptive premiss is the same as the antecedent of the connective premiss, the connective premiss expresses what we call 'complete connection' or 'complete implication', and the conclusion is the same as the consequent of the conditional premiss. Let us see now what happens to this kind of exceptive syllogisms in case the connective premiss expresses chance connection and in case it expresses implication. We say: If the connective proposition expresses chance connection, then nothing new will be known *10*   from the syllogism; for the consequent in this case is not something implied by the assumed antecedent, rather it is taken to be connected [by chance] with the antecedent. The reason is that it is known that the consequent in itself, as well as the antecedent, are true; and what is known to correspond with reality does not need to be deduced syllogistically. Therefore, the consequent must be in itself something unknown, but we need to know that it follows or that it is implied by the antecedent. Thus, when we know that the antecedent corresponds with reality, we will know that the consequent corresponds with reality – as when we say 'If A is B, then C is D', where 'C is D' is already known. If we assert 'A is *15*   B', we conclude that 'C is D'. But in this case nothing new is known. However, if 'C is D' is unknown, and we know that it follows 'A is B', then, when 'A is B' is found to be true, 'C is D' will also be true. Therefore, if the conditional premiss in the exceptive syllogism is a connective proposition, then it must be one which expresses implication.

[*When the connective is incomplete implication; (i) we assert the antecedent deducing the consequent*]

[*391*]   In the second indemonstrable mood the exceptive premiss is the same as the antecedent (of the connective premiss), and the connective premiss expresses 'incomplete connection' or 'incomplete implication'. This mood is the same as the first except that in this mood the implication expressed is incomplete. It is unnecessary to distinguish between this mood and the first and, therefore, treat it as a new mood. In case the

antecedent (of the conditional premiss) is excepted [i.e. asserted], it is irrelevant to point out the distinction between the connective proposition which expresses complete implication and the one which expresses in-
5 complete implication. It will be more correct to say: the exception [i.e. assertion] of the antecedent of the connective premiss, whatever kind of connection this premiss expresses, produces the consequent of the con-nective premiss. The reasoning in this case is evident and the syllogism is perfect (*kāmil*). The distinction between complete and incomplete im-plication is to be noticed in case we except the contradictory of the antecedent; or when we except the consequent (of the conditional pre-miss).

[*The connective is complete implication; (ii) we assert the consequent de-ducing the antecedent*]

In the third indemonstrable mood the excepted premiss is the con-sequent (of the connective premiss), and the connective premiss is sup-posed to express 'complete implication'. In this mood we produce the antecedent (of the connective premiss). *They said:* In this mood the pro-
10 duction is not self-evident, it is rather an imperfect syllogism. It will be-come perfect if we bear in mind that 'complete implication' is the case where implication is convertible. Thus, we are allowed to turn the con-sequent into an antecedent and the antecedent into a consequent. There-fore, we can assert what was before a consequent and is now an antecedent producing what was an antecedent and is now a consequent. But what the just man must believe is that when we discuss the form of the syllogism, we must discuss the premiss as an assumed premiss with no regard to its
15 subject-matter whether it is this particular thing or that; since this kind of discussion is not concerned with the premiss as such. When we make the statement 'If A is B, then C is D' a premiss in a syllogism, we must
[92] study the form of this premiss and what this form requires. But to say that its consequent can be converted into an antecedent is something which does not concern the form of the premiss but its content. It is the same as the discussion whether the predicate in a universal affirmative proposition is identical (*musāwin*) with the subject or not. If this kind of discussion is relevant to the inquiry into the rules which govern the pre-
5 misses and the syllogisms, then it can be argued that it is also relevant, when treating predicative syllogisms, to say that some universal affirma-

tive propositions express 'complete predication' and others express 'in-complete predication' or something of this sort; or to say that when the predicate and the subject are identical, we could convert them without changing the quantity or the quality of the proposition, while when they are not identical, the universal affirmative becomes a particular proposition. One could also say that in the third figure of [predicative syllogisms] if the subject and predicate in the minor premiss are identical, then the conclusion will be a universal affirmative proposition. Again, one could say that in the third and fourth moods of the first figure if the minor term is not distributed in the middle, then the conclusion will be a universal proposition. No inquiry of this kind was carried out because they treated the premiss as a proposition consisting of a subject and a predicate and has a certain quality and quantity; and paid attention to those things which are determined by these considerations. They refused to discuss any of the considerations which are determined by something which is not part of the premiss as such, or which concerns certain subject-matters and not others. The same applies to connective-conditional propositions. What is to be considered in these propositions is the protasis, or the antecedent, and the consequent as such; and what follows in a general way from this with no regard to the subject-matter. We should not pay any attention to that which is neither contained in nor is it an inseparable (part) of the preserved form of the connective premiss – when this is regarded as one which has an antecedent and a consequent – and which changes without making a necessary change in that form. For to know that a statement is a connective proposition which has an antecedent and a consequent and whose consequent is connected with its antecedent in this or that way, does not entail any knowledge of whether the consequent and the antecedent are convertible or not, since this is not known from the form of the premiss but it can possibly be known from outside. It is also not one of the necessary relations which we know from outside, like the necessary following of the converse from the convert; but only a possible characteristic that may belong to one subject-matter and not to the other. Therefore, we must not pay any attention to these proliferations. If someone knows from outside, and not from the form of the premiss, that the consequent and the antecedent are convertible, then he does not need this kind of syllogism, since he is allowed to make the implicate the antecedent of the (conditional premiss).

This situation is different from [the one we met in predicative syllogisms] where the second and the third figures are used[2] in spite of the fact that they were reduced to the first. For as you learned there, what usually comes first to the mind is that 'Nothing of A is B' and afterwards it may or may not come to the mind that it must be[3] 'Nothing of B is A'. In any case that one comes first to the mind. Therefore, we do not need conversion here, since (the proposition) will be in itself productive once another premiss is added to it. The same applies to the particular affirmative premiss. Therefore, what we said shows that it is useful to use the other two figures [i.e. the second and the third]; though the converse follows necessarily from the convert, as we already explained to you. But here when we say 'If A is B, then C is D' the form of the proposition does not require that when 'C is D', then it necessary that 'A is B', since this is not a necessary characteristic which belongs to the form of the above proposition. Rather it is something which you already knew, and which does not follow necessarily from the premiss. Thus, if this [namely that if C is D, then it must follow necessarily that A is B] is known in itself and it is in your mind, then when you except 'C is D', you will actually except the antecedent; since ('C is D') is what came first to your mind, without the mediation of anything else. If whenever the statement 'If every A is B, then C is D' comes first to your mind, its converse, namely the statement in which the antecedent is produced by the consequent which is actually the antecedent of what came first to your mind, will follow necessarily, then you will say that since this came first to the mind it will be followed necessarily by another and a third. But the third follows necessarily from the first. Therefore, I should not trouble myself by allowing my mind to move to the first and from the first to the third, which is the second in our chain of reasoning; but, in using it, I will let it move once to the second, as though it is the first, without paying any attention to the first syllogism. Though I need to (move to the first) in case I want to prove that it is a conclusive syllogism. Thus, by so doing, apart from cutting short part of your reasoning, you will learn something, and the process will be the same as that used in the moods of the second and the third figure [of predicative syllogisms]. But this is not the case at all. For you need to attend to this conversion in order to be able to construct the syllogism, because you need to know that the implication is complete; which is to say that you need to know and to make yourself aware of the fact that this thing which is a consequent takes precedence of that which is now the antecedent. Thus, what you brought to your mind would be the statement 'If C is D, then A is B'. And when you except 'C is D', you except the antecedent of the first premiss that came actually to your mind. Therefore, one cannot ignore stating the first premiss as part of the syllogism. The cases where we mostly ignore[4] it are those in which the premiss can only remind us of something which does not follow necessarily from it, but it happened to be with it by accident.

[*The connection is incomplete implication; (ii) we deny the consequent deducing the denial of the antecedent*]

In the fourth indemonstrable mood, we assert the contradictory of the consequent in the conditional premiss that expresses 'incomplete implication'.[5] In this case we produce the contradictory of the antecedent – as when you say

> If C is D, then A is B,
> but A is not B,
> therefore C is not D.

This is not a perfect syllogism. We prove it in the following way: If the (conclusion) is not 'C is not D', then it will be 'C is D'. But if 'C is D', then 'A is B'. Therefore, if it is not the case that 'C is not D', then 'A is B'. But we assumed that if 'C is not D', then 'A is B'. Therefore, we assert both 'A is B' and 'A is not B'. This is a contradiction.

There is no need to remind you again, after the long discussion we held before, that if the connective premiss expresses chance connection, then the conclusion of the above mood will not necessarily follow.

Some said: The consequent can be sometimes compounded of many parts though we can consider them as one thing – as when they say 'The planet is neither heavy nor light'. Thus, when we assert its contradictory, we assert the whole sentence, namely neither heavy nor light. Our view on this point is that if by saying 'Neither heavy nor light' we want to negate both (that it is heavy and that it is light), then it is enough to assert the contradictory of the one to produce the contradictory of the other. But if we mean that the planet's weight is in between, a fact which is expressed by negating both heavy and light, then the consequent must be considered as one and not many things. However, it is enough to except

5   one of them. For if you affirm one of them, you must deny the case that
its weight is in between; as when we deny one of the conditions, we must
deny the rest of the parts together. For the negation of one of the parts
is potentially the negation of the rest taken together as such.

[*The connective is incomplete implication. No production when the ante-*
cedent is denied]
    In the fifth indemonstrable mood we except the contradictory of the
antecedent in the connective premiss which expresses 'incomplete implication'. The widely-accepted view is that this mood is inconclusive.
For in case the consequent is implied not only by the antecedent but also
by other statements, then it will not be necessary to deny the consequent
whenever the antecedent is denied, since in this case the consequent exists
0   with either statements – as when they say 'If Zayd is moving, then he is
changing' and except that 'He is not moving'. We cannot conclude from
this that he changes or not. For if he is not moving he may or may not
change in quality.

[*Or when the consequent is asserted*]
    In the sixth mood we except the consequent of the connective premiss
which expresses 'incomplete implication'. This mood is inconclusive. As
when we say (if Zayd moves, then he changes) and except that he does
not change. For we can neither conclude that he moves nor that he does
not.

[*The connective is complete implication; (iii) we deny the antecedent de-*
ducing the denial of the consequent]
5   In the seventh mood we except the contradictory of the antecedent in
the connective premiss which expresses 'complete implication'. The conclusion must be the contradictory of the consequent. For, as we know
from what is said before, (the antecedent) becomes the consequent and
what was a consequent becomes an antecedent. The rules which apply
to the third (mood), apply also to this mood.

[*(iv) we deny the consequent deducing the denial of the antecedent*]
7]   In the eighth mood we except the contradictory of the consequent in
the connective premiss which expresses 'complete implication'. This is in
fact the same as the previous mood.

You must know (a) that no conclusion follows from excepting the contradictory of the antecedent, (b) that when we except the antecedent, the conclusion will be the consequent, (c) that no conclusion follows from excepting the consequent, and (d) that when you except the contradictory of the consequent, the conclusion will be the contradictory of the antecedent.[6]

5   All the above proliferations result from the fact that the work of the first teacher [i.e. Aristotle], in which he discussed in detail the conditional syllogisms, was lost. Thus, they were obliged to take up the subject by themselves. Add to this that they were unaware of that part of conditional syllogisms which deals with conjunctive syllogisms, and so they came across these exceptive syllogisms. They found that the number of syllogisms which appeared to them is small. They also found it infamous that these syllogisms should be parallel to those which the first teacher explained in his treatment of predicative syllogisms. Thus they sought to sharpen the difference (between their logic and that of the first teacher) by contradicting (his methods).

10   We want to finish this chapter with the following remark, that you should not pay any attention to those who say that the exceptive premiss must be a predictive proposition. The exceptive premiss is what the antecedent or the consequent of the conditional premiss, or the contradictory of any of them, is. Since these can be of any kind (whether predicative or conditional), the exceptive premiss can be of any of these kinds. If someone says 'If, if the sun rises, then day follows necessarily from the rising of the sun', and he wants to except the antecedent, the exception will

15   be a conditional proposition. Some thought that (the relation) of implication can be regarded as if it expresses a possible connection between things – as when they say 'If this is an animal, then it is possible that it is a man', and that in this case the rules that govern the exception of any part of the conditional premiss are the opposite of those which we explained before.

[398]   They were misled by this kind of example, for possibility here is only mental and not factual. For nothing in the external world is 'animal' and can possibly be 'man'. 'Animal' is either necessarily 'man' or it is necessarily 'not man'. It cannot become 'man' at all while its substance is at it is, namely something which is taken to be a possibility. To show that this mood, contrary to what they believed, is inconclusive we say: If you say

5   'If this is animal, then it can possibly be white', then nothing will follow

whether you assert that he is white or not white, animal or not animal. Though it may be conclusive if possibility here is taken to be a mental possibility which is concerned with the relation of the general to the particular, namely the particular which is part of the general. But this is something which goes beyond the idea of possible implication. It is also something which concerns the subject-matter of the proposition not its form. They were led to this view by a strange reason. For in his *De Anima* the first teacher says that if the soul does not have an action proper to it, then it will not have an independent existence; and if it has an action proper to it, then it will have an independent existence.[7] A man who is strong in medicine but weak in logic claimed that so-and-so is mistaken when he excepted the contradictory of the consequent. Some zealous followers of the first teacher answered saying that the first teacher is not mistaken because the implication here is only a possibility, and, therefore, he is permitted to except the contradictory of the antecedent to produce the contradictory of the consequent. Some other people may reply to them saying that the implication here is complete and therefore one can conclude the contradictory of the antecedent. But the truth is that the first teacher did not mention this sentence in the form of an exceptive premiss to reach a certain conclusion; rather he stated the two premisses together in such a way as to show that one of them is the converse of the other. As though one starts saying that 'Every creature-that-laughs is a man' and 'Every man is a creature-that-laughs' so as to indicate that both the subject and the predicate are identical. He does not want to show that the second is proved by the first. He only wanted to mention them together. And that is why he mentioned the second preceded with the word used with the protasis (of a conditional premiss) while in the exceptive premiss this word should not be mentioned. The exceptive premiss is stated as a complete discourse and not as part of a discourse. He first put the premisses together; then he showed in another place that the soul has an action proper to it and from this produced that it has an independent existence. Therefore, he did not except the contradictory of the antecedent in the first premiss but the antecedent of the second. Thus, the critic was misled in thinking that (the first teacher) produced the contradictory of the consequent from the contradictory of the antecedent; while the person who tried to solve it thought that the critic was right in what he claimed and, therefore, tried to find an outlet for him [i.e. the first teacher] by a useless device. Thus, the critic committed one mistake, and the one who tried to anwer him committed two mistakes – the first is to believe the critic in what he said and the second is to answer saying that exceptive syllogisms can be productive if the conditional premiss is a possible statement.

NOTES

[1] Reading *muqaddaman* for *tāliyan*.
[2] Reading with H *idh*.
[3] Reading *yajib* for *lā yajib*.
[4] The B.M MS. reads *ghinā'ihi*. The edited text reads *'ināyatan*.
[5] Reading *al-luzūm* with D.
[6] All this is true when the connective premiss expresses incomplete implication.
[7] See *De Anima* 403a10–15. The Arabic translation of the *De Anima* by Isḥāq ibn Hunayn reads: *fa'in kāna fi'lun min af'āli 'l-nafsi khāṣṣun huwa aw mina'l-taghayyuri 'l-'āriḍi lahā fa bima'nā 'l-imakāni an takūna mubāyinatan li'l-jismi, wa in lam yakun shay'un khāṣṣun lahā falaysa bi-mubāyina.* Cf. *Fī'l-Nafs* (ed. by A. Badawi), Cairo 1954.

CHAPTER TWO

ON THE ENUMERATION OF THE EXCEPTIVE SYLLOGISMS [WHICH HAVE A SEPARATIVE-CONDITIONAL PREMISS]

[When the conditional is separative expressing complete conflict; (i) we assert any part deducing the denial of the other]

The exceptive syllogism which is compounded of conditional premisses that express a real separative proposition can either have two or more than two parts. Those which have two parts may have one affirmative and one negative parts, namely contradictory parts – as when we say 'Either so or not-so'. If we except [i.e. assert] any one of them we produce the contradictory of the other. In this case the conclusion will be the same as the exceptive premiss. For if your exception is 'but it is so' you will produce 'therefore it is not not-so'. This conclusion does not tell us anything more than what the conclusion, which we got when the exceptive premiss was identical with one of the parts in the conditional premiss, tells us. Also, if we except 'But not not-so' we produce 'therefore it is so'. It is not unlikely that the exceptive premiss is not more known than the conclusion, and that it does not come to the mind before the conclusion. This kind of reasoning is useful when the syllogism is compounded of a connective and a separative proposition – as when they say 'So is either so or not so, and if it is not so, then A is B; but A is not B; therefore it is so'. In this case the exceptive premiss is not the contradictory of one of the parts, but a statement implied by it. This syllogism will also be complete if its conditional premiss is a connective proposition. It is not unlikely that the separative will not be needed at all. Therefore, this kind of separative propositions are not very useful when used as premisses in an exceptive syllogism, for the parts (of the separative premiss) must not be opposed to each other in the above way. They should be opposed in this way: 'If this is a number, then it is either even or odd'. When one of the parts is excepted, the contradictory of the other will be produced. If we except that it is even we produce that it is not odd. And this is the first mood.

[(ii) or denying any part deducing the other]

In the second mood we except the contradictory (of any one of the parts) – as when you say 'but not even' and produce 'it is odd' or (assert) 'not odd' and produce 'it is even'.

[*When the real separative has more than two parts, then* (i) *if we assert one part we* (a) *deny everyone of the others or* (b) *deny the separative consisting of the others*]

In the real separative propositions which have many parts, the parts are either actually or potentially finite. The rule which applies to this case is the same as the rule which applies to the previous case. For example, you say 'This number is either equal to or more or less than (another)'. If you except any one of the parts, you produce the contradictory of all the rest. When we say 'the contradictory of all the rest' we mean one of two things: (a) that the conclusion is not one proposition but, as it is the case in this example, two propositions. For example, in the above example we say 'therefore, it is not more and it is not less than (another)'. This conclusion is in fact two propositions. There are examples in which the parts (of the separative premiss) are more than they are in the above example and therefore the conclusion will be more than two propositions. (b) That the conclusion is the contradictory of all of the parts taken as parts of one separative proposition – as when we say 'therefore, it is not either more or less than (another)'.

Someone may object to this and say that the case described in (a) cannot be considered a syllogism, for if the conclusion is two or more than two propositions, then you allow that one particular syllogism produces two or more than two conclusions taken together at one and the same time not one of them preceding the other. And if the case described is (b), then you produce a false conclusion. For it is not true that this number is not either more or less than (another), since when it is equal (to another) it can neither be more nor less (than it). But if you say 'Either this or that or something else', then your exceptive premiss does allow it, and it will not be the contradictory of the exceptive premiss; since the predicative premiss does not contradict the separative.

In answering this we say: First, it is not one of the conditions for the syllogism that it should not produce two conclusions. The condition is that it should produce one conclusion. Thus, if it produces two conclusions, this does not mean that it did not produce one conclusion. Second, it produces two conclusions because the syllogism is, in fact, potentially

two syllogisms. For the separative premiss produces these many predicative conclusions with the force of other premisses. For when you say 'but
it is equal to (another number)' you need to mention to yourself another premiss which is 'what is equal to (a certain number) cannot be
more than it', from which you produce one of the conclusions; and you
also need to mention the premiss 'what is equal to (a certain number)
cannot be less than it', from which you produce the other conclusion.
Though you did not say or utter these premisses, you certainly say them in
your mind for what they state must come to your mind. For if someone
says: Why should it be neither less nor more than (a certain number)?
You will say: Because it is equal to it, and what is equal to (a certain
number) can neither be less nor more than it. In this case you would be
analysing your discourse into its component parts. You must have these
(premisses) in mind even if you were not faced with the above objection,
for you can never prove the validity of the conclusion if your mind does
not recognize them. Thus, the conclusion is in fact produced from the
separative premiss with the help of another conjunctive syllogism. Therefore, the combination which leads to the conclusion 'It is not more than
(a certain number)' is different from that which leads to the conclusion
'It is not less than it'. There are things here that need to be discussed but
which we will leave to al-Lawāḥiq. Further, the statement 'Not: either
more or less' is true and its contradictory is false. For when you say 'Not:
either' what you want to say is that 'It is not the case that the thing which
is equal to (something) is either so or so'. Thus, it is true to say 'That thing
which is equal to (a certain number) is not either greater or smaller than
it', because it is equal to it. Also, 'Never: what is equal to (a certain number) can be either smaller or greater than it'. Thus, 'This thing is not either
greater or smaller than (a certain number)'. To prove the truth of the
major premiss we say: If it is not true, then its contradictory 'Some of what
is equal to (a certain number) is either greater or smaller than it' is true.
This means that the truth regarding some of the things which are equal
to (other things) is that they are either greater or smaller; and this is clearly
false. You have known before this law. Therefore, there is no objection to
saying that this is the real conclusion, and that the two conclusions[1]
follow necessarily from it[2] alone; since from saying that 'A is not either
B or C' it does not follow that 'It is neither B nor C'. When you say 'Zayd
is not either man or rational' it does not follow necessarily from it that

[*404*] he is neither man nor rational. We produce two conclusions because we have in mind another consideration combined with that which is 'Not: either greater or smaller, but something else'. And if the thing is always like that, then it cannot be any one of the two. This is the discourse concerning the case in which we affirmatively except one part of the separative premiss.

[(*ii*) *If we deny one of the parts, we produce a separative consisting of the others*]

5   We turn now to the case where we except the contradictory of one part (of the separative premiss). If you except the contradictory of anyone of the parts, you produce the whole of the rest taken as a separative proposition. For example, when you say 'But it is not equal to (a certain number)' you produce 'Therefore, it is either greater or smaller than it', and this is the proximate conclusion (*al-natīja al-qarība*). If you continue (your reasoning) by constructing another syllogism from the above conclusion and the exception [i.e. assertion] of the contradictory of one of its parts, then you will produce one part only. The number of syllogisms in this kind will be the same as the number of the parts (in the separative

10   premiss). There will be no difference between this case and the previous one if the separative premiss is compounded of two parts. What is common to both cases, is that when we except one of the parts we produce the contradictory of the rest, whether it is one or more than one part; while in the case of excepting the contradictory of one part, we produce the rest whether this is compounded of one or more than one part.

         If the parts are potentially infinite, then there is no use in constructing a syllogism from this conditional premiss. Nor is the work on their pro-

15   duction approved of. For if one excepts one of the parts, then he will not be able to put all the other parts together in order to except their contradictory, or to construct from them a negation of a separative proposition. Except if you put the conclusion in the following form: 'Therefore, all but

[*405*] what we asserted (is false)'. In this case the conclusion will have two parts. As if he said: 'Either the number is two or what is not-two; but it is two; therefore, it is not not-two'. Also, if we except the contradictory of some of the parts of the separative premiss, we produce an infinite number of parts. And these cannot be stated except if we say 'Therefore, it is one of the rest'. This is in fact produced from a syllogism compounded of a

separative premiss which has two parts. As if he said: 'Either it is two or whatever number that comes after it'. We must add that when excepting the parts of the separative premiss the last conclusion is reached by constructing successive syllogisms each of which excepts one of the parts (of the separative premiss) until we end up with one part, i.e. one conclusion. But this cannot be achieved when we construct an exceptive syllogism from a separative premiss which has an infinite number of parts. This is the exceptive syllogism compounded of real separative premisses.

[*Both parts of the separative may be true. If one of the parts is denied the other must be asserted*]

When the separative premiss is unreal, it will be (1) a separative whose parts can both be true; which means (a) that they are in themselves true – as when we say 'Either ʿAbd Allāh does not sink or he is in the water' which is nearly the same as saying 'It is not the case that "ʿAbd Allāh is sinking and he is in the water'. When we except the contradictory of any one of them we produce the rest. But there is no production from excepting anyone of the parts. (b) That they are true by chance – as when you say 'Either ʿAbd Allāh does not talk or ʿAmr permits him to talk'; which is nearly the same as saying 'It is not the case that ʿAbd Allāh talks and ʿAmr does permit him to do so'. What applies to (a) applies also to (b). There are other two statements which are nearly the same as those we mentioned in (a) and (b). For example 'It is not the case that ʿAbd Allāh sinks and he is not in the water' and 'It is not the case that ʿAbd Allāh talks and ʿAmr does not permit him to do so'. But the conclusion here differs from the conclusion there, for if you except the contradictory of one of the parts you produce the contradictory of the other. In (a) and (b) we can have negative separative premisses – as when you say: 'Either it is not plant or it is not inanimate'. It gives the same conclusion. What comes near to it is to say "ʿAbd Allāh cannot be plant while he is inanimate' and "ʿAbd Allāh cannot be plant or he cannot be inanimate'. In the first example the two parts are the same as those in the original proposition ('Either it is not plant or it is inanimate'). But in the second example one of the parts is the same as in the original ('Either it is not plant or it is inanimate') and the second part is the opposite of the other. In the example where the two parts are the same as those in ('Either it is not plant or it is inanimate') we produce the consequent when we except the contradictory (of the antecedent). In the other, when we except the contradictory (of the antecedent) we produce the contradictory (of the consequent); and this (syllogism) is called the one which starts with a negation and ends with a negation. The parts in all these cases may happen to be more than two as you know from (the discussion of separative) premisses. The case here is the same as stated in the mentioned (discussion).

[Both parts of the separative may be false]
(2) The other kind of unreal separative proposition, namely the separative whose parts can be false, is not used in the sciences – as when you say 'Either it is plant or inanimate'.

[When one of the parts is asserted, the other must be denied]
When we except one of parts it will produce the contradictory of the other. This kind resembles the (exceptive syllogisms compounded of a) restricted connective premiss in excepting one of the parts; while the first kind resembles these syllogisms in excepting the contradictory of any one of the parts.
We say: All syllogisms compounded of real separative premisses become complete (*tatimmu*) by syllogisms compounded of connective premisses. The same is true of those syllogisms compounded of unreal separative premisses. You will realize that if you remember what we said of them before. The words 'it is exclusively' indicate the meaning of the real separative (premiss) which can be reformulated in the following way: If a thing is exclusively either this or that, namely that both cannot be true, and the thing is not this; therefore it is that. Or it is that; therefore it is not this. Thus, you necessarily conceal a connection of which (one of the parts or its negation) is excepted, but you do not state it explicitly. How can one fail to see this knowing that the *quaesitum* is necessarily implied by the premisses; while what is in conflict with another is not actually implied by it, since it either implies the contradictory of what is in conflict with it, or it will be implied by the contradictory of what is in conflict with it. Therefore, implication is the first and real way of proof which is self-dependent. But in the case of conflict, implication works as an intermediary between it [i.e. the proposition which expresses conflict]

and what necessarily follows from it. The reader must represent and ex-
pound this with the help of the faculty he acquired through the exercises
he did to achieve this end.

NOTES

[1] Reading *natījatan* with D.
[2] Reading *'anhā* with H.

BOOK IX

ON EXPLAINING THAT EXCEPTIVE SYLLOGISMS CANNOT BE COMPLETED EXCEPT BY CONJUNCTIVE SYLLOGISMS

Every syllogistic discourse from which a predicative (proposition) is produced is completed by one of the three figures of predicative (syllogisms). On the whole, exceptive (syllogisms) are completed by the conjunctive, if the intention is to have a productive syllogism. We say: It has been shown that the *reductio ad absurdum* proof is completed by conjunctive and exceptive-conditional syllogisms.[1] And it has been made clear that the conditional syllogism is completed by the conjunctive.[2] Since the *Prior Analytics* talks of the syllogisms producing a predicative (proposition), thus, in it, the conjunctive is meant to be the same as the predicative. We say: It has been made clear to you that in the exceptive syllogism from a separative (premiss) we except (i.e. assert) when we become aware of the connective.[3] And that the (exceptive syllogism from) a connective (premiss), where the contradictory of the consequent is excepted, is shown by the one in which what is excepted is the antecedent itself.[4] If, then, it becomes clear that the (syllogism) in which we except the antecedent itself does not give a conclusion except by a conjunctive syllogism, this [i.e. the completion of the syllogism by means of the conjunctive] will be evident to you in the case of any syllogism: conditional or predicative. The best effort made to explain this is what one of the scholars (*muḥaṣṣilīn*) said, that if the antecedent were evident and clear, what follows it and is implied by it would be evident and clear. And that means that it [i.e. what follows] cannot be proved by a syllogism, since the syllogism shows the unknown, and what is evident need no syllogism to lead to it. *He said:* If the antecedent were evident, we would not attach to it the word which indicates doubt, i.e. the word which characterizes the protasis, ['if']. When we say 'If such is such, then such is such', this requires that the antecedent is subject to doubt. When this (doubt) is removed, the consequent, then, will be true. So, if the antecedent were self-evident, there would be no reason for attaching to it the word which indicates doubt.

What we should do is to examine this statement. We will complete it if we find it defective; and if we find that it is false, we will move to another.

We say: As to what he said, that the antecedent is doubtful or not doubtful, we have made our view clear on this before.[5] The weakness of this claim can be known from what is said there. As to (his saying) that what is evidently related to what is evidently true would be evidently true, this is something which is not to be conceded. For we might have

15 something which is self-evident and which evidently implies another without the implicate being self-evident, such as when we know the implicate through the mediation of a third party. It is not one and the same thing to say that something is self-evident and to say that it is evidently

[417] implied by something which is self-evident. Unknown things are reached on stages. And that is by their being implied by things which are either self-evident or made evident though their implication is not immediately evident in which case a mediator is required that will lead us, in the last analysis, to the implicate which would then be evidently implied. But if (the proposition) reached at the end were self-evident; and the (mediating) one, i.e. that which implied the last one without the mediation of anything else, were self-evident – since it is evidently implied by what is self-evident [i.e. the first proposition from which we started] – then all the things involved in this would be self-evident. From this it would follow that the

5 first mood of the first figure (in predicative syllogisms) would be un-informative. For we would, then, analyse it as having two self-evident premisses and a conclusion which is evidently implied by them, as ex-plained. What we did here is to take the relation between the syllogism[6] and the conclusion to be like the relation between the antecedent and the consequent.[7] (When we say that) the antecedent is evident (it will be like saying so of), for example, (the premisses) 'Every C is B' and 'Every B is A'. And when we say that the consequent is evidently implied by the ante-cedent, it will be like saying that 'Every C is A' (evidently follows from the above premisses). Thus, the statement 'Every C is A' must be evident.

10 And so also with the infinite number of conclusions we may have.

But to say that much will not reveal the real objective. For one can also say that it is not the case that a connective premiss is not considered connective unless the consequent is evidently implied. For it may not be evidently implied but shown to be so. When it becomes evidently implied through a proof, and, then, the antecedent itself is excepted, the consequent will be produced. This will be a conclusive syllogism. So, it is possible for the antecedent to be self-evident and the implication not to be evident but proved. When we prove that, the exception of a self-evident antecedent will lead to something unknown.

What we should say on this – and we will try to support (our view) – is that when a single evident thing, which is evidently related with something else, comes to the mind, it will help the mind grasp the truth of the implied consequent. Thus, when 'A is B'[8] is evident, and the following of 'C is D' from it is evident, then once 'A is B' comes to the mind, the consequent will be implied without constructing a syllogism at all. When you bring to your mind the case 'A is B', as you say 'If A is B', it will be as though you said to yourself 'If A is B, which is, then C is D'. There is no need to repeat and put 'But A is B'. For that had been done implicitly when you brought the antecedent 'A is B'. For you do not take it as an antecedent but as something which came to your mind; and it does not come to the mind except as something posited. In such a case, positing it as an antecedent will help you know the truth of the consequent. You have in fact excepted [i.e. asserted] the antecedent as an assumption, but this exception is included in the process of bringing forward the antecedent and is already made, and, therefore, there is no need for you to initiate a separate exception since you are already aware of (the assertion). This picture would change if (the antecedent) is not evident; for, then, you have to except it separately in your mind.

The same is true of the conjunctive syllogism [i.e. the two premisses of a predicative syllogism], if you regard them as the antecedent (of a connective proposition). For you don't need to resume excepting them when they are evident. Since the conclusion, which you will regard as the consequent, will necessarily follow from the syllogism which you regard as the antecedent of a (connective-)conditional (proposition). Accordingly, if the implication is perfect, the soul need not resume excepting (the premisses) and say: But every C is B and every B is A. For this is implicit in the process of bringing the antecedent (which is these two premisses) to the mind. Of course before constructing the syllogism and before positing it, (the conclusion) does not evidently follow, otherwise we would not need the syllogism. For the conclusion does not necessarily follow from one evident thing, but from two and their combination; and the form of this combination is not fixed in the mind. An assertion of one of

[419] the propositions might come to the mind without being accompanied by an assertion of the other, because the second did not come to the mind not that it is not evidently true. And the difference between these two things has been explained to you somewhere else before.[9] So what might be present is an assertion of the first (alone), or of both but without their being ordered together the kind of order that will lead to the conclusion. In which case you will not be conscious of the part they share [i.e. the middle term]. A single assertion may be considered enough. This is so because whenever the first comes to the mind the second must come with

5 it. But if more than one assertion is considered necessary, then they ought to be combined together (in a particular order). In either case when what comes to the mind is the complete (set), there will be no need to resume this exception [i.e. assertion], for we have done that implicitly when we introduced the first premises. To resume excepting them as though this is done for the first time is a redundant act. So, in one of them the implicant is one assertion; and in the other, the implicant is two assertions with certain conditions (laid down for their combination). All this

10 is true not only of the antecedent which is self-evident, but also of that which becomes evident through a syllogism and knowledge. Here too the exception would be redundant. The same is also true in case the antecedent is self-evident and the implication is proved. Therefore, if it is redundant to resume excepting (the premises), it will be redundant to form a complete syllogism based on this (process). That is why in the various sciences this kind of conditional premises are not used in a syllogistic form. What one says is 'Whereas (*lamma*) such, it is such', not 'If

15 such, then such; but such therefore such', for this is taken for granted.

[420] One cannot say, as a result, that self-evident major premises [i.e. the second premiss] in syllogisms are redundant; and that it is enough to have the implicitly stated proposition in (the first premiss) for that is how [the latter] is used. We say: A discourse can be redundant in two ways. It can be redundant and dispensable (a) in the sense that it already came to the mind, though implicitly. So if it is uttered, it will be as though we are

5 bringing it again to the mind, i.e. repeating it. (b) It can be redundant in the sense that the soul does not need to seize it [through the utterance]; not that if it were made explicit it would be as though it was brought twice to the mind. It is as though when made explicit, we brought to the mind something which would come to the mind without (its being necessary for us) to utter it. And that which is brought to the mind without (the necessity of being) uttered is brought once to the mind. If it were made explicit, it will come to the mind in a second instance after (the utterance). And what comes to the mind as a result will be as though it is brought once to the mind. In the sense (b) redundancy applies to the utterance not the meaning. Thus, (the discourse) involved in (b) is not redundant and is necessary to get the full meaning. And this is (what applies to) the major premiss as we have shown. To state something [i.e. the first premiss] and then follow it by the *quaesitum*, which is, for example, 'Every B is A', will bring to the mind that the speaker has left something implicit. If (the implicit premiss) is self-evident, there will be no need to state it explicitly in order to make the conclusion follow from the (first) premiss. It will be enough to bring it to the mind. If it were not self-evident, the addressed will ask for it and say: why every B is A? If he did not understand what the person he is addressing had explicitly and implicitly stated, he would not have asked him why every B is A? There will be no use whatsoever of this discourse if the major [i.e. the second] premiss does not come to the mind when the above conclusion is brought following (the first) premiss. Therefore, (this discourse in which) the major premiss is implicit will be useful (in bringing forward the conclusion) if the major premiss is brought to the mind independently of bringing the minor [i.e. first] premiss to the mind, and if the time (in which both premisses occur) is connected. It is as though the major (premiss) is explicitly stated. If it does not come to the mind, it will not be useful at all and (the discourse in which the major premiss) is stated implicitly will not lead to any knowledge at all. If it does, the implicit statement will be useful in bringing to the mind something which will inevitably come to the mind and at the same time in which it is made explicit. Therefore, the meaning indicated by the utterance of the major premiss is needed. But it will be enough to bring it to the mind to know it, in which case we can dispense with the utterance. For though the meaning expressed by the words is needed, the words can be dispensed with.

Now if we look at (this discourse) as a conditional (proposition), we find that when we say 'If every A is B' the posited thesis comes to the mind and so also its assertion. And the assertion, for example, comes to the mind at an instance of time which precedes that in which the mind moves to the consequent, let alone the time in which we except [i.e. assert] it.

When the exception comes, it will either not bring anything to the mind, or repeat what has already occurred, and, therefore, be dispensable. Here the time in which (the exception) is made is not the same as that in which it is uttered; as is the case when the major (premiss), which need not be uttered, is made explicit at the time it occurred to the mind. Therefore, the exception here does not produce anything essential for leading us to what we are aiming at: it is something which is already asserted. And what has been already asserted is redundant in its utterance and meaning, because the time in which it is uttered is not the same as the time in which it is needed. It neither informs us of anything new nor does it inform us of what is dispensable. This cannot be said of that which, when uttered, gives the needed information at the same time we needed it and whose significance corresponds with what is needed at that time.

It is clear, then, that treating such premisses [i.e. the 'If – then' propositions] as a form of a syllogism is a useless effort, and that it ought to be treated in the mentioned way. They put it this way: 'Whereas such is such, such is such'. But not everything which takes the form of a syllogism produces like a syllogism. For when someone says 'Every man is a creature-that-laughs' this is true; and when he adds 'And every creature-that-laughs is an animal' this is true. But from this we do not get a new information. For we know that every man is an animal, but not after we were informed that he is a creature-that-laughs. This is how we should understand what the first teacher [i.e. Aristotle] says. It should not be thought that his view is that whatever is evidently implied by something which is evidently true, is evidently true. Or that the antecedent is not to be posited as an antecedent unless it is doubtful. As though the proposition is not connective unless its antecedent is doubtful. Which means that when one says 'If man is an animal, then he is a body' the antecedent must be something doubtful, otherwise the proposition will not be connective. What (he says) amounts to saying that it is not syllogistic, or that it is not a case where the significate corresponds with what is needed, to except the antecedent in a proposition whose antecedent is doubtful when the consequent is evidently implied or shown to be evidently implied or it is itself self-evident. If the consequent is not evidently implied, it will then be remote and need necessarily a conjunctive syllogism to show it. So, in order that the connection be evident and, therefore, useful, it must lead to a conjunctive syllogism. Thus, we cannot except the antecedent of a connective premiss unless the antecedent is doubtful, and the consequent is evidently implied by or connected with (the antecedent) or proved to be so.

It is evident and clear that the *reductio ad absurdum* proofs and the connective-hypothetical (propositions) cannot be used in a syllogistic form unless the antecedent is doubtful and that the connection in them is either self-evident or made evident by a conjunctive syllogism. As to the antecedent, it is shown either by an exceptive or a conjunctive syllogism. If it were shown by an exceptive (syllogism), we will end up with an exceptive syllogism in which the premisses are doubtful. These are shown by conjunctive (syllogisms). If it was shown start from the beginning by a conjunctive syllogism, it will be clearer that (they cannot be shown except by the conjunctive). Therefore, all conclusive syllogisms, when used in a syllogistic form, are reduced to the conjunctive. We do not exclude the possibility of ending up with an exceptive which need not be used in a syllogistic form. But that is rare, and the majority of cases are what we said.

Someone might say: What do you say of a conditional premiss whose antecedent is a conjunctive syllogism? How can one show its antecedent by a conjunctive syllogism? We say: What we are discussing here is the thing proved by an exceptive (syllogism) from a premiss which can be related to a conjunctive syllogism. If the antecedent itself were a conjunctive syllogism, then (it is obvious) that an exceptive argument is related to the conjunctive syllogism. If the relation between them is not clear, we can show it by another syllogism. However, I have shown before that (the process) of showing the consequent, which we regard as the conclusion, through the antecedent, which we regard as the syllogism, is not a syllogistic process from which a conclusion is derived.

Someone might say: What do you say of the exceptive syllogism used in proofs *per impossible* where the contradictory of the consequent is excepted to produce the contradictory of the antecedent? We say: This is not of the same kind as that in which the antecedent is evident, and the consequent is evidently implied by the antecedent. How can the antecedent be evident when it is what we want to falsify? And how can the consequent be evidently implied by the antecedent when that needs to be shown by a conjunctive (syllogism)? If, however, the consequent is shown to be implied with the help of a conjunctive (syllogism), it will be correct to produce the contradictory of the antecedent when the contradictory of the consequent is excepted. Someone might say: Such an argument, where we except the consequent, is an indispensable syllogism. In other words, he is saying that we have here a conditional syllogism in which the excepted part is self-evident and is not shown by a conjunctive (syllogism). As though he says: Let us assume that when the excepted part is the antecedent the case is what you have described. But what do you say of the case in which the excepted part is the consequent? For this can be com-

15   pleted without reducing it to the conjunctive at all. We say: This syllo- gism is either of the kind in which the implication is concealed or not. If the implication is concealed, it will need the conjunctive to prove it. If the

[425]   implication is evident, which is to say that the implication of the contra- dictory of the antecedent by the contradictory of the consequent is evident, then there will be no new information given through (the process) of ex- cepting the contradictory of the consequent to produce the contradictory of the antecedent in a connective (proposition). For if we put the contra- dictory of the consequent in place of the antecedent, and express its pre- cedence by 'whereas', it will produce in the way explained before. Thus, it will be redundant (to assert the antecedent) in this converted connective

5   premiss which we have as the first premiss; and there will be nearly the same kind of repetition mentioned earlier. We do not forbid that syllo- gisms be compounded of connective (propositions) in the way mentioned before. What we mean is that (arguments made from connective pre- misses) will not be conclusive though the implication of the consequent by the antecedent is evident. But the implication of the contradictory of the antecedent by the contradictory of the consequent is not evident. So we cannot say that the statement 'If A is B, then C is D' is self-evident and that 'Not C is D' may be asserted and with it 'Not A is B'.[10] Except

10   if we consider with it the first proposition. If we use it with the first proposition, then in order to show that it is conclusive we need a con- junctive in the form of a proof *per impossible* as you know it. If it were not put with the first proposition there will be need for the syllogism to show the implication.

This is the most I can say to support the view of whoever regards the (exceptive argument made from) a connective (premiss) as being com-

15   pleted only by a predicative (syllogism). However, the predicative here should not be seen as predicative but as a conjunctive as opposed to

the exceptive. Since the only conjunctive mentioned in the *Prior Analytics* is the predicative, the conjunctive and the predicative there follow the same route.

Since we reached our objective, with all the effort it took us, we should add that the predicative is not completed except by two premises, and that a single *quaesitum* need no more than two premises. You can transfer everything said about the predicative to the conjunctive, if you have the capacity to do it.

NOTES

[1] *Al-Qiyās*, 408–11.
[2] *Ibid.*, Book VI.
[3] *Ibid.*, 400 and 401; 406–07.
[4] *Ibid.*, 395, 8–13.
[5] *Ibid.*, 236, 12–18.
[6] A syllogism to Avicenna is the two premises without the conclusion. See pp. 216–17.
[7] Reading *al-muqaddam ilā al-tālī* instead of *al-tālī ilā al-muqaddam*.
[8] Reading with the majority of MSS. *alif bā'* instead of *kullu alif bā'*.
[9] See 394–95.
[10] Reading *laysa alif bā'* instead of *alif bā'*.

COMMENTARY

BOOK V

CHAPTER ONE

231, 5. The word *shartiyya*, which literally means conditional, is used by Avicenna to describe both the so-called connective (If ..., then) and separative (Either ..., or) propositions. The problem that concerns us here is how to translate the word *shartiyya*. In the Arabic translation of Aristotle's *Prior Analytics* one finds the phrase *al-maqāyīs al-shartiyya* being used as a translation for οἱ ἐξ ὑποθέσεως συλλογισμοί.[1] It is no doubt tempting to think that perhaps the word hypothetical would be the correct rendering of *shartiyya*, especially in a context such as logic.[2] However, there are evident reasons which induce us not to follow this premature conjecture. In *Mantiq al-Mashriqiyyīn* Avicenna shows that he feels ill at ease in using the word *shartiyya* for both the connective and the separative propositions. He says there that the word *shartiyya* in Arabic refers only to the 'If ..., then' type of propositions, since in this case we have first a condition, which is the antecedent of the connective proposition, and an apodosis that follows the condition being hypothesized.[3] As to separative propositions, it is not clear why they also should be called *shartiyyāt*, he adds. This new usage of the term, which is not ordinary in Arabic, needs to be explained and Avicenna provides his own explanation. It seems, he says, that they (meaning Greek philosophers) use the word conditional in this context to indicate the dependence of the antecedent and the consequent on each other in both types of propositions. For neither the antecedent nor the consequent is in itself a statement-making sentence and therefore true or false. This is so because we attach to the antecedent the particle 'if', in the case of the connective, and the particle 'either', in the case of the separative; while in the case of the consequent, 'then' is added in the first type of propositions and 'or' is added in the second. To say, for example, 'If the sun rises' would be an incomplete statement which is neither true nor false. So also when we say 'Then it is day'.[4] This understanding of the matter gives Avicenna the clue to the solution of the problem why the above two types of propositions are called *shartiyyāt*. For in both the connective and the separative the antecedent (the consequent) is to be taken as a condition for turning the consequent (the antecedent) into a complete statement.[5] This makes it clear that 'conditional' is the word that Avicenna had in mind when using the word *shartiyya*. We can also add here that when Avicenna speaks of a hypothesis (or any of its derivations) he puts the word *wadˁ* or *fard* (or any of their derivations) and not *shart*[6]

In this rather clear picture there is one thing left. In *Mantiq al-Mash-riqiyyīn* Avicenna says that the 'If – then' proposition is either called *shartiyya muttasila* or *wadˁiyya*.[7] But when, in the same source, he refers to the 'Either – or' type he says that it is called *shartiyya munfasila*.[8] Now if we take the conclusion we reached above as a guide, we can simply say that the 'If – then' proposition is either called 'connective-conditional' or 'hypothetical'; and that the 'Either – or' type is named 'separative-conditional'. Therefore, while 'conditional' names both types of propositions, 'hypothetical' seems to be exclusively indicative of connective propositions. If we go back to Greek sources we find in Alexander of Aphrodisias' commentary on the *Prior Analytics*[9] and in Galen's *Institutio Logica*[10] both the Stoic and the Peripatetic terms used for the above types of propositions. The 'If – then' proposition is called by the Peripatetics hypothetical 'by connection' κατὰ συνέχειαν, and the 'Either – or' proposition is called hypothetical 'by separation' διαιρετικαὶ προτάσις. The Stoics, however, called the first 'conditional' συνημμένον and the second 'disjunctive' διεξευγμένον. This seems to indicate that the Peripatetic word 'hypothetical' is the one used to refer to both types of propositions while the Stoic term 'conditional' is only indicative of the 'If – then' type. We were not able to find any evidence in Arabic sources that would help us explain this incongruity between the Avicennian and the Greek terminology.

231, 6–12. Earlier in this work Avicenna discusses what he describes as two ways of looking at predicative (categorical) syllogisms. The first sees the syllogism as two premises sharing one common term (the middle term). The second considers the syllogism as a pair of premises with a given conclusion. (Cf. *al-Qiyās*, 106–07.) Avicenna himself adopts the first view in all his known writings; and there are reasons to believe that this view applies not only to predicative but also to conditional syllogisms.[11] It is clear that for Avicenna a conditional syllogism is a syllogism having at least one conditional premiss. Avicenna does not explain the words 'pure' and 'mixed' as ascribed to conditional syllogisms, nor does he use the words again in the text. The 'pure conditional' (*sharṭī ṣirf*) is possibly the one whose premisses are all of the same type of conditionals ('If – then' or 'Either – or'). Or, one can also say, it is the one made up of conditional premisses, even if these differ in type. The 'mixed conditional' (*sharṭī mukhtalaṭ*) can be either a syllogism in which the premisses are a mixture of both types of conditional propositions, or a mixture of predicative and conditional premisses.

The text discusses one type of syllogism (called conjunctive-conditional) in which the premisses are made up of either two connective or two separative or one connective and one separative proposition. These syllogisms are carried out by means of figures and moods in the Aristotelian manner. The schema which Avicenna gives for the first mood of the first figure (in which the connective premisses are universal affirmative propositions) is:

(1)   Always: when A is B, then C is D,
and always: when C is D, then H is Z,
therefore always: when A is B, then H is Z.[12]

This schema bears no resemblance to the Stoic 'arguments from two conditionals' ὁ διὰ δύο τροπικῶν of which Origen gives the following example:

If you know that you are dead, you are dead.
If you know that you are dead, you are not dead.
Therefore, you do not know that you are dead.

Origen mentions its Stoic schema:

(2)   If the first, then the second.
If the first, then not the second.
Therefore, not the first.[13]

Nothing much is known about (2), but the difference between (1) and (2) is quite obvious.

We must, therefore, look for another source for (1). In his commentary on Aristotle's *Prior Analytics*, Alexander of Aphrodisias gives the following example as one of five arguments which, he says, were arranged by Theophrastus:

(3)   If A then B.
        If B then Γ.
        Therefore, if A then Γ.[14]

According to Alexander, Theophrastus used the expression 'syllogism by analogy' ἐξ ἀναλογίας to designate (3) while Philoponus says he used the expression 'pure hypothetical syllogism' δι ὅλων ὑποθετικοί. It is relevant to note that Avicenna never uses the expression 'syllogism by analogy', and that the name given to (1) seems to be 'pure conditional syllogism'. This may be an important point in determining Avicenna's sources. But we must also add that there is a significant difference between (1) and (3). In (1) each of the parts (antecedents and consequents) of the premiss is always and consistently expressed in the form 'A is B'. In other words each of the parts of a conditional proposition is in (1) always a proposition. While in (3) the variables A, B, and Γ "are apparently intended to mark places which can be filled by general terms".[15] One can also add that while all the examples cited by Alexander of syllogisms by analogy are compounded of the 'If – then' propositions, this, as we said before, is not true of Avicenna's (1). In spite of these differences, it is clear that (1) is an elaboration on (3) and not on (2).

In the anonymous scholium published by M. Wallies in the preface to his edition of Ammonius' *Commentary on Aristotle's Prior Analytics*, the author speaks of two kinds of hypothetical syllogisms. He calls the first kind simple ἁπλῶς or pure hypothetical ὅλως ὑποθετικός. The example he gives for this kind is:

(4)   If the sun is over the earth, then it is day.
        If it is day, then it is light.
        Therefore, if the sun is over the earth, then it is light.[16]

Unfortunately nothing more in the scholium is said about this kind of syllogism. But one at once sees that (4) is an example of (1).[17]

The case of the mixed conditional is more complicated. As said above it can mean two things: (a) The syllogisms which are compounded of a mixture of the two types of conditional propositions; or (b) the syllogism

whose premisses are a mixture of conditional and predicative propositions. The example for (a) is

(5)   Always: when H is Z, then C is D,
           and always: either C is D or A is B,
           therefore, always: when H is Z, then A is not B.[18]

Under (b) comes what he calls 'exceptive syllogism' (*istithnā'ī*), which is
of the same type as the Stoic indemonstrables. The following is an example of one of its forms:

(6)   If A is B, then C is D.
           But A is B.
           Therefore C is D.[19]

There is also what he calls 'syllogisms compounded of conditional and
predicative premisses'. An example of this is the following:

(7)   If A is B, then C is D,
           and D is H,
           therefore, if A is B, then C is H.[20]

The context in which the mixed conditional syllogism is mentioned seems
to exclude (6) because Avicenna is talking of conditional syllogisms
leading to conditional conclusions, and the conclusion in (6) is a predicative proposition.

In the anonymous scholium mentioned above (*loc. cit.*) there is a discussion of what is called the mixed μικτός hypothetical syllogism. In
this discussion five syllogisms are treated in which the premisses are
sometimes a mixture of 'If – then' and 'Either – or' propositions or a
conditional and a predicative premisses. These syllogisms are by no
means identical with (7). An analysis of these syllogisms shows that they
are identical with Chrysippus' five indemonstrables.[21] Thus the expression mixed conditional syllogisms as used by Avicenna has a different
meaning from that which the scholium gives.[22]

231, 12–14 and 232, 1–5. In this passage a definition of both predicative
as well as conditional (connective and separative) propositions is given.
What it all amounts to is this: (a) Both the predicative and the conditional propositions are statement-making sentences in which a *meaning*

can be allocated; and this meaning is what we relate to or correspond with the external world. (b) In both types of propositions a judgment is expressed that relates one part of the proposition to the other. The only difference between the predicative, on the one hand, and the conditional, on the other, is in the form which this judgment takes.[23] In the predicative the judgment has the form 'A is B', while in the conditional the form is 'If p, then q' (connective) or 'Either p or q' (separative). The two points need further explanation.

(a) "... Not every sentence is a statement-making sentence", Aristotle declares[24], "but only those in which there is truth or falsity. There is not truth or falsity in all sentences: a prayer[25] is a sentence but is neither true nor false." A sequence of words will have a truth-value, i.e. be true or false, if it tells us something or if it asserts something. This, for Avicenna, is true of both predicative and conditional propositions.[26] Avicenna, however, goes further than this and tries to answer an important question, namely what is it that makes a statement true? Avicenna's answer, in Quine's words, is that there are two factors: (1) The meaning which the sentence in question has; and (2) The state of affairs as is found in the world. The sentence 'The sun has set' would be true because the sentence means that the sun has set and as a matter of fact the sun *has* set. Therefore, it is the meaning of a sentence rather than the sentence itself which is true or false.[27] Indeed logic deals not with the words said or written but with the meaning which these words reveal, Avicenna says.[28]

To turn to (b), it is obvious that in any statement-making sentence the statement made is about some kind of relation between two elements in the proposition. If the proposition is predicative, then the elements are the subject and the predicate (terms); and the relation is that of belonging. In the case of the conditional proposition the elements are called the antecedent and the consequent (propositions); and the relation is that of following (in case the propositions is connective) or of conflict (in the case of separative propositions). Thus the only difference between predicative and conditional propositions is in the form which these propositions take. In the predicative proposition the judgment has the form 'A is B', while in the conditional the judgment has the form 'If p, then q' or 'Either p or q'. From this passage alone it is not clear whether in a conditional proposition, say, 'If the sun rises, then it is day', one or more

than one judgment are made. It is, however, clear that in this example
we made at least one judgment, namely that something is implied by or
follows from another. Later on in this chapter Avicenna says that the
antecedent and consequent, as parts of a conditional proposition, are
not propositions. In other words they are neither true nor false. For the
expression 'If the sun rises' in itself is neither true nor false, nor is the
expression 'then it is day'.[29] Therefore, as he says in his al-ʿIbāra (On
Propositions), a conditional proposition is a single statement-making
sentence.[30] This is an important point, since it explains Avicenna's conception of conditional propositions on which his whole treatment of
conditional propositions and syllogisms is based.

As a modern writer on the subject puts it, the question as regards conditionals (Avicenna's connective propositions) is whether "the form of
language 'if p, then q', when used for asserting q on the condition p, itself
expresses a proposition"[31] and if so, whether this proposition is to be
asserted categorically or conditionally.[32] The writer's answer to the first
question is in the negative. The reason which he gives for his answer is this:
"To assert q on the condition of p is to assert that p materially implies q
without asserting or denying the antecedent or the consequent of the
material implication". Hence, "although part of what we do in thus
using 'if p, then q' is that we assert a certain proposition, it is equally a
part of what we do that we leave some propositions unasserted. Therefore the whole of what we do in asserting q on the condition p is not that
we assert some proposition (or combination of propositions) categorically."[33]

To sum up. The form 'if p, then q' consists of three propositions though
the assertion made is only one. The reader will remember that Avicenna
thought that the form 'if p, then q' consists of one proposition (since the
antecedent and the consequent for him are not propositions) in which
only one assertion is made. As a result, he considers the form 'if p, then q'
as being itself a proposition asserted categorically viz. unconditionally.
For he speaks, for example, of the negation of that which is asserted,
when q is asserted on the condition p, namely 'Not: if p, then q'. This, as
we said before, is a fundamental point in his conception of conditional
propositions. It also explains how Avicenna was able to apply Aristotle's
theory of the syllogism, a theory which is applicable to categorical propositions, to conditional propositions as well.

232, 5–18 and 233, 1–4. The words 'following' and 'conflict' are introduced here for the first time without being defined. But afterwards conflict is divided into complete and incomplete. A proposition expressing complete conflict is defined as one having two contradictory parts. In other words, if the first is true, the second is false; and if the first is false, the other is true. A proposition expressing complete conflict can, therefore, be represented by the following table:

If the first part is	and if the second part is	the proposition expressing complete conflict will be
True	True	False
True	False	True
False	True	True
False	False	False

A proposition expressing incomplete conflict is defined as one which does not have contradictory parts. This, as Avicenna says, means that both its parts can be false though they can never be together true. The following table represents this relation:

If the first part is	and if the second part is	the proposition expressing incomplete conflict will be
True	True	False
True	False	True
False	True	True
False	False	True

In another place, Avicenna seems to be saying that conflict means that the parts of the proposition cannot be both true (al-Qiyās, 244 and 247). Therefore, when it is qualified and called complete another property is added, namely that the parts of the proposition cannot be both false. While in the incomplete forms both parts can be false.

Avicenna's treatment of separative propositions is, in fact, based on the concept of conflict and its divisions as explained here; and it is natural for a systematizer of conditional inferences to start with an explanation of his basic concepts. It is not possible to determine with certainty Avicenna's source for the ideas of complete and incomplete conflict, since he makes no reference to any writer or book here. But his source might well be Galen. In Galen's *Institutio Logica* (Ch. IV) conflict [34] μάχη is given the same definition as in Avicenna. It is also divided into complete τέλειος and incomplete ἐλλιπής. Both divisions are given the same definition explained above. In father Stakelum's view, the fact that Aristotelian opposition appears to correspond so nicely to Galen's explanation of Stoic idea of conflict suggests that Galen tried to identify the two mutually exclusive systems of logic.[35] Galen's complete conflict, Stakelum continues, "could very easily have been suggested by Aristotle's contradictory opposition, which for the Stagirite was the only complete or perfect opposition. For contradictory or perfect opposition Aristotle generally reserves the term ἀντικεῖσθαι as Galen also does."[36] In opposition to the above view, J. S. Kieffer says that the concept of conflict "belongs to the Stoic view of hypothetical propositions as a unity, rather than to the Peripatetic view that they are combinations of categorical propositions".[37] He concludes saying that the doctrine of conflict "must therefore have been worked out by reflection on Chrysippus' indemonstrables".[38] Avicenna's text seems to support Kieffer's position. For although Avicenna uses the word 'contradictory' (*naqīd*) to explain the idea of complete conflict, in his explanation of incomplete conflict he simply says 'not contradictory' and not 'contrary' as he might be expected to if his source was influenced by Aristotle's theory of opposition. It is also important to note that the conception of a conditional proposition in Avicenna's work is that of a single statement-making sentence in which only one assertion is made.

In the same passage there is also a division of 'connection' and not of 'following', as one would expect, into complete and incomplete. Complete connection, as Avicenna says, is that in which the antecedent and the consequent imply each other. Later in this work (cf. *al-Qiyās*, 390, 391 and 396) he says that in a proposition expressing complete connection[39] we derive the consequent when we assert the antecedent, or the antecedent when we assert the consequent. Also, in the same proposition when the negation of the antecedent is asserted, the negation of the consequent will be derived, and when the negation of the consequent is asserted, the negation of the antecedent will be derived. The following table represents the relation of complete connection:

If the first part is	and the second part is	the proposition expressing complete connection will be
True	True	True
True	False	False
False	True	False
False	False	True

Incomplete connection is the same as implication. For Avicenna describes it as that in which the antecedent implies the consequent and not vice versa. An implication, according to Avicenna (cf. *al-Qiyās*, 260–61) is true when both the antecedent and the consequent are true, or when both are false, or when the antecedent is false and the consequent is true. And it is false when the antecedent is true and the consequent is false. The following table represents this relation:

If the first part is	and the second part is	the proposition expressing incomplete connection will be
True	True	True
True	False	False
False	True	True
False	False	True

In Galen's *Institutio Logica* (XIV, 10–11) there is a reference to what is called incomplete ἐλλιπής ἀκολουθία and complete consequence τελεία ἀκολουθία, but Galen gives no explanation of these words.

233, 4–9. These lines contain the following information: (a) Some group of philosophers assert that connection is the same as affirmation and that separation is identical with negation. (b) Some other group of philosophers maintain that the conditional (connective and separative) proposition has no quality, i.e. can neither be affirmed nor negated. (c) This same group would include among separative propositions those 'Either – or' statements whose parts (antecedent and consequent) can both be true; and (d) they treated with conditionals a category of propositions Avicenna calls 'indeterminables'.

As they stand these statements of Avicenna do not tell us much. Some explanation of (a), (b) and (d) can be found in *al-Qiyās*, 256–59. Therefore our commentary will be based on the passage commented on here in addition to those which appear in *al-Qiyās*, 256–59. First of all there

seems to be some incongruity between what he says here and in 258. In
our passage (a) and (b) are reported as though they were held by two
different groups. However, in 258 he refers to both doctrines as if they
are related and therefore belong to one doctrine which, as he says, is
advocated by the majority of philosophers. Whether they are related or
not depends very much on how we understand them. For reasons that
will appear below we favour considering them as reflecting two aspects
of the same doctrine. Avicenna himself rejects both (a) and (b). For rejecting (b) he simply reiterates the view he held elsewhere that the form
'If p, then q' itself expresses a single proposition and assertion, and therefore it can either be affirmed or denied.[40] He immediately adds that the
quality of the antecedent or the consequent of a conditional proposition
in no way affects the quality of the conditional form 'If p, then q' or
'Either p or q'. To explain this he says that some people thought that 'If p,
then not-q' is equivalent to 'Not: if p, then q'. However, he declares,
what is meant by the form 'Not: if p, then q' is not that the negation of q
is asserted on asserting p, but that q is not asserted at all on the condition p. What is puzzling here is that the view described under (b) denies
that the conditional proposition can be affirmed or negated. And in the
last point made it is clear that what is denied is a certain idea of negation
which Avicenna gives the form 'Not: if p, then q'. Thus, when talking
about the negation of a connective proposition, the exponents of (b)
would refer to 'If p, then not-q'.[41] As to (a) it seems that those who
identified separation with negation were in fact talking about an equivalence between the 'Either – or' proposition and the negation of the connective proposition. Thus while connection is expressed by the form 'If p,
then q', separation can be expressed by the negation of the connective
proposition.[42] What is not clear here is whether the mentioned negation
is the Avicennian 'Not: if p, then q' or the negation discussed before,
namely the negation of either the antecedent or the consequent of the
connective proposition. The problem could be left at that except for what
we find in Galen in reference to this question. Galen says that one class
of hypothetical (Avicenna's conditional) propositions is 'the hypothetical
by connection', whenever one says, "if some other thing is, necessarily
this thing is"; the other class, the separative, "whenever, if one thing is
not, another is, or, if one thing is, another is not".[43] According to Galen,
then, the separative proposition can in fact be considered as a connective

proposition with either the antecedent or the consequent negated.[44] This might well be the view described in (b).

We will have another chance to discuss (c) in detail.[45] What is significant in this context is to draw the reader's attention to the fact that the propositions discussed under (c) are very similar to Galen's paradisjunctives παραδιεξευγμένον (ἀξίωμα)[46] Avicenna explains (d) in 256–58. These so-called indeterminables are also 'If – then' and 'Either – or' propositions. Except that their antecedents and consequents are predicative propositions which share one and the same subject, and the subject is put before the conditional word ('Either' or 'if'). E.g. 'Number is either even or odd'. This proposition, according to Avicenna, is indeterminable; meaning that it can be treated as a conditional or as a predicative proposition. You can treat it as a predicative proposition if you take 'number' as the subject and 'either even or odd' as the predicate. Never mind that the predicate is complex in this case. For one can give the complex predicate one single sign, e.g. *Alpha*, and say 'Number is *Alpha*'. Examples of this type of propositions can also be found in Galen's *Institutio Logica*[47] though Galen does not call them indeterminables nor does he say about them anything comparable to what Avicenna says.

233, 12–17 and 234. A distinction is made here between two kinds of 'following' – implication (*luzūm*) and chance connection (*ittifāq*). Avicenna understands implication to be a relation in which the truth of the consequent depends on the truth of the antecedent (cf. *al-Qiyās*, 282). In the case of chance connection the proposition is considered true simply because the antecedent and the consequent are true. The truth of the consequent in such a case does not depend on the truth of the antecedent. Thus, Avicenna says, a proposition which expresses chance connection is true when both is parts are true and false otherwise (cf. *al-Qiyās*, 238, 10–17).

In this text Avicenna refers to the antecedent and the consequent of a proposition expressing implication by the words *shart* (protasis) and *jazā'* (apodosis). Later in this passage he says that if the first part of a connective proposition is a *shart* and the second is *jazā'*, then this connective proposition is an implication. The words *shart* and *jazā'* are used in Arabic grammar as technical terms referring to the parts of a conditional sentence: the first refers to the condition and the second to the sentence depending upon it. It seems that, in calling the antecedent and the consequent of an implication *shart* and *jazā'*, Avicenna wanted to point out the peculiar characteristic of such propositions: that the subject-matter of the antecedent and that of the consequent are related. (Or, as modern logicians would put it, that they express formal implication.) Throughout the text these terms were never used to refer to the antecedent and the consequent of a chance connection; that is the kind of connective propositions in which the subject-matter of the antecedent and that of the consequent are not related. Another set of terms used frequently in the text is *muqaddam* (antecedent, that which precedes) and *tālī* (consequent, that which follows or comes after). These Avicenna used without restriction to refer to the antecedent and the consequent of the 'If – then' and 'Either – or' propositions of any type.

In Greek sources the antecedent and the consequent of an 'If – then' proposition is indicated by two sets of terminology: one Peripatetic and the other Stoic.[48] The Peripatetic and the Stoic word for the antecedent (the proposition which immediately follows the connective 'If') is τὸ ἡγούμενον (interchangeable with ἀρχόμενον). The Peripatetics, however, used τὸ ἑπόμενον (interchangeable with ἀκόλουθον) for the consequent (or the proposition which does not immediately follow the connective 'if'), while the Stoics introduced for it the term λῆγον. Clearly Avicenna's two sets of terms cannot be compared with those found in the Greek sources.

In this passage a distinction is also made between two kinds of implication. The first is the implication which is necessary in thought and existence, and the second is the implication which is necessary in existence only. The concept 'man', for example, implies the concept 'rational' in existence and thought. It implies it in existence because there is no man in the world which is not rational. Also, 'man' implies 'rational' in thought because rationality is part of the essence of man; for we cannot think of man without thinking of his being rational. But the concept of 'a creature-that-laughs' is implied by 'man' only in existence; because, though being a creature-that-laughs is something which is peculiar to man, and, therefore, it enables us to distinguish him from other existing creatures, it is not part of the essence of man.[49] The above distinction does not, of course, belong to formal logic. But it is important to note that this distinction is part of his theory of definition and demonstration; and logic, for Avicenna, is only a step towards the more important aim, namely demonstration. Therefore if science is concerned with demonstration, then it is important to know not only the formal conditions which govern the following of the consequent from the antecedent, but also whether the consequent is related to the antecedent in the way a genus is related to the essence, or in the way an inseparable accident is related to the essence.

Although Avicenna does not mention Plato in name, he is no doubt referring to Plato's theory of Ideas in this passage. Avicenna asserts that Ideas are the ultimate nature of things. He also says that these Ideas are necessarily connected. The question which he raised here is whether it is possible to accept Plato's Ideas and the necessary relation between them and at the same time speak of things as being connected by chance. His answer is that the realm of Ideas cannot be a subject for human inquiry. Neither reasoning nor immediate thought, Avicenna says, can hit upon Ideas or the relations between them. The conclusion seems to be that our inquiry here concerns our world and the different ways the human mind grasps it. And to our limited intellect certain events and objects do seem to be connected by chance though their Ideas, which our minds cannot grasp, are not.

235, 1–12. According to Avicenna some words used in connective propositions indicate the relation of implication, and others do not. *Idh, Kullamā* and *lammā* are of the second kind, while *in, idhā* and *matā* are of the first. Avicenna also distinguishes between the last three words according, as he says, to their strength in indicating the relation of implication. He considers *in* as being very strong in indicating implication, *matā* is very weak in this respect and *idhā* is in between. The distinctions introduced here have no linguistic basis. The question now is whether there is a Greek source for these distinctions. In the *Institutio Logica* Galen refers to εἰ and ἐπεί as the two particles used in Greek to make conditional propositions (III, 3)'[50] But Galen tells us that "it makes no difference whether you say εἰ or ἐπεί in conditional propositions ... because they signify one and the same thing".[51] However, Diogenes Laertius says that the difference between εἰ, ἐπεί and διότι, according to Stoic doctrine, is a difference between hypothetical, inferential and casual propositions. The first, Diogenes says, is true if the contradictory of its consequent is incompatible with its antecedent. The second is true if its antecedent is true and the consequent follows from it. While the third is true if the consequent follows from the antecedent and not vice versa.[52] There is no way of comparing Diogenes' distinctions with those of Avicenna, since the latter does not explain what he means by the strength of the implication.

235, 12–16 and 236. This passage gives a clear explanation why Avicenna considers the conditional proposition to be a single statement-making sentence. Considering first the antecedent of the connective-conditional proposition, he says that it is only a hypothesis which can neither be affirmed nor denied. In other words it is not a statement-making sentence which can be true or false. The same is also true of the consequent of these propositions. Avicenna's argument for this view is that the sentence 'If the sun rises' can neither be affirmed nor denied and, therefore, it is neither true nor false. Also, the sentence 'then it is day' is neither true nor false. According to Diogenes Laertius, Chrysippus in his *Dialectical Definitions* considered a hypothetical ὑποθετικός as neither true nor false.[53] Unfortunately, Diogenes does not give an example of the hypothetical. However, as father Stakelum says, it appears that hypothetical expressions are like the cause 'If it is day'.[54]

In his *De Interpretatione* Aristotle says that

A single statement-making sentence is either one that reveals a single thing or that is single in virtue of a connective. There are more than one if more things than one are revealed or if connectives are lacking. (17a 15. The translation is Ackrill's.)

Commenting on this passage in Aristotle, J. L. Ackrill says that

On Aristotle's scheme a compound expression of a suitable sort would seem to qualify both as a single statement ('single in virtue of a connective') and as more than one statement ('If more things than one are revealed').[55]

Al-Fārābī, who also commented on this passage in Aristotle's *De Interpretatione*, explains Aristotle's text saying that though the conditional proposition consists of two predicative propositions, these two propositions become one when connected by a conditional word.[56] Avicenna, who seems to agree with al-Fārābī's view, gives a reason for such an interpretation. He says that the sentence 'The sun rises' is either true or false,

and so also the sentence 'It is day'. But when both predicative propositions become parts of a conditional sentence, neither of them will remain
a statement-making sentence. (See above pp. 220–21.)

237. A close examination of the truth-conditions of the connective
proposition is what occupies Avicenna from this passage right to the end
of the chapter. Avicenna regards the connective proposition as true in
the following cases: (a) When both the antecedent and the consequent
are true, (b) When both are false, and (c) When the antecedent is false and
the consequent true. It is false when the antecedent is true and the consequent false. The passage begins with the distinction made before between what is called implication (formal implication) and chance connection. The distinction amounts to this: In connective propositions whose
antecedents and consequents are true, if the antecedent formally implies
the consequent, the proposition would be an implication (luzūm).[57] But
if no such relation exists between the antecedent and the consequent,
except on a very abstract level as to say that the fact that the antecedent
and consequent are always found to be true is a kind of relation, then the
proposition is said to express chance connection.

A new classification of connective-conditional propositions is also
given. Avicenna distinguishes between the restricted (ʿlā'l-tahqīq) and
the unrestricted (ʿlā'l-iṭlāq) connective propositions saying that in the first
what concerns us is the relation between the antecedent and the consequent, namely the relation of formal implication. While in the second we
are only interested in the fact that the antecedent and the consequent are
true. This means that the unrestricted connective proposition can be
either a formal implication or a chance connection, since in both cases
the antecedents and consequents are true. The restricted connection
is of course the same as the formal implication. This point is made clear
at the end where the unrestricted proposition is described as being
more general than the restricted. For the restricted, i.e. the formal
implication, can also be unrestricted. But the contrary is not true, since
the unrestricted proposition can either be a formal implication or a chance
connection (Cp. al-Qiyās, 238, 10–17).

237, 16; 238 and 239, 1–8. This is a very difficult passage. What Avicenna
says here is that a proposition with a false antecedent and consequent is

true only if the consequent is formally implied by the antecedent.[58] If the proposition does not reveal such a relation, then it is false. Thus, according to this viewpoint the proposition 'If man is not animal, then he is not sensitive' is true; while the proposition 'If man is a creature-that-caws, then the raven is an articulate creature' is false.

The difficulty in the passage arises in connection with what is said in defending a view contrary to the above. It is clear that Avicenna subscribes to the line of thought which says that in the proposition 'If man is not an animal, then he is not sensitive' one can assume the antecedent to be true in which case the consequent would be true by implication (in his sense of implication). This cannot be said of the second example 'If man is a creature-that-caws, then the raven is an articulate creature'. For even if we assume that the antecedent is true, the consequent will remain false since it is not formally implied by the assumption. That would leave us with a connective proposition whose antecedent is true and its consequent false. It seems that at one point he thought that by applying the concepts of restricted and unrestricted connection he would be able to regard propositions similar to his second example as true. The absurdity of this method is quite clear and Avicenna himself must have realized that, for he comes back at the end to his original position which we summarized above.

239, 9–17 and 240, 1–16. Until now Avicenna has given an analysis of two cases in which the connective proposition is considered true. The first is the case in which the antecedent and the consequent are true; and the second is the case in which the antecedent and the consequent are false. In this passage he discusses the only case remained, namely that in which the antecedent is false and the consequent is true. He must have felt that unlike the others this case is not readily acceptable, and therefore needs to be explained. This has been done with the help of the theory of the syllogism with which the reader is supposed to be acquainted. Avicenna says that in a proposition like 'If five is even, then it is a number' the statement 'Five is a number' follows from 'Five is even' and another statement which we omit, i.e. 'Every even is a number'. Thus, Avicenna continues, we can treat 'If five is even, than it is a number' as a syllogism whose premises are 'Five is even' and 'Every even is a number', and whose conclusion is 'Five is a number'. In other words, what Avicenna is

saying is that the logical principle which allows us to deduce a true conclusion from a false premiss applies not only to the syllogism but also to
connective propositions.

To understand his objection to this case of true connection, i.e. the case
in which the antecedent is false and the consequent is true, we must bear
in mind the fact that for Avicenna the last aim in logic is demonstration.
A formal inference in his view is to be judged according to whether it can
help us in constructing what Avicenna thinks to be a demonstrative
argument. And for Avicenna a demonstrative argument is a valid inference in which the conclusion is established with the help of premisses
which are already proved or evidently true. Therefore, though from a
formal point of view, it is logically valid to deduce a true proposition from
a false proposition, such an inference will not be of any help in demonstration.

240, 18 and 241, 1. The only case in which a connective proposition would
be false is the one in which the antecedent is true and the consequent is
false. Avicenna adds nothing more to that, for the case must have looked
obvious to him and therefore needed no explanation. It is interesting to
note here that al-Jubbāʾī, as reported in al-Ashʿarī's *Maqālāt al-Islāmiyyīn*, Vol. I, p. 204, refers to this case in his own way and says that

If what is decreed (*maqdūr*) is connected (*wuṣila*) with what is impossible (*mustaḥīl*), the
speech would be impossible.

CHAPTER TWO

242, 4–8. There are several ways in which one can express a relation of
conflict. One way is to use a non-conditional form of language. This
means that the proposition should be expressed in neither an 'If – then'
nor an 'Either – or' sentence. Avicenna's example for such propositions
is '*p* is in conflict with *q*'. Another way is to express conflict in the form
of a connective-conditional proposition [59], such as 'If *p*, then not-*q*'
which is equivalent to 'Either *p* or *q*' provided the latter is used in the
exclusive sense (see below). The third way of expressing conflict is to put
it in the 'Either – or' form. In the following passages Avicenna concen-
trates on the third way of expressing conflict, that is on separative propositions, referring briefly to the second and completely ignoring the first.

242, 9–14; 243 and 244, 1–15. There are three kinds of separative propositions: (1) The separative proposition which expresses real conflict. In these propositions it is necessary that one of the parts should be true and the other false. Thus, when both parts are true or when both are false the separative expressing real (or complete) conflict will be false. Avicenna adds the words *lā yakhlū* ('it is exclusively') before the sentence expressing this kind of conflict to distinguish it from the other two kinds of separative propositions all of which have the form: 'Either – or'. This proposition can be expressed in the following matrix:

If the first part is	and the second part is	the separative expressing real conflict will be
True	True	False
True	False	True
False	True	True
False	False	False

(2) The separative proposition which does not exclude the possibility of having both its parts false. Avicenna says that this proposition also expresses conflict; but conflict in this case is incomplete. This proposition can be represented in the following matrix:

If the first part is	and the second part is	the proposition expressing incomplete conflict will be
True	True	False
True	False	True
False	True	True
False	False	True

What Avicenna is trying to do is to explain the context in which such propositions exist or may be used. The example he gives is of a situation where a person mistakenly states that a certain thing is inanimate *and* animal and someone else corrects him saying that it cannot be both but either the one or the other, without getting involved in the question of what that thing is. For in that case he would be considering the possibility of the thing being either inanimate or animal or plant, and it is likely that the thing is a plant. Thus in Avicenna's view, there are cases in which we use the 'Either – or' form to show that though it is impossible for the antecedent and the consequent to be true, the possibility of the antecedent and the consequent being false cannot be excluded.

In trying to underline the idea that both parts of such separative propositions can be false, Avicenna remarks that these propositions are equivalent to the negation of a connective proposition. (Cp. *Institutio Logica* IV, 4.)

(3) The separative proposition in which both parts can be true. In this case it is not possible for both parts to be false. This proposition can be represented in the following table:

If the first part is	and the second part is	the separative proposition will be
True	True	True
True	False	True
False	True	True
False	False	False

The Stoics did not recognize except (1) and they called it διεξευγμένον (ἀξίωμα). Galen, however, mentions the three above kinds. In dealing with (1), he gives the above Stoic name in addition to the Peripatetic name, namely διαιρετικαὶ προτάσις. He calls (2) παραπλήσια διεξευγμένοις and (3) παραδιεξευγμένον. Unfortunately, Avicenna does not give specific names to any one of the above three kinds. But he agrees with Galen in taking (1) as a proposition expressing complete conflict τελεία μάχη and (2) as expressing incomplete conflict ἐλλιπὴς μάχη. However, it should be noted that Avicenna's example of (3) is of a separative proposition whose parts are negative propositions which is not so in Galen's work.

245, 9–17 and 246, 1–5. It should be remembered here that the order which the parts of an 'If – then' proposition take, i.e. one being specifically the antecedent and the other the consequent, does affect the truth-value of the compound proposition for it is obvious that when the antecedent is true and the consequent false, the compound proposition is false; while if the antecedent is false and the consequent true the compound is true. The same thing is not true of the 'Either – or' proposition, since it is true in case the antecedent is true and the consequent false or vice versa.[60] Thus, while the order of the parts (antecedent and consequent) of the 'If – then' proposition is essential for establishing its truth-value, the truth-value of the 'Either – or' proposition is not affected at all by this order. Therefore, Avicenna concludes, while the words 'Either – or' do not necessitate that the propositions joined by them have a certain order – one being *the* antecedent and the other *the* consequent – the words 'If – then' do. In the sense that once we choose a certain proposition to be the antecedent and another the consequent, the order cannot be changed unless we intend to form a new proposition. This is what Avicenna means by saying that the antecedent and the consequent of the 'Either – or' proposition are equivalent, i.e. interchangeable; while this is not so in the case of the 'If – then' proposition.

The word Avicenna uses for 'equivalence' is *takāfu'*. Here as well as in the other two places in *al-Qiyās* in which the word is mentioned, 251, 4–7 and 383, 15–16, the meaning of *takāfu'* is clear. Two propositions are said to be 'equivalent' if they are interchangeable. In all its occurrences in Aristotle's *Categories* ἀντιστρέφειν is translated into *takāfu'*. It may well be that Avicenna or his source imported the word from the *Categories*. But it should be clear that ἀντιστρέφειν, as used in the *Categories*, is said of terms which reciprocate. As J. L. Ackrill, *Aristotle's Categories and De Interpretatione* (p. 100), explains it

The claim that *A* and *B* reciprocate is the claim that 'X is A of (to, than, etc.) Y' entails 'Y is B of X' and 'Y is B of X' entails 'X is A of Y'. (See the commentary in pp. 266–67.)

246, 6–17 and 247, 1–5. This is the beginning of Avicenna's own analysis of the three kinds of separative propositions described above. Here he compares the first kind with the other two. The first kind, as is said earlier, is true when the antecedent is true and the consequent is false, or when the antecedent is false and the consequent true. When both the antecedent and the consequent are true or when both are false, the compound proposition is false. He sees such propositions as presenting us with only two alternatives or possiblilities one of which is necessarily true and the other is necessarily false. This peculiar characteristic is indicated by using the words 'It is exclusively' which are supposed to be added at the beginning of every such proposition to distinguish it from the other two. Avicenna says that if the antecedent of such propositions is false, the consequent is necessarily true; and if it is true, the consequent is necessarily false. This is not so in either the second or the third kind of separative propositions. For in the second kind, if the antecedent is false, the consequent could either be true or false, since in this kind of separatives the proposition can be true when both the antecedent and the consequent are false. (See the table in p. 233). In the third kind if the antecedent is true, the consequent could be either true or false as is clear in the table at p. 234. But is it necessary that the first kind of separative propositions should be constituted of two parts only? Avicenna's answer, as this passage reveals, is in the negative. He allows for propositions such as 'It is exclusively either p or q or r'. What Avicenna does in such cases is to treat the first part as the antecedent and the rest, taken together as a separative proposition, as the consequent. It is obvious that if the first part of such propositions is true, everyone of the others would be false. For suppose we have the proposition 'It is exclusively either p or q or r' in which p, the antecedent, is true. In this example 'q or r' should be false. This leaves us with two possibilities: either both q and r are false or they are both true. The second possibility is excluded since p is true, as already said, and in the first kind of separative propositions the proposition would be false if both its antecedent and consequent are true. Therefore, in such compound propositions, if the first part is true, everyone of the other propositions will be false. This means that there is complete conflict between the first part of the proposition (p) and everyone of the others: be it q or r. But what if the first part is false? Here, the only way to establish complete conflict is to treat the first part as the antecedent and the rest, taken together as a separative proposition, as the consequent. Take the same example: 'It is exclusively either p or q or r'. If p is false, then 'q or r' is necessarily true. Of course this would mean that either q is true and r is false or vice versa. Avicenna refers to this (second) case when he talks of objections raised against including propositions with more than two parts in the first kind of separative propositions. For when p is regarded as false, neither q nor r can be said to be necessarily true. This is the reason why he wants the consequent to be 'q or r'. Otherwise we would not be able to talk here of complete conflict.

247, 6–17; 248; and 249, 1–9. The second and the third kind of separative propositions are compared and analyzed this time. Avicenna says that while in the third both the antecedent and the consequent can be true, this is not so in the second. Thus, as we said above, if the antecedent of the third is true, the consequent can either be true or false. But if it is false, the consequent will necessarily be true. (See pp. 233–34.) This is what he means by saying that when the contradictory of the antecedent is affirmed, the consequent will necessarily be true. This of course is not true of the second kind as Avicenna remarks. For the compound proposition is true if the falsity of the antecedent is affirmed. Another difference between the two is that in the third the parts are both expressed in the negative form, while this is not so in the second or the first.[61] Does this mean that all separative propositions in which the antecedent and the consequent can be true are of this type? A few lines before (al-Qiyās 245, 5) Avicenna gives an example of a separative proposition with both its parts expressed in the affirmative and in which the antecedent and the consequent are true. But these, as far as one can see, are another type of separative propositions which Avicenna, for some reason or another, wanted to distinguish from the second kind which he is discussing here. Avicenna goes on with his comparison between the second and the third kind of separative propositions saying that the two have the following in common: First both do not take the words 'It is exclusively' which is characteristic of the first kind. Second both are not pure and simple separative propositions. This means that, unlike the first kind where the compound proposition is true only when one of the parts is true and the other false, their parts can both be false (the second kind) or both true (the third kind). Thus both the second and the third are given one common label, 'defective conflict'. Third both are in essence two propositions expressed in a single separative proposition. Take the third kind of separative propositions. According to Avicenna when one says 'Either this thing is not a plant or not inanimate', what he is in fact saying is 'Either this thing is not a plant or it is; if it is, then it is not inanimate'. That is to say, the first kind of separative propositions presents us with a choice between two contradictory alternatives. But in the third kind of separative propositions the second alternative (the consequent) is no longer the contradictory of the first (the antecedent). For only when the negation of the first alternative is affirmed (i.e. when the first alternative itself is false) can we say that the second is true (since in this kind of separatives the possibility of both being false is excluded). In the case of the second kind of separative propositions we can be sure that the second alternative is false only when the first is true. But if it is false the other may or may not be true.

249, 10–15. This passage contradicts the previous one in which it was clearly stated that the third kind of separative propositions should have

negative antecedents and consequents while the antecedent and consequent of the first kind must be in the affirmative. In fact this was regarded
as one distinctive mark for both. Here Avicenna does not exclude the
possibility of having negative antecedents and consequents in the first
kind of separative propositions. He even says that one of their parts can
be negative and the other affirmative. The opening sentence says that
a separative proposition with two negative parts can be treated in the
same way as the one with negative and affirmative parts. This means
that the third kind of separative propositions can also have negative
and affirmative parts, which again seems to contradict what he said
earlier.

250, 5–17 and 251, 1–11. The question being raised is whether we can
have a real separative proposition in which the subject-matter of its
antecedent and that of its consequent are not related. In other words, is it
necessary that the antecedent and the consequent of a real separative
proposition should be statements about one and the same subject? The
main idea underlying Avicenna's answer is that in the real separative
(which is the first kind of separatives discussed above) the antecedent and
the consequent must be contradictory statements, that is to say should
express contradictory judgments about one and the same thing. And that
it is necessary for it to be so is clear from what he said before, viz. that this
is what distinguishes if from the other kinds of separative propositions.
Avicenna gives another reason for rejecting a so-called 'chance relation'
between the antecedent and the consequent of a real separative. He says
that in the case of the proposition expressing chance connection one can
argue that the antecedent and the consequent are in fact connected in their
ultimate natures and that it is due to the limitations of our minds that we
are incapable of detecting the connection.[62] (See also al-Qiyās, 234.) This,
he thinks, does not apply to the proposition expressing conflict. For if we
do talk at all about conflicting statements which are in no way related, we
can only have in mind statements which are impossible in themselves, as
for example 'Either two is not even or man is not a rational animal'.
According to him these impossible statements are not related at all not
even by what he calls 'chance relation'. This is certainly not so if we agree
that as Forms things are ultimately related, except if one says that impossible things have no Forms.

251, 12–17 and 252, 1–8. Two things emerge from this passage: (a) What is essential to conditional propositions is that they join together *propositions* and not single *concepts* (which is the case with predicative propositions). (b) Though there are several devices for joining propositions into one unit, all such devices can be reduced to two basic forms – the 'If – then' or/and the 'Either – or'. In his view a proposition such as 'A is not B unless C is D' is equivalent to 'If C is D, then A is B' and to 'Either C is D or A is not B' (if we take the separative here as belonging to the third kind). The same applies to conjunctive propositions, namely those in which the connective 'and' occurs. This is a very important remark. It is no doubt puzzling to the reader that Avicenna completely disregard such statements. It is clear now that he recognizes such types of propositions but he thinks that they can be reduced to the main types to which these chapters are devoted. On this point Avicenna might have simply taken the view of some Latin-Greek commentators.

CHAPTER THREE

253; 254 and 255, 1–2. Avicenna distinguishes here between simple and compound conditionals. The simple conditional is the one whose antecedent and consequent are predicative propositions. The compound is constituted of (a) conditional and predicative propositions, and (b) of conditional propositions alone, whether they are of the same type as the original proposition or of a different type or even of a mixture of the two conditionals – the connective and the separative. It should be noted that Avicenna does not use brackets or any such notation to enable the reader to figure out the way in which the author wants him to read these compound propositions. All Avicenna did is to differenciate between, on the one hand the main propositions, and, on the other, the subsidiary propositions, which are the antecedent and the consequent of the main proposition. Perhaps the reason for not introducing any kind of notation is that he did not make any use of compound propositions in this work. The only ones he deals with are those whose antecedents and consequents are single predicatives, and these, of course, are manageable by his device The following is a list of the compound propositions which Avicenna mentions in this passage. We will use modern notation to make it easier for the reader to follow his examples.[63]

(1) $(p \rightarrow q) \rightarrow (r \rightarrow t)$
(2) $(p \rightarrow q) \vee (r \rightarrow t)$
(3) $(p \vee q) \rightarrow (r \vee t)$
(4) $(p \vee q) \vee (r \vee t)$
(5) $(p \rightarrow q) \vee (r \vee t)$
(6) $(p \vee q) \vee (r \rightarrow t)$
(7) $(p \rightarrow q) \rightarrow (r \vee t)$
(8) $(p \vee q) \rightarrow (r \rightarrow t)$
(9) $(p \rightarrow q) \vee r$
(10) $p \vee (q \rightarrow r)$[64]
(11) $p \rightarrow (q \rightarrow r)$
(12) $(p \rightarrow q) \rightarrow r$
(13) $(p \vee q) \vee r$
(14) $p \vee (q \vee r)$[65]
(15) $p \rightarrow (q \vee r)$
(16) $(p \vee q) \rightarrow r$[66]

255, 3–20 and 256, 1–5. The distinction he makes in this passage is between the two truth-operators he has been discussing since, namely 'If –
then' and 'Either – or'. While the first, he says, joins two parts: the
antecedent and the consequent, whether they are predicative or conditional propositions[67], the second can join more than two, in fact an
infinite number of propositions. What he has in mind is propositions
where several possibilities are being given in the form 'Either p or q or ...
etc.'. This cannot be done in the case of the 'If – then' proposition. Avicenna adds promptly that this does not mean that the antecedent or/and
the consequent of the connective propositions cannot be a conjunction
of several propositions, i.e. propositions connected by 'and'. The last
point is important because a conditional proposition, though itself a
combination of more than one proposition, is nevertheless considered in
this work as a single statement-making sentence. But a conjunctive proposition is not. Avicenna examines the case (a) when the antecedent of the
connective proposition is a conjunctive proposition and (b) when the
consequent is a conjunctive proposition. For (a) he gives the following
example: 'If this man has chronic fever, hard cough, laboured breathing,
proding pain and saw-pulse, he has pleurasy'. This he says is a single

proposition because the five symptoms listed in the antecedent compliment each other and are all required in order to reach the conclusion that the man has pleurasy, which is to say that in this case the parts of the conjunctive propositions cannot be taken separately and should be taken as a whole. But in (b) the same example, when converted, can show that the connective proposition is not a single proposition but several propositions. For one can say 'If this man has pleurasy, then he has chronic fever' and what he says is a complete statement. So also if he says 'If this man has pleurasy, then he has hard cough' ... etc. For every one of these propositions would be a complete statement. At least (b) gives a counterevidence for his thesis that the connective cannot have more than two parts. For here we have an example of a proposition which, admittedly, has five distinct consequents.

256, 11–17; 257 and 258, 1–12. In these lines the main theme is the reduction of conditionals to predicative propositions. Not all conditionals, however. For, though the opening lines assert that conditionals are reduceable to predicative propositions, later on in this passage a certain kind of connective and separative propositions is specifically excepted from this general statement. The conditionals which are not reduceable to the predicatives are the propositions which Avicenna had been mainly occupied with, such as 'If the sun rises, then it is day' and 'Either this number is even or it is odd'. The passage is on the main devoted to specifying the conditionals which are so reduceable. First, the connective propositions which are reduceable to the predicatives are those in which the antecedent and the consequent (which are there taken to be predicative propositions) share the same subject. He further adds that the class of connective propositions which are more similar to predicative propositions are those in which the subject is put before the truth-operator e.g. 'The sun, always when it rises, then it is day'. (Notice that these two characteristics are absent from 'If the sun rises, then it is day'.) For, to him, 'The sun, always when it rises, then it is day' is similar to 'The sun is something of which one can say that when it rises it will be day'. The latter is a predicative proposition with a complex predicate. But never mind this complexity, for it is possible to give the whole of the predicate a single name, e.g. *Alpha*, and therefore end up with a predicative proposition with a single subject and predicate. Second is the separative proposition.

All that Avicenna says is that the reduction in this case is possible when the shared subject is put before the truth-operator. For in this case a proposition like 'Every number is either even or odd', can be reduced to 'Every number is something which can be described as being either even or odd'. As in the previous case, the complex predicate in the last proposition can be given a single name like *Gama*, and the proposition becomes 'Every number is *Gama*', which is a predicative proposition with a single subject and predicate.

258. 13–19; 259;260 and 261. See the Commentary on 233, 4–9.

CHAPTER FOUR

262 and 263. The underlined thesis here, repeated in more than one place in this work, is that in conditional propositions what is to be considered as universal, particular, singular or indefinite is the judgement that a proposition *follows* from or is in *conflict* with another. The reason behind Avicenna's emphatic language is that some Greek logicians, whom Avicenna does not name, allegedly regarded such labels (universal, particular, affirmative and negative), when applied to conditional propositions, as being indicative of the quantity and/or quality of the antecedent and consequent. (Or when they are absent, to the absence of quantity and/or quality in the antecedent and consequent as in the case of the indefinite proposition.) To support his view, he reminds his reader of what is said about predicative propositions in which the quantity of the judgement of predication, rather than the quantity of the subject and predicate, determines the quantity of the proposition. If in a predicative proposition the judgement is universal, then the proposition is universal; whether the subject and the predicate are singular or universal terms. Thus according to Avicenna's opponents, the connective proposition 'If every C is B, then every H is Z' is a universal connective proposition simply because the antecedent and the consequent are universal propositions. But, to Avicenna, it is indefinite, because of the absence of any of the quantifiers which are always put before the conditional proposition. In this passage, he mentions only the universal quantifier 'always' which he uses for both the connective and the separative propositions. (The quantifier for particular conditional propositions is 'sometimes'.) There is a brief explanation

of what he means by the universal quantifier. (The quantifiers are explained fully in this and the succeeding chapter.) A universal quantifier when annexed to a connective proposition indicates that the consequent follows from the antecedent under any condition we may state or posit. The same is true of the separative proposition. In this case the universal quantifier is meant to show that the consequent is in conflict with the antecedent under any condition. The indefinite proposition, which contains none of the quantifiers, can have two forms each of which has a peculiar sense. The first is the 'If – then' form and the other is the 'When ..., ...'. Avicenna says that when we say 'When A is B, H is Z' what is meant is that at all times 'H is Z' will follow from 'A is B'. But when we use the form 'If – then' what is indicated is that 'H is Z' will follow from 'A is B' even if that happened at one particular time, say t_1. Out of these remarks an important distinction is drawn between the forms 'Always: when ..., ...' and 'When ..., ...'. Both forms tell us that the consequent follows from the antecedent at any time. But it is peculiar to the first that it indicates as well the following of the consequent from the antecedent under all conditions. (See the Commentary in pp. 244 and 247.) What is not clearly defined is the singular conditional. All he gives is a negative definition. He says that the singular conditional is not the one whose antecedent and consequent are singular predicative propositions, i.e. propositions whose subjects are singular terms. But what could a singular conditional so defined be?

264. This passage deals with the view that the universal connective proposition is, in fact, a universal predicative proposition. In his brief statement of this view, Avicenna says that its advocate asserts that the proposition 'Always: when this is a man, then he is an animal' is the same as the proposition 'Every man is an animal'. Avicenna rejects this view for the following reasons: (1) The subject of both the antecedent and the consequent of the universal connective proposition is a singular term, while the subject of the predicative proposition is a universal term. (2) The above universal predicative and universal connective propositions are not logically equivalent because there are instances in which the universal connective is true and the universal predicative is false. (3) Even if the two propositions are equivalent, still they are different in form; for the predicative says that 'animality' belongs to 'man', while the con-

nective says that the sentence 'this is an animal' is true whenever the sentence 'This is a man' is true.[68]

265, 1–8. Avicenna's treatment of the quantifiers begins here with a definition of the universal connective proposition (when it is in the affirmative). He repeats what he said at the beginning of this chapter that what is meant by a universal quantifier in this context is that the consequent follows from the antecedent at any time and under any condition. There is little more said about what he means by the following of the consequent from the antecedent under any condition. He says that that is meant to indicate the following of the consequent from the antecedent no matter what conditions we may add to the antecedent. Less essential is the other feature of the universal connective, namely that the consequent follows from the antecedent at any time. For, Avicenna says, the antecedent could describe something which cannot be repeated or does not recur in which case there will be no reference to time.

265, 9–19 and 266, 1–8. Having defined the universal quantifier as applied to conditional propositions, Avicenna proceeds with another task, viz. of applying the universal quantifier to those connective propositions to which the universal quantifier seems less intuitively applicable. In doing so he also hopes to explain much more clearly what he means by saying that in a universal connective proposition the consequent follows from the antecedent under any condition. The kind of connective propositions he has in mind is the one in which the relation expressed is that of chance connection, i.e. the case where the consequent, though not formally implied by the antecedent, is nevertheless true as well as the antecedent. Before going into the universal forms of such propositions he talks briefly about their indefinite forms. The proposition he analyzes is 'If man talks, then the donkey brays'. Evidently the consequent here is not formally implied by the antecedent, but both the antecedent and the consequent are admittedly true. Oddly enough Avicenna says that once the consequant in such propositions is known to be true, the proposition as a whole must be true. Now what if one says 'Always: when man talks, then the donkey brays'? What are the conditions for regarding such propositions as true? To be regarded as true two conditions must be fulfilled. One is that it should be true of every donkey that it brays. The second is that the consequent must follow from the antecedent under any condition or at any time we may stipulate. What if one stipulates a time in which no donkey exists? Would it not be true to say that at such a time and under such condition the consequent would be false? This of course would mean that the above connective proposition could not be universally asserted. But, to Avicenna's mind, this is not so. Because when we say that the donkey brays we do not refer to any existing donkey. This, to him, is clear because we can still consider the statement 'The donkey brays' as true though none of the existing donkeys is braying at the time the statement is made.

266, 9–15 and 267, 1–6. What if we have a universal proposition like 'Always: when every donkey talks, then every man brays' where both the antecedent and the consequent are false propositions, Avicenna asks. Some people, he claims, think that such a following is valid, because if we assume that every donkey talks, then (for no clear reason) we should assume the truth of the consequent, i.e. that every man brays. Avicenna rejects this view. His reason for this rejection can be stated as follows: The above proposition can either be taken as expressing chance connection or a formal implication. It cannot be the former, since a proposition expressing chance connection is by definition true only in case both the antecedent and the consequent are true. It also cannot be a formal implication, simply because the consequent is not formally implied by the antecedent. Therefore, the above proposition does not express a relation of following in any sense of the word.

267, 6–18, 268; 269 and 270, 1–8. In the previous passage Avicenna stated the fact that the proposition 'Always: when every donkey talks, then every man brays' does not represent a formal implication. In these lines he is trying to prove this point. It must be said at the outset that his trial is relevant in as much as it reveals his own understanding of the logic of propositions. His argument, though no doubt intended to prove the above mentioned point, only shows that the proposition 'Not every donkey brays' would formally imply 'Not every man talks' if and only if 'Every man talks' formally implied 'Every donkey brays'. Since this is not so, the desired conclusion would not follow. What is interesting to point out in all this is that for him the rule of inference, which he explains later on (al-Qiyās, 395) and which he assumes in the argument, namely

If p, then q
but not q
therefore, not p,

is applicable only in case the first premiss expresses formal implication.

Still Avicenna seems to be ill at ease as regards his original view that the proposition 'Not every donkey brays' does not formally imply 'Not every man talks'. For he defends it this time against some feigned objection which is put in the following way: If it is agreed that in the proposition 'Always when every man talks, then every donkey brays' (which expresses chance connection), both the antecedent and the consequent must be true, and that every time the antecedent is found to be true, the consequent should also be true, (without, of course, the consequent being formally implied by the antecedent), then the proposition 'Not every donkey brays' should not be connected with 'Every man talks'. Otherwise a contradiction would follow thus:

Sometimes when every donkey does not bray,
then every man talks,
and always when every man talks,
then every donkey brays;
therefore, sometimes when not every donkey brays,
then every donkey brays.

It seems that Avicenna thinks that if such a contradiction can be established, then 'Not every donkey brays' would be connected with 'Not every man talks'; and the only kind of connection they can have is formal implication. So Avicenna's job is to challenge this contradiction and to show that it is not what it is taken to be. He says that the conclusion reached above is not a contradiction. On the contrary it is a true statement; since its antecedent is nothing but an assumption, and the consequent is a true statement. And if we have a false assumption connected by chance with a true consequent the proposition, Avicenna declares, would be true. Avicenna underlines this view, and says that this is what we do in arguments *per impossible*. In such arguments we assume the contradictory of a true proposition, and this assumption is connected by chance with another true proposition. (See p. 277.)

270, 9–13. This passage repeats what is said in the one immediately before it. It says that in chance connection when the antecedent is a false assumption and the consequent a true proposition, the whole connective proposition would be true.

270, 14–17; 271 and 272, 1–12. One should bear in mind, Avicenna says, that the antecedent of a connective proposition is nothing but an assumption. This is indicated by the words 'if' and 'when' which precede the antecedent. What we should know about an assumption is that its truth or falsity may have nothing to do with the actual state of affairs it describes. For we might assume that it is true knowing (or discovering later on) that it is not. If the assumption turns out to be in fact true, then what follows validly from it would be true. But if it is actually false, then what follows validly from it is undecidable, i.e. can be true or false. The consequent, on the other hand, is not an assumption. And in case it follows from a false antecedent, it should be judged in itself and independently of the antecedent, though it might be formally implied by that antecedent. Then he goes on to say that in a true connective proposition when the antecedent is in fact true, the consequent must also be true whether it is connected with the antecedent by chance or it is formally implied by it. But when the antecedent is actually false, the consequent which follows [69] would be either true or false. Now suppose we were faced with the case in which the antecedent is false and the consequent is true. He says that in such a case the proposition would be true if the consequent is formally implied by the antecedent. When both the antecedent and the consequent are false, the proposition as a whole would be true when the relation of following expressed is that of formal implication.

272, 13–18 and 273, 1–6. After a lengthy digression Avicenna is coming back to his original topic which he started in 265. He repeats here the definition of the universal connective proposition with more information this time on what he means by 'conditions' or 'cases'. To repeat, we say of a connective proposition that it is universal if (a) every time the antecedent is stated the consequent necessarily follows from it. And (b) when the consequent follows from the antecedent under any condition. What he is trying to clarify here is (b). He says that the conditions or cases he is thinking of are those which we attach to the antecedent, either to specify it, or to limit its application ot to make explicit some of its implications so that more is known about it. Such conditions or cases should never contradict the original antecedent, he adds.

273, 7–17; 274 and 275, 1–14. The question raised is what if the conditions which we might add to specify the antecedent are contrary to known facts? Would the universal connective in this case cease to be universal? For example, would a universal connective proposition like 'Always: when this is a man, then he is an animal' cease to be universal when we add to the antecedent conditions like 'Man is neither a creature-that-senses nor a creature-that-moves'? Avicenna's answer is that with such conditions the proposition can no longer be described as universal. This is not, he says, because the antecedent is false or impossible, for the truth of the antecedent is not in question here.[70] What is in question is whether the consequent follows from the antecedent or not.[71] And as the above example shows the consequent does not follow from an antecedent conditioned by contrary-to-fact statements. Avicenna's next problem is to try to find a way out since his definition of the universal connective states clearly that the consequent must follow from the antecedent under *any* condition; and in this form the definition cannot be fulfilled. His answer to this is that we should add to the antecedent of the formal implication a statement to the effect that no conditions like those mentioned above are to be allowed.

275, 15–17; 276 and 277, 1–15. Avicenna turns now to particular connective propositions. He distinguishes here between two kinds of particular connective propositions (a distinction which turns up to one between two ways of establishing the truth of such propositions). In the first the truth of the particular proposition is derivative. What he means by this is that a connective proposition with a particular quantifier ('sometimes') will be true if that same proposition is true when stated universally. I.e. if we established that a certain consequent follows from a certain antecedent under any condition and at any time, then that consequent will follow from the same antecedent under some condition(s) and at a certain time. It is derivative in the sense that we do not need to verify the proposition to establish its truth, all we do is to derive the particular form of that proposition from its universal form (which is established as true). The second kind of particular connective proposition is the one whose truth is not derivative. There are propositions which are true only under certain conditions and at certain times. In this case the particular proposition is to be judged independently of its universal form and its truth is to be established without any reference to its universal form. Then Avicenna goes on to say that in the second kind the case can be that (a) the consequent follows necessarily from the antecedent as in 'Sometimes: when something is animal, then he is a man'. Or (b) the consequent would possibly follow from the antecedent as in 'Sometimes: when this is a man, then he is a creature-that-writes'. Avicenna says that in the example given for (a) the consequent follows necessarily from the antecedent under one condition, namely when an animal is rational. In this case, he says, it is necessary that the consequent should be formally implied by the antecedent. In the example given in (b) when the man referred to in the antecedent is capable of expressing himself in written words, he will be a creature-that-writes but not necessarily so, for it is conceiveable that he might not express himself at all in that form.

277, 16–17 and 278. The problem raised here is whether the particular quantifier can be applied to propositions with universal antecedents and consequents. His answer is in the affirmative. He says that there are cases in which it is not impossible to assume the universality of something which is ordinarily not so. This possibility can be expressed in particular connective propositions whose antecedents and consequents are universal propositions. For example in normal conditions a man moves his hands for doing one thing or another and it is not normal to think of men moving their hands for one and only one purpose, for instance writing, though that is not impossible. Such a possibility, Avicenna says, is expressed in a proposition like 'Sometimes: when every man moves his hand, then every man is writing'.

CHAPTER FIVE

279; 280 and 281, 1–2. The negative connective proposition is defined as that in which we deny the following of the consequent from the antecedent. We are reminded here that the relation of following is divided into chance connection and formal implication. Thus, Avicenna says, we can use the negative form either (a) to deny chance connection, and this happens when the proposition in question expresses formal implication; or (b) to deny formal implication which is the case with propositions expressing chance connection. Then he talks about universal negation. If we are universally denying chance connection, then what we are stating is that under no condition can the antecedent and the consequent be true.

281, 3–16 and 282, 1–8. The question asked is whether in propositions expressing chance connection the negation of implication can be universal. E.g. in a proposition like 'If man exists, then void does not exist' where we have a true chance connection (knowing that in Avicenna's philosophy void is taken to be non-existant) can we universally deny implication and say 'Never: if man exists, then void does not exist'? The reason for asking the question is that under some conditions which we may add to the antecedent, the consequent might then follow by implication; and of course in such cases we cannot say that under no condition the consequent can be formally implied by the antecedent (which is what universal negation means). Avicenna's answer to this is simple. He says in such cases and whenever we intend to make a universal negation of such propositions we add to the antecedent a new proposition in which all such conditions are negated.

282, 9–16 and 283, 1–9. The question now is whether we can universally negate a false connection, i.e. a proposition whose antecedent is true and consequent false, such as 'If this is a number, then it is a line'. It should be remembered here that the universal negation of a connective proposition is obtained if under no condition will the consequent follow from the antecedent. Avicenna says that one can think of some conditions under which the consequent in the above example would follow from the antecedent, namely when we take number to be the extremity of the plane. The above example will then be understood thus: 'If this is a number and it is the extrimity of the plane, then it is a line'. Such an example, Avicenna thinks, would be a counterevidence for the view that false connective proposition can be universally negated.

283, 10–18; 284 and 285, 1–4. The subject under discussion now is the universal separative proposition. First Avicenna talks very briefly about the universal affirmation of separative propositions saying that such an affirmation is obtained if, whenever the antecedent is stated, a relation of conflict should occur between it and the consequent. He leaves,the question of universal affirmation at that adding that what needs attention is the universal negation. All he does after that is to examine a subclass of these universal negative propositions which, he says, is more difficult to grasp than other types of such propositions. This turns to be the universal negation of separative propositions whose antecedents and consequents are universal affirmative propositions. Avicenna lists the conditions under which such propositions are considered true. It should be stated at the outset that in the following the words 'Either – or' are used to express complete conflict (see p. 222). The first case in which the universal negation of the above mentioned separative propositions is obtained is when we have an antecedent and a consequent which are universally true. When we say 'Never: either every man is a creature-that-talks or every donkey is a creature-that-brays', we deny that the antecedent and the consequent can be in complete conflict, since the antecedent and consequent of an 'Either – or' proposition which expresses complete conflict cannot be both true. Nor can they be both false. Which brings us to the second case: that in which the antecedent and consequent are universally false. When we say 'Never: either every man is a creature-that-brays or every donkey is a creature-that-talks', we deny that the antecedent and the consequent are in complete conflict. The third case is when the subject-matter of the antecedent and consequent are not related. In such a case no relation of conflict can be contemplated. Even if one of the parts (antecedent or consequent) is universally true and the other universally false, the separative proposition cannot express complete conflict, he says. Therefore, the universal negation of this case would be true; as when one says 'Never: either man is an animal or void exists'.

285, 4–16; 286; 287 and 288, 1–2. The topic has changed, and Avicenna's concern here is with indefinite separative propositions which have universal antecedents and consequents (whether affirmative or negative). Avicenna starts voicing doubt as to whether we can make statements of the type 'Either A is B or C is D' or 'Either none of A is B or none of C is D' at all. He does not state clearly the reason behind this doubt; but goes on to say that the problem arises mostly in connection with those cases

where the antecedent and the consequent have one common subject –
such as 'Either every A is B or every A is C'. In this case Avicenna's
doubt as to the possibility of ever having a true statement of this form
seems to be based on the following: If we were at all sure that for every
instance of A the alternatives are necessarily that it is either B or C and
nothing else, then what we do is to put the subject of the antecedent and
consequent ('A') before the word 'either', in which case we say 'Every A
is either B or C'. In case we are not sure of this, what we say is 'Either every
A is B or every A is C or some A is B and some A is C'. In spite of all this
Avicenna still thinks that we can make statements like 'Either every A
is B or every A is C' even though it is not certain that the alternatives
for A is that it is necessarily B or C. His main argument is that the truth
of some statements sometimes depends on the context in which they
occur. E.g. In a context where it is taken for granted that the actor in any
event is one, one can correctly argue that either every action is determined
by God or every action is determined by man. In which case the limitation
of the alternatives into two is correct in so far as the previous belief is true.
He also says that the truth of a proposition sometimes depends on a widely-accepted opinion and need not be true in itself. Thus one would accept
as true a separative proposition in which the alternatives are limited into
two even if that is based on a widely-accepted opinion. (See also the Commentary on 289 and 290).

288, 3–19 and 289, 1–2. This and the succeeding passage deal with
particular separative propositions. It is clear, he says, that the particular
quantifier can be applied in cases where separative propositions express
incomplete conflict (where both the antecedent and the consequent may
be false).[72] When we say for example 'Sometimes: either A is B or A is C'
what we are saying is that A might neither be B nor C. Avicenna discusses
another case where the particular quantifier can be applied to separative
propositions. E.g. if the possibilities for A is that it either be B or C or D
and that in a certain context or as a result of some assumption we make
one of the propositions can no longer be contemplated, then we can say
that sometimes either A is B or A is C.

289, 3–19 and 290. The question now is about the occasions or situations
in which one can construct particular propositions with universal ante-

cedents and consequents.[73] He says that such propositions are used in cases where we deviate from, or make an exception to, a general rule. For example though as a rule every line should be either equal to or larger or smaller than some other line, there are certain situations, such as when every line is compared with the diameter of the universe [74] which is larger than any other existing line, where one can say that every line is either smaller than or equal to some specified line. Thus the general rule would be 'Either every line is equal to or smaller or larger than a certain line'. And one of the exceptions could be expressed as a particular separative thus: 'Sometimes: either every line is equal to or smaller than a certain line'. He ends the passage saying that an indefinite separative proposition with universal parts such as 'Either every A is B or every A is C' might become universal if we add a third alternative which says that some A is B and some A is C. This would mean that all the possibilities are taken into consideration. Of course if the proposition is introduced in a context where we have a certain assumption which would not allow us to have except two parts, then we would have a particular separative such as 'Sometimes: weither A is B or A is C'. Avicenna goes on to say that if the alternatives are absolutely true, not because in a certain context they are assumed to be true, then we can construct a universal separative such as 'Always: either A is B or A is C'.

291 and 292. Avicenna does not discuss modal conditional propositions except very sketchily, and these lines are all that he had to say about the subject.[75] He first says, without giving reasons for it, that the appropriate thing to do is to discuss modality only with regards to connective propositions. Then he explains that a connective proposition is modal not because its parts are so. What we describe as necessary, possible ... etc. is the judgement that a certain consequent follows from a certain antecedent.[76] Saying this he goes on to explain what is meant by the modal notion 'necessity'. A universal connective, according to him, is necessary if the consequent follows (in any of the senses of following) the antecedent every time we posit the antecedent and so long as the antecedent remained posited. The only objection that might be raised is to say that in the case of the universal connective which expresses chance connections, the connection between the antecedent and the consequent must be necessary and cannot be otherwise. His answer is that there is nothing necessary

about their connection and it might happen that no such connection between them have taken place. As to 'possibility' the only thing said is that it means that the consequent might follow the antecedent and it might not. He adds however that a universal connective expressing implication is possible if there are conditions under which the consequent would not be implied by the antecedent. The odd thing about this is that, according to his early analysis, the proposition would then be particular rather than universal.

NOTES

[1] A. Badawi (ed.), *Manṭiq Arisṭū*, Vol. 1, pp. 197 and 216; also pp. 177 and 179–80 (*Prior Analytics*, I, 45b16, 50a16, 40b25 and 41a22–40). However, in the translation of the *Topics*, Abū ʿUthmān al-Dimashqī (ca. 860 – ca. 920) renders οἱ ἐξ ὑποθέσεως συλλογισμοί as *qiyāsāt al-Waḍʿ* (*Manṭiq Arisṭū*, Vol. II, p. 500). Cf. the Arabic text of the *Posterior Analytics* where ὑπόθεσις is translated as *al-aṣl al-mawḍūʿ*. (*Ibid.*, Vol. II, pp. 315, 340, 366 and 390.) The first thing to be said is that though the Arabic translation of the *Prior Analytics*, done by Tadhārī (ca. 790 – ca. 850) is an early one, it was selected by Abū Bishr Mattā (ca. 870 – ca. 940), the translator of the *Posterior Analytics*, from among several others as the standard translation of the Aristotelian text. (See Walzer, *Greek into Arabic*, p. 78.) The second point concerns the importance and relevance of the *Prior Analytics* to our subject vis-à-vis the other two texts. For it was in their commentaries on this book that Peripatetic philosophers discussed the subject of conditional propositions and inferences. It is important to note here that Abū Bishr Mattā, who commented on the *Prior Analytics*, is reported by Ibn al-Nadīm (*al-Fihrist*, p. 264) to have written a book entitled *al-Maqāyīs al-Sharṭiyya* (*Conditional Syllogisms*).

[2] See also below for what might seem to be another reason for such rendering. It should be noticed here that Aristotle's *Organon* is one of the very few translations of logical works from Greek that survived in Arabic.

[3] *Manṭiq al-Mashriqiyyīn*, p. 61. This of course shows that *sharṭiyya* for him means conditional.

[4] *Ibid.* It is of course clear that the same argument is true of separative propositions. For to say 'Either the sun has risen' is not a complete statement; nor if you say 'Or it is dark'. Cf. what Avicenna says on this point in *al-Qiyās* 236; also 289–90.

[5] *Manṭiq al-Mashriqiyyin*, p. 61.

[6] Cp. Bergsträsser (ed.), *Hunain Ibn Ishaq, Über die syrischen und arabischen Galen-Übersetzungen*, p. 48, where the title of a logical work of Galen is translated *Fī'l-Qiyāsāt al-Waḍʿiyya* (*On Hypothetical Syllogisms*).

[7] *Ibid.* Another name given to the 'If – then' proposition in *Manṭiq al-Mashriqiyyīn* (*ibid.*) is *al-majāziyya* (the figurative). This, Avicenna claims, is the name given to it by the Orientals. Cp. al-Yaʿqūbī's *Tārīkh*, ed. by M. Th. Houtsma, Leiden 1883, Vol. I, p. 104, where an 'If – then' proposition is given the same name. Al-Yaʿqūbī's example of *al-waḍʿ* (hypothesis) is "Let this landed estate be an endowment to the poor" (*takūnu hādhihi al-ḍayʿatu waqfan ʿalā al-masākīn*), *ibid.*

[8] *Loc. cit.*

[9] Alexander of Aphrodisias, *Commentarium in Aristotelis Analyticorum Priorum Librum I* (ed. by M. Wallies), Berlin 1883, pp. 262–63.

[10] *Galeni Institutio Logica*, Ch. III, Sec. I.

[11] In some places the schema of a conditional syllogism consists of two premisses without the conclusion. Also some of the examples he gives of conditional syllogisms have no conclusions. Sometimes he speaks of the unproductive moods meaning two premisses from which no conclusion can be derived. (Cp. *Galeni Institutio Logica*, VII, 5, where the conclusions of two syllogisms are omitted in the original text and supplied by the editor.)

[12] *Al-Qiyās*, 296, 3–4.

[13] Benson Mates, *Stoic Logic*, Berkeley 1961, pp. 80–81.

[14] W. and M. Kneale, *The Development of Logic*, Oxford 1962, p. 110.

[15] *Ibid.*

[16] Ammonius, *In Aristotelis Analyticorum Priorum Librum I Commentarium, Commentaria in Aristotelem Graeca*, IV (VI) (ed. by M. Wallies), Berlin 1899, p. IX. Cf. the example given in Alexander of Aphrodisias *op. cit.*, p. 374.

[17] It goes without saying that while in (1) the premisses (including the conclusion) are quantified this is not so in (4).

[18] *Al-Qiyās*, 305.

[19] *Al-Qiyās*, 390. Notice that while the Stoic use the ordinal numerals as variables, the only variables Avicenna uses are the letters (A, B, ..., etc.) which are substituted by terms.

[20] *Al-Qiyās*, 326.

[21] Karl Durr, *The Propositional Logic of Boethius*, Amsterdam 1951, p. 14.

[22] In Alexander, *op. cit.*, p. 262, μικτός seems to refer to the Chrysippian indemonstrables.

[23] It is clear that the difference in form accounts for the difference in the relation expressed. In the predicative proposition the relation is that of belonging, while in the conditional it is either that of following or of conflict. For an analysis of the last two relations see below.

[24] Aristotle, *De Interpretatione*, 17a1-6. The translation here is from J. L. Ackrill's *Aristotle's Categories and De Interpretatione*, Oxford 1962.

[25] Other examples are commands and questions.

[26] From the opening lines of this chapter it is clear that predicative and conditional propositions are the only statement-making sentences which Avicenna recognizes.

[27] For Aristotle's position see A. J. Ackrill's commentary on the above passage from Aristotle in *Aristotle's Categories and De Interpretatione*, pp. 124–25. A modern attack on such theories of meaning as we find in Avicenna is found in W. V. Quine, *Philosophy of Logic*, Englewood Cliffs, New Jersey, 1970, Ch. 1.

[28] "The primary occupation of a logician as a logician is not with words, except in so far as conversation and debate are concerned", Avicenna stresses. "And if it were possible to learn logic by a simple idea, where only meanings are observed, then that would be sufficient. And if it were possible for the debater to inspect what is in his soul by other means, then that would dispense completely with the word. But since necessity requires the use of words, especially since it is difficult for reflection to order meanings without imagining with them the corresponding words – and reflection is almost an inner conversation between man and himself through imagined words – it is inevitable that words, which have different states, will affect the states of those corresponding meanings in the soul, and as a result they (meanings) will have certain characteristics which would not exist but for the words. Therefore, it was necessary that parts of the art of logic be a study of the states of words." *Al-Shifā'*, *al-Madkhal*, pp. 22–23.

[29] *Al-Qiyās*, 235–36.

[30] *Al-ʿIbāra*, British Museum MS. Or. 7500, 40ʳ.

[31] G. H. Von Wright, *Logical Studies*, London 1957, p. 131.

[32] *Ibid.*

[33] *Ibid.*, p. 135.

[34] Cp. Alexander of Aphrodisias, *op. cit.*, pp. 264–65.

[35] J. W. Stakelum, *Galen and the Logic of Propositions*, Rome 1940, pp. 39–40.

[36] *Ibid.*, p. 40.

[37] J. S. Kieffer, *Galen's Institutio Logica*, p. 13.

[38] *Ibid.*

[39] 'Complete connection' is sometimes called 'complete implication' (*al-Qiyās*, 391 and 396); and 'incomplete connection' is also called 'incomplete' or 'defective inplication' (*al-Qiyās*, 396).

[40] See above pp. 220–21.

[41] Perhaps 'If not *p*, then *q*' is also considered by these people as a negation of the connective proposition 'If *p*, then *q*'.

[42] Probably the doctrine was held by later Platonists who took Plato's identification of connection with affirmation and separation with negation (the *Sophist*) as a starting point for developing a theory on the nature of conditional propositions to encounter Peripatetic and Stoic theories on the subject.

[43] Galen's *Institutio Logica* (J. S. Kieffer's translation), Ch. III, 1.

[44] The reader realizes that 'If *p*, then *q*' is equivalent to 'Either not-*p* or *q*' only if we take the second to be of the kind where both the antecedent and the consequent can be true. And that 'If *p*, then *q*' is equivalent to 'Either *p* or not-*q*' if in the latter both parts can be false.

[45] See below pp. 234–38.

[46] Cf. *Institutio Logica*, Ch. V. Galen did not include the paradisjunctives in his general division of separative propositions (see Ch. III), but later on he gave a definition of the paradisjunctives and compared them with the two kinds of separative propositions he first introduced.

[47] Ch. V, 2 and VI, 3.

[48] J. Philoponus, *Commentaria in Analytica Priori Aristotelis* (ed. by M. Wallies), Berlin 1905, pp. 242–43. See Sextus Empiricus, *Against the Logicians*, trans. R. G. Bury, The Loeb Classical Library, London and Cambridge, Mass. 1967, II, 110–17, and Diogenes Laertius' *Lives of Eminent Philosophers*, trans. R. D. Hicks, The Loeb Classical Library, London and Cambridge, Mass. 1965, VII, 73–74 and 80–81. We owe the information on what the Greek sources say on these terms to B. Mates' *Stoic Logic*. See especially p. 128 and his Glossary.

[49] *Al-Madkhal*, pp. 29–30.

[50] In fact the word ἐπεί is a conjecture of Prantl and does not exist in the text. Prantl's conjecture, however, is based on Diogenes' distinction between εἰ and ἐπεί (see below). Further support for Prantl's conjecture can be found in Sextus Empiricus' *Adv. Math.*, VIII, 109.

[51] *Institutio Logica*, III, 22.

[52] Diogenes Laertius, *Lives of Eminent Philosophers*, (trans. by R. D. Hicks), The Loeb Classical Library, London and Cambridge, Mass. 1965, VII, 71 ff.

[53] *Ibid.*, VII, 66–67.

[54] J. Stakelum, *Galen and the Logic of Propositions*, p. 19.

[55] J. L. Ackrill, *Aristotle's Categories and De Interpretatione*, p. 126.

[56] Al-Fārābī, *Sharḥ Kitāb al-ʿIbāra*, p. 54.

[57] The Avicennian *al-Luzūm* is the formal implication of modern logic. For him *al-Luzūm* indicates the dependence of the consequent on the antecedent. We can show that such a dependence exists between the antecedent and the consequent if, for example, the antecedent is shown to be a cause and the consequent its effect.

[58] In al-Ashʿarī's *Maqālāt al-Islāmiyyīn* (ed. by H. Ritter), Vol. I, Istanbul 1929, p. 204,

al-Jubbā'ī (d. 915/916) is said to have claimed that "If an impossible (*muḥāl*) is connected (*wuṣila*) with an impossible the speech will be true". The example given is "If (*law*) at a certain state the body were moving and at rest, then it would be possible that in (this) state it would be alive and dead". Notice the use of the word *wuṣila*, since Avicenna calls the 'If – then' proposition *muttaṣila*.

[59] See *al-Qiyās*, 376–79.

[60] This view applies also to the other kinds of separative propositions which Avicenna deals with: the one which does not exclude the possibility of having both its parts false and that which could have both its parts true.

[61] See next passage.

[62] He seems to imply here that this is why chance connection is regarded as a relation.

[63] It should be noted that none of these forms can be compared with the first premiss of a homogeneous non-simple argument mentioned in Sextus' *Against the Logicians*, II, 229–33: "If it is day, then if it is day then it is light." Needless to say that Avicenna's simple and compound conditionals do not correspond to the atomic and molecular propositions mentioned in Sextus, *op. cit.*, II, 93. See also Diogenes' *Lives of Eminent Philosophers*, VII, 68.

[64] This form is not in the text.

[65] This form is not included in Avicenna's list.

[66] This is the same as the first premiss of the pseudo-conditional mentioned in the anonymous scholium published in Ammonius' commentary on the *Prior Analytics*, *op. cit.*, p. IX.

[67] The conditional can itself be compounded of conditional propositions which may, in turn, be compounded of conditional propositions ... etc.

[68] What Avicenna is referring to here, when he speaks of the view according to which the universal predicative proposition is equivalent to the universal connective, is perhaps the equivalence between the prosleptic (an implication preceded by the universal quantifier) and the universal categorical proposition. According to Alexander of Aphrodisias, this view was held by Theophrastus (*In Aristotelis Analyticorum Priorum Librum I Commentarium* (ed. by M. Wallies), *C.I.A.G.*, II (I), p. 378). For a discussion of prosleptic syllogism see C. Lejewski, 'On Prosleptic Syllogisms', *Notre Dame Journal of Formal Logic* II, No. 3 (1961), 158–76.

[69] The only kind of following which might occur in this case is that of formal implication.

[70] As a matter of fact the falsity of the antecedent indicates the truth of the connective proposition irrespective of what truth-value the consequent has.

[71] Of course following here means formal implication.

[72] His examples show that he is thinking of those separative propositions whose antecedent and consequent have one common subject.

[73] The examples he gives are of propositions whose antecedent and consequent have one common subject.

[74] Avicenna like Aristotle believed that the universe is finite.

[75] At one point he promised to discuss it in detail in *al-Lawāḥiq*, a book which he never wrote.

[76] Of course the antecedent and the consequent themselves might be modal, but their modality has no bearing on the modality of the connective proposition of which they are parts.

BOOK VI

CHAPTER ONE

This chapter is entirely devoted to those syllogisms which are solely compounded of connective propositions. These syllogisms take the form of the three figures which Aristotle applied to predicative premisses. The analogy from predicative syllogisms can be easily seen once it is realized that Avicenna replaces the subject-predicate pattern, which applies to predicative propositions, with an antecedent-consequent one. Avicenna regards all propositions as being composed of two parts which are linked together either by the relation of predication, conflict or following. According to this view the difference between a connective and a predicative proposition is that (a) the parts in a connective proposition are themselves propositions, while in the predicative the parts are single terms. (b) The relation in both cases are different. In the case of connective propositions, the relation which links the parts together is that of following; while in the second case it is a relation of predication. (See *al-Qiyās* 232, 2–5.) Therefore, as in predicative syllogisms, we will have here a major, minor and middle parts except that in this case these parts will be propositions rather than terms. Remembering that Avicenna puts the minor premiss before the major, it becomes obvious that the first figure will have the following form;

> If *p*, then *q*
> and if *q*, then *r*
> therefore, if *p*, then *r*

which is to say that the middle part is the consequent of the minor premiss and the antecedent of the major. In the second figure the middle is the consequent of both premisses thus:

> If *p*, then *q*
> and if *r*, then *q*
> therefore, if *p*, then *r*

when the middle is the antecedent of both premisses, this becomes the third figure:

> If q, then p
> and if q, then r
> therefore, if p, then r.

Again as Aristotle did with syllogisms from predicative premisses Avicenna divides every one of the three figures into moods according to the quality and quantity of the premisses. The first and the second figures each has four moods, and the third has six. In the first figure the conditions for production are that the premisses should not be both particular or negative or that the minor be negative and the major be particular. In the second there can be no production when both premisses are affirmative or particular, or when the major is particular. In the third it is necessary that the minor be affirmative and that either one of the two premisses be universal.

Avicenna, as we know, divided the connective proposition into that which expresses chance connection and the one which expresses implication. It is clear from what he says that in the first figure the premisses are all implications. He says that if the premisses were connective propositions expressing chance connection, we will then have a *petitio principii*. This is evident, he says, because we already learned that in the two premisses the antecedents and consequents are true, i.e. we know that p, q, and r, in, say, the syllogism:

> If p, then q
> if q, then r
> Therefore, if p, then r

are true, and that any chance connection between any two of the three parts is true. (One such connection would be 'if p, then r'.) Another point he makes is that in the first figure there can be no syllogism when the minor premiss is an implication and the major a chance connection and vice versa.

CHAPTER TWO

This chapter deals exclusively with those syllogisms which have one connective and one separative premisses. In these syllogisms the former distinction, made earlier in this work, between real and unreal separative propositions is taken into consideration. But Avicenna fails to mention the other distinction, which is between connective propositions expressing chance connection and those expressing implication. Anyway, Avicenna refers to four types of syllogisms in this chapter: (a) Where the minor (first) premiss is connective and the major (second) premiss is real separative; (b) where the minor premiss is a connective proposition and the major is unreal separative; (c) the minor is real separative and the major is a connective proposition; and (d) the minor is unreal separative and the major is connective. In the case of (a) and (b) there are two figures. The first is the one where the middle part is the consequent of the minor premiss and the antecedent of the major; and the second is the one in which the middle part is the antecedent of both premisses. But in (c) and (d) the two figures in which the premisses are formed are not quite the same as before. The first figure in their case is the one in which the middle is the consequent of the minor premiss and the antecedent of the major; but the second figure is the one in which the middle part is the consequent of both premisses. And as expected everyone of these figures is divided into different moods according to the quality and quantity of the premisses.

For the word *rujāꜥ* (reduction) see p. 267.

CHAPTER THREE

The last kind of syllogisms constructed out of conditional propositions alone is the one in which both premisses are separative propositions. This chapter reveals the following information. First of all there is no syllogism from real separative premisses alone. Second, since, as said before, the antecedent and the consequent in a separative proposition are interchangeable in any particular case, which amounts to saying that the truth of the separative proposition is not affected by the placement of its parts, it will not be necessary to distinguish between different figures. (This is only true of those syllogisms which are constructed solely of separative propositions.) Thus, the chapter contains inferences which take as premisses either a mixture of real and unreal separatives or a combination of unreal separative propositions alone.

CHAPTER FOUR

Here the discussion turns to those syllogisms which have one of their premisses a connective proposition and the other a predicative proposition. The middle term, through which the conclusion is reached, is to be established between the predicative premiss and, the antecedent of the connective proposition or its consequent. This chapter deals with the second case, viz. the one in which a middle term is established between the predicative premiss and the consequent of the connective. Now the predicative premiss can either be the minor or the major premiss, and so Avicenna treats the different syllogisms which arise in both cases. For everyone of them there are three figures, and these are the three figures of the predicative syllogism; since the propositions in which the middle term occurs are predicative propositions. The first figure is where the middle term is the predicative of the minor and the subject of the major, the second where the middle term is the predicate of both propositions and the third where the middle term is the subject of both. The different moods are determined by the quality and quantity of the propositions in which the middle term occurs.

CHAPTER FIVE

In the previous chapter the syllogisms treated were those in which a middle term is established between the predicative premiss and the consequent of the connective premiss. Now Avicenna is trying to tackle the other case, i.e. where the middle term is established between the predicative premiss and the antecedent of the connective proposition. As is said in the preceding chapter the predicative proposition could be either the minor or the major premiss. And in either case the three classical figures, which Aristotle discusses in relation with predicative syllogisms, are to be constructed according to the placement of the middle term. (See the previous chapter.) The three mentioned figures are established in both cases with different moods in each one. In the first case the first figure has 16 moods, the second figure 15 and the third 21. In the second case, the first figure has eight moods, and each of the second and the third has 16 moods.

CHAPTER SIX

Under what he calls the divided syllogism, four different kinds of inferences are discussed.

(a) The syllogisms which consist of a predicative proposition (the minor premiss) and a separative proposition (the major premiss). Two conditions are stipulated. First that the separative premiss must express complete conflict; and secondly, that the parts of the separative premiss (which are themselves predicative propositions) must share one of their parts – the subject or the predicate. For this kind of syllogism only two figures are productive, the first and the third. The first is:

>   C is B
>   and B is either H or Z
>   therefore, C is either H or Z.

The other productive figure, which he calls the third for the simple reason that the middle term is the subject of both premisses has the following schema:

>   B is C
>   and B is either H or Z
>   therefore, C is either H or Z.

The only mood which he discussed in connection with the first figure is that in which both premisses are universal affirmative. The other figure is not discussed.

(b) This is the kind of syllogism which consists of a separative premiss and more than one predicative premiss. The condition for such a construction is that the parts of the separative premiss, which as before consists of predicative propositions, share one of their parts (the subject or the predicate). The second requirement is that the separative premiss must express complete conflict. Now with (b) two cases are taken into consideration. The first is where the predicative premisses share one of their parts, the subject or the predicate; and the second where these propositions have nothing in common. In the first case three figures are established. The first is:

>   B is either C or H or Z
>   and C, H and Z are A
>   therefore, B is A.

As usual Avicenna considers also the quality and quantity of the premisses and gets four different moods for this figure. The second figure is:

> B is either C or H or Z
> and A is C and H and Z
> therefore, B is A.

For this figure Avicenna establishes only three moods. The third figure is:

> Either C or H or Z is B
> and C and H and Z are A
> therefore, B is A

There seems to be only four moods for this figure. There are also three
figures in the second case where the predicative premisses do not have
anything in common. The first figure is:

> D is either C or B
> and C is H and B is Z
> therefore, D is either H or Z.

The second figure is:

> D is either C or B
> and H is C and Z is B
> therefore, D is either H or Z.

The third figure is:

> Either C or B are D
> and C is H and B is Z
> therefore, D is either H or Z.

No moods are established in the last three figures.

(c) This kind consists of a minor connective premiss and a separative
major premiss. Avicenna gives two figures here. In the first, which has
four moods, the sharing occurs between the consequent of the connective
and the separative premiss:

> If C is B, then H is Z
> and Z is either D or A
> therefore, if C is B, then H is either D or A.

The second figure has eight moods. Here the sharing occurs between the consequent of the connective premiss (which is itself a separative proposition) and the separative major premiss. What is common to both these separative propositions is that the predicate of their antecedents and also that of their consequents are identical:

> If C is B, then H is either Z or D
> and A is either Z or D
> therefore, if C is B, then H is A.

(d) The last kind consists of two separative premisses. The first figure is:

> Either C is D or H is D
> and D is either B or A
> therefore, either C is D or H is B or A.

For this figure he gives four moods.

The second figure is not clear to me. He gives it as follows:

> Either C is D or C is H
> and either D or H
> therefore, C is A.

There is an interesting remark which he makes at the beginning of the chapter where he tries to point out briefly the similarities and dissimilarities between this kind of syllogism and what he calls induction or inductive reasoning. Like Aristotle before him (*Prior Analytics*, II, XXIII) Avicenna sees induction as being syllogistic in nature. Avicenna's example for induction is this:

> Every gall-less animal (A) is either man, horse or mule (C)
> every long-lives animal (A) is man, horse and mule (C)
> therefore (if B is no wider than C) all gall-less animals (B) are
> long-lives (A).

(Except for some minor changes like putting the minor premiss before the major and expressing the first as a separative proposition, this is the same example which Aristotle gives.) It is important to note here that we cannot infer that all gall-less animals are long-lived unless it is definite that man, horse and mule are the only gall-less animals there are, i.e. unless the minor premiss is convertible. From what Avicenna says it is clear that that is not always the case. For this reason a distinction between complete and incomplete induction is introduced. In the first case a complete enumeration of the particulars should be given but this is not so in the second. (*Al-Qiyās*, 557–67.) This brings us back to the divided syllogism which is said to consist also of several predicative propositions and a separative expressing complete conflict. This in simple words means that the separative premiss enumerates all the possibilities. And that is nothing but what he calls complete induction. But he still does not want to call it complete induction because, as he says at the outset, in the divided syllogism the predication is real while in the case of induction (complete or incomplete) it is not. What is puzzling is that this last point is not made at all in Avicenna's account of induction. All he says there is that induction is a generic name which refers to both the complete and the incomplete kinds, while the label 'divided syllogism' specifies the syllogism as being that in which the specific cases mentioned in the separative premiss are all the possibilities we have. (*Al-Qiyās*, 559)

BOOK VII

CHAPTER ONE

The whole of Book VII deals with a new subject and that is the so-called immediate inference. In so doing Avicenna is in fact following the same method which Aristotle used in treating predicative propositions. First of all Avicenna makes it clear that he intends to deal only with necessary conditional propositions. And among them only those whose parts (antecedent and consequent) are quantified. Then he proceeds with his account of the kind of inferences that can be established in this way. One such inference is that of getting the universal affirmative connective from the universal negative one. (Whatever quantity and/or quality their antecedents and/or consequents may have.) As Avicenna puts it, to turn the universal negative into a universal affirmative, (a) we change the quality from affirmation to negation while keeping the quantity (universality); and (b) while the antecedent of universal negative is kept as it is, the consequent should be negated. Avicenna also adds that this is true in case the connective expresses implication or when it is used in a generic sense. The same is true of connective propositions when they are particular. I.e. we can infer the particular affirmative from the particular negative, or, to put in his words, we can turn the particular negative into particular affirmative, by changing the equality of the first (namely turn it from a negative into an affirmative proposition) and negating its consequent. At the end he says that it is clear that when the universal is true, the particular must also be true. This is of course true of those propositions which have identical quality.

The word *talāzum*, used here and in the next two chapters, is translated as 'equipollence' but could also be rendered 'mutual implication'. There is no ambiguity as to what it means. Two propositions are said to be 'equipollent' if we can infer either one from the other. It is important to note that '*talāzum*' is only used in the context of Avicenna's treatment of immediate inference. It is never used, as one would expect, to describe the relation named elsewhere in the text (Book VIII, Ch. 1) 'complete implication'. It should be further noted that the relation of 'equipollence' is never stated in an 'If – then' proposition as is the relation of 'complete implication'. Another word Avicenna uses here is *rujūʿ*[1], translated here as 'reduction'. The Arabic translator of Aristotle's *Prior Analytics* used *rujūʿ* to translate in some places the word ἀντιστρέφειν. W. D. Ross in *Aristotle's Prior and Posterior Analytics* (Oxford 1949, p. 293), gives six different meanings for ἀντιστρέφειν as occurs in the *Prior Analytics*. (1) It is used of the conversion or the convertibility of premisses. (2) It is used in the closely related sense of the conversion or convertibility of terms. (3) It is used of the substitution of one term for another without any suggestion of convertibility. (4) It is used of the inference (pronounced to be valid) from a proposition of the form 'B admits of being A' to one of the form 'B admits of not being A' or vice versa. (5) It is used of the substitution of the opposite of a proposition for the proposition without any suggestion that this is a valid inference. (6) By combining the meaning 'change of direction' (as in (1) and (2)) with the meaning 'passage from a proposition to its opposite', we find the word used of an argument in which from one premiss of a syllogism and the opposite of the conclusion the opposite of the other premiss is proved.

All the references for (1) Ross gives in his index are rendered by the Arabic translator as *ʿaks*, conversion. In all the references given for (2) the Arabic word used is *rujūʿ* except in 57b32–58b12 where both *ʿaks* and *rujūʿ* are used. (3) and (4) are always rendered *rujūʿ*. (5) becomes sometimes (45b6) *rujūʿ* but mostly *ʿaks*, while (6) becomes *ʿaks*. (4) is very close to the usage of *rujūʿ* in this chapter; and to avoid confusion we translated it as 'reduction' and kept 'conversion' for *ʿaks*. It should be noted that in Aristotle's *Categories* πρὸς ἀντιστρέφοντα λέγεται is translated *tarjiʿu baʿḍuhumā ʿalā baʿḍin fi'l-qawli bi'l-takāfuʾi*. See p. 235.

CHAPTER TWO

In this chapter Avicenna continues with his exposition of immediate inferences which he began in the previous chapter, but this time the cases under discussion are (a) immediate inference between separative propositions and (b) immediate inference from a separative to a connective premiss and vice versa. Under (a) he treats two kinds of inferences. First, he says, a universal affirmative proposition with affirmative parts can be turned into a universal negative with the antecedent negated. (Avicenna says that the antecedent of the inferred proposition can be the consequent of the first and so also with the consequent.) E.g. from 'Always: either every A is B or every C is D' we infer 'Never: either not every A is B or every C is D' or 'Never: either not every C is D or every A is B'. The second case is that of the particular affirmative among separative propositions. These, he asserts, can be turned into particular negative with the antecedent negated. E.g. from 'Sometimes: either every A is B or every C is D' we infer 'Not always: either not every A is B or every C is D'. As to (b) two cases are discussed: (1) inferring the connective from the separative premiss, and (2) the separative from the connective. (1) Here he discusses only the universal affirmative among real separative propositions, first when their parts are affirmative. And from these he infers a universal affirmative connective with a negated antecedent. He also asserts that it does not matter whether the antecedent of the connective is the antecedent of the separative or its consequent; and the same is true of the consequent. E.g. from 'Always: either every A is B or every C is D' we infer 'Always: when not every A is B, then every C is D' or 'Always: when not every C is D, then every A is B'. But when the parts of the separative are negative, the only difference from the case above is that the antecedent is not simply negated but is the contradictory of the antecedent of the separative. E.g. from 'Always: either none of A is B or none C is D' we infer 'Always: when some of A is B, then nothing of C is D' or 'Always: when some of C is D, then nothing of A is B'. This inference, Avicenna declares, is mutual. This brings us to (2) where only two cases are treated. First, he says, from a universal affirmative connective premiss we infer the universal negative separative which agrees with the first in both the antecedent and the consequent. E.g. from 'Always: when some A is B, then nothing of C is D' we infer 'Never: either some A is B or nothing of C is D'. The second case is the universal negative among the connective propositions. From these we infer a universal negative separative proposition with the antecedent negated. E.g. from 'Never: when every A is B, then every C is D' we infer 'Never: either not every A is B or every C is D'.

CHAPTER THREE

This chapter treats only the conversion of the connective premiss. And the two kinds of conversion treated are the *conversion simpliciter* and *conversion contrapositionem*. In the first the antecedent and the consequent exchange their places without touching the quality or the quantity of the main proposition or its parts. In the second the conversion is accomplished by keeping the quality and quantity of the proposition the same but this time both the antecedent and the consequent are the contradictories of the antecedent and consequent of the original proposition.[2]

NOTES

[1] See also *al-Qiyās*, 310, 6 and 11.
[2] In Chapter VI, Section 4 of the *Institutio Logica* Galen refers only to the conversion of the premiss 'If it is day, it is light' to 'If it is not light, it is also not day'. He also says that when inverted it becomes 'If it is light, it is day'.

BOOK VIII

CHAPTERS ONE AND TWO

Avicenna distinguishes between two kinds of syllogisms. The first he calls conjunctive (*iqtirānī*) and the second is called exceptive (*istithnā'ī*). The conjunctive syllogism, in turn, is divided into (a) predicative (*ḥamlī*) and (b) conditional (*sharṭī*). In (a) both premisses (and the conclusion) are predicative propositions; while in (b) at least one of the premisses is a conditional proposition and the conclusion is always a conditional proposition. In both (a) and (b) the premisses are supposed to share one of their parts with each other (which is a single term in the case of the predi- ·cative and some types of the conditional syllogisms, and a proposition in the case of most types of conditional syllogisms). The placement of this shared part (called in the text the middle) determines the figure of the syllogism. The predicative syllogism is compounded of three figures. In the first figure the middle part is the predicate of the minor premiss and the subject of the major. (Remembering that Avicenna puts the minor premiss before the major.) In the second it is the predicate of both premis- ses; while in the third it is the subject of both premisses. Most types of conditional propositions are also divided into three figures. If both premisses are conditional propositions, then the middle part will either be the antecedent of the minor premiss and the consequent of the major, and this is called the first figure; or the consequent of both premisses, and this is called the second figure; or the consequent of both premisses, and this is called the third figure. If the conditional syllogism is compounded of a conditional and a predicative syllogism, then the middle part is either (1) the consequent of the conditional premiss and the predicative premiss or (2) the antecedent of the conditional premiss and the predicative premiss. In both (1) and (2) the figures are divided into three. The middle part in the first figure will be the subject of the predicative premiss and the predicate of the consequent (or the antecedent) of the conditional pre- miss [1], and this is called the first figure; or the predicate of both, and this is called the second figure; or the subject of both, and this is called the third figure. All the figures in (a) and (b) are divided into moods according to the quantity and the quality of the premiss.

In the case of the exceptive syllogism, the minor premiss is a conditional proposition, and the major is a predicative proposition. We start first with the syllogisms in which the conditional premiss is a connective proposition. As we explained before, the connective proposition reveals either complete or incomplete connection. In case it reveals complete connection, we will have the following moods.

(1)   If A is B, then C is D,
        but A is B,
        therefore, C is D,
(2)   If A is B, then C is D,
        but C is D,
        therefore, A is B.
(3)   If A is B, then C is D,
        but A is not B,
        therefore, C is not D.
(4)   If A is B, then C is D,
        but C is not D,
        therefore, A is not B.

The moods when the connective proposition expresses incomplete connection are the following:

(5)   If A is B, then C is D,
        but A is B,
        therefore, C is D.
(6)   If A is B, then C is D,
        but C is not D,
        therefore, A is not B.

What if the conditional premiss is a separative proposition? The reader remembers that Avicenna has three kinds of such proposions. The first he calls the real separative. This is true when one of the parts is true and the other is false and false otherwise. He says that there are two moods when the real separative is compounded of two parts. These are:

(7)   Either A is B, or C is D,

but A is not B
therefore, C is D.

or

Either A is B or C is D
but C is not D,
therefore, A is B.

(8)   Either A is B or C is D,
but A is B,
therefore, C is not D.

or

Either A is B or C is D,
but C is D,
therefore, A is not B.

In case the real separative has more than two parts we will have two moods.

(9)   Either A is B or C is D or E is F,
but A is B,
therefore, C is not D *and* E is not F.

However, Avicenna adds, one can also conclude 'Therefore, not: either C is D or E is F'.

(10)   Either A is B or C is D or E is F,
but A is not B,
therefore, either C is D or E is F.

In this case we, for the second time, deny any of the parts, saying for example 'But C is not D' and conclude that 'E is F'.

The second kind of separative premisses are those in which both parts can be true. In this case we get one mood.

(11)   Either A is B or C is D,
but A is not B,
therefore, C is D.

or

Either A is B or C is D,

but C is not D,
therefore, A is B.

The third kind of separative premisses are those in which both parts may be false. These propositions, Avicenna claims, are not used in science. From such premiss we get one mood.

(12)   Either A is B or C is D,
        but A is B,
        therefore, C is not D.

or

        Either A is B or C is D,
        but C is D,
        therefore, A is not B.

To help the reader compare Avicenna's list with that of Chrysippus we will give here the five indemonstrable arguments attributed to the latter.

(1)   If the first, then the second.
        The first.
        Therefore, the second.
(2)   If the first, then the second.
        Not the second.
        Therefore, not the first.
(3)   Not both the first and the second.
        The first.
        Therefore, not the second.
(4)   Either the first or the second.
        The first.
        Therefore, not the second.
(5)   Either the first or the second.
        Not the first.
        Therefore, the second.

(See Benson Mates, *Stoic Logic*, pp. 67–74.) Galen says that Chrysippus' (1) and (2) are syllogisms "deriving from complete consequence τελεία ἀκολουθία" " and that (4) and (5) are syllogisms deriving "from complete conflict". (*Institutio Logica*, XIV, 11; Kieffer's translation.) Galen does not say what is meant by complete consequence, and as it stands the phrase does not tell us how Galen wants us to interpret Chrysippus' (1) and (2). If, however, we understand complete consequence to mean what Avicenna calls complete implication, then it is easy to see that Chrisippus' (1) and (2), as Galen sees them, would correspond to Avicenna's (1) and (4). We have shown earlier that complete conflict means the same thing for both Galen and Avicenna (see pp. 222–24). Surely, then, Crysippus' (4) and (5), as Galen understands them, would be similar to Avicenna's (8) and (7) respectively. Galen condemns (3) as "useless for demonstration" (*ibid.*, XIV, 8) and adds that it should be understood as a syllogism "from deficient conflict". (*Ibid.*, XIV, 11.) He says that unlike the case in complete consequence and conflict, the second premiss in the syllogism from deficient conflict can only be affirmative (*ibid.*). This corresponds with Avicenna's (12). Then in Chapter XV (see the different interpretations given to it by Kieffer and Mau) Galen adds two more syllogisms to the above five. In the sixth the first premiss is a paradisjunctive (where all the parts can be true) consisting of more than two parts. Here we deny one of the parts producing a separative proposition consisting of all the others. In the seventh we deny everyone of the parts but one, producing the one we did not deny. There is nothing in Avicenna's list which corresponds to any of these two syllogisms.

One last word about the terms *darb* (mood), *mashhūr* (which I translate as indemonstrable and which literally means widely-accepted) and *qiyās* (syllogism).

The use of *darb* here conforms with what we find in Greek sources. Galen, e.g. says "And the dialecticians apply the name 'mood' τρόπος to the schemata of arguments." Then he says that in Chrysippus' first indemonstrable

the mood or schema σχῆμα is as follows:

> If the first, then the second.
> The first.
> Therefore, the second.[2]

The only difference between the above mood and Avicenna's *darb* is that the latter replaces the numerals (first, second) by letters (A is B, C is D).

It took me a long time to decide on a translation for *mashhūr*. Avicenna does not even hint at what is meant by it in this context. However, there is enough evidence to show what he means by *mashhūr* when used to describe premisses. In this case *al-mashhūrāt* (pl. of *mashhūr*) are a category of first principles (*mabādi'*) whose truth is postulated (*tusallam*) because they are widely-accepted. Such as "Justice is good" and "Injustice is bad".[3] These are premisses used in dialectical arguments.[4] He contrasts them with another type of first principles whose truth is known *a priori* (*awwalī*), and which cannot be subject to doubt, such as "The whole is greater than the part."[5] Sextus Empiricus says[6] that ἀναπόδεικτος (indemonstrable) has two senses. It is used (a) of arguments which have not been demonstrated; and (b) of those which have no need of demonstration, because it is at once obvious that they are valid. Then he goes on to say that Chrysippus' five indemonstrables are called indemonstrable in the second sense.[7] It may well be that the term *mashhūr* here translates ἀναπόδεικτος in the second sense referred to in Sextus' text.[8] It is important to note that none of the syllogisms which have a separative proposition as a minor premiss is called *mashhūr*. This is significant because these syllogisms are said to be proved by the exceptive syllogism which has a connective minor premiss (see *al-Qiyās*, 406, 15 and 407).

Qiyās istithnā'ī (exceptive syllogism)[9] is a label he gives to Chrysippus' five indemonstrables and arguments of the same type. In using the word *qiyās* to describe this type of arguments Avicenna seems to be following the Peripatetic commentators. For this is how Alexander of Aphrodisias calls Chrysippus' indemonstrables in his *Commentarium in Aristotelis Analyticorum Priorum Librum* I (pp. 18 and 19). And so does J. Philoponus in *Commentaria in Analytica Priora Aristotelis*, p. 244.[10]

NOTES

[1] I.e. when the conditional proposition is the minor premiss and the predicative is the major. Avicenna discusses also the case when the conditional is the major premiss and the predicative is the minor. He gives three figures for this case also.

[2] Galen, *Institutio Logica*, Ch. VI, 6 (B. Mates' translation). See also Diogenes Laertius' *Lives of Eminent Philosophers*, VII, 76, where he says that a mood τρόπος is a sort of outline of an argument, like the following "If the first, then the second; but the first, therefore the second". Cf. Sextus Empiricus' *Against the Logicians*, II, 227.

[3] *Al Shifā'*, *al-Burhān* (ed. by A. Affifi), Cairo 1956, p. 66. *Al-Qiyās*, pp. 453–54.

[4] *Al-Shifā'*, *al-Jadal* (ed. by A. Ehwani), Cairo 1965, p. 34. See *al-Najāt*, p. 63.

[5] *Al-Burhān*, pp. 64–66.

[6] Sextus Empiricus, *op. cit.*, II, 223.

[7] ἀναπόδεικτος occurs also in Aristotle's *Prior Analytics*, 53b2 and 57b33. The Arabic translation renders it *ghayr mubarhana* (not demonstrated). But the word there refers only to premisses not arguments.

[8] For the perfect τέλειος categorical syllogism, as Aristotle calls it, to which imperfect ones are reduced, the word Avicenna uses is *kāmil*. This word occurs also in the context of his discussion of conjunctive-conditional syllogisms as well as in his discussion of the exceptive syllogism.

[9] The term *istithnā'ī* is discussed in note 110 to the Introduction.

[10] Cp. Diogenes Laertius, *op. cit.*, VII, 78–79 and Sextus Empiricus, *Outlines of Pyrrhonism*, trans. R. G. Bury, The Loeb Classical Library, London and Cambridge, Mass. 1961, II, 149.

BOOK IX

CHAPTER ONE

415–16, 1–3. Avicenna's view here is that we would not reach a conclusion from any given pair of premisses unless we can show, directly or indirectly, that the given pair are related by a middle part which combines them together; and that this middle part must take the form of the three figures explained in the section dealing with predicative syllogisms. In Book VI the idea of the middle part arranged in three figures is directly applied to a pair of conditional premisses as well as a combination of a conditional and a predicative premiss. This is the syllogism called conjunctive-conditional. The passage also claims that this is true of *reductio ad absurdum* proofs. In both *al-Qiyās*, 408–11 and *al-Najāt*, pp. 55–56, the *reductio ad absurdum* proof is explained in the following way: Suppose that what we want to prove by *reductio ad absurdum* is the conclusion in the syllogism

> Every A is C
> and every C is B
> therefore, every A is B.

First we construct a conjunctive-conditional syllogism thus:

> If it is not the case that every A is B, then every A is not B,
> and every A is C (which is the first premiss in the above syllogism)
> therefore, if it is not the case that every A is B, then every C is not B.

The second step will be to detach the above conclusion and put it as the first premiss in an exeptive syllogism:

> If it is not the case that every A is B, then every C is not B,
> but every C is B (which is the second premiss in the first syllogism)
> therefore, every A is B.

Avicenna further says that the exceptive syllogism can also be shown by the conjunctive (which would then show that the *reductio ad absurdum* proof is entirely reduced to the conjunctive). This remark seems to echo a similar one made by Galen and Alexander of Aphrodisias. In the *Institutio Logica*, VII, 2–3, Galen talks of the primacy of the categorical syllogism to the hypotheticals, if it is granted, he says, that the propositions of which the first is composed are prior; "for no one will doubt that the simple is prior to the composite". Alexander of Aphrodisias, *op. cit.* (pp. 262 ff), also argues that if the hypotheticals are to yield knowledge, the second premiss must be true. And since these premisses are categorical propositions, there truth must be established by categorical syllogisms. (See J. S. Kieffer, *Galen's Institutio Logica*, p. 94.)

To prove his point, Avicenna first states that the fundamental form of exceptive syllogism (which we use to show the others) is

> If A is B, then C is D,
> but A is B,
> therefore C is D.

Exceptive syllogisms from a separate first premiss as well as those whose first premiss is an 'If – then' proposition but in which we assert the contradictory of the consequent to produce the contradictory of the antecedent, are all shown by the above exceptive syllogism.[1] So all we have to do is to show that the above exceptive syllogism is shown by the predicative.

416, 4–11. This passage contains a qoutation from a scholar who held the above view but whose defence of it is not acceptable to Avicenna. As quoted, the scholar wants to show that in the syllogism

> If A is B, then C is D,
> but A is B,
> therefore C is D

'A is B', as occurs in the first premiss, must be in question. And the fact that this is so, is indicated by the word 'if' at the beginning of the connective premiss. If 'A is B' were self-evident, the argument continues, and so were the implication, the conclusion would be self-evident; which means that there would be no reason to construct a syllogism to produce it. From what Alexander said, *loc. cit.*, one would add to the above that since 'A is B' is a categorical proposition, and these are proved by categorical syllogisms, this will, supposedly, show that the exceptive syllogism is shown by the predicative.

416, 12–17, and 417, 1–10. To refute the above view the passage refers us to an earlier statement made in the book that in an 'If – then' proposition what concerns us is not whether the antecedent is doubtful or not, but whether it implies the antecedent or does not imply it. Avicenna also attacks the other view made in the previous passage, namely that what is evidently implied by what is self-evident, must also be self-evident. He says that something may be evidently implied by another thing, which is itself self-evident, through the mediation of a third party. In which case a syllogism will be needed to lead us to the conclusion. He makes a further point on this issue saying it is not one and the same thing to say that something is self-evident and to say that it is evidently implied by what is itself self-evident. Otherwise, the first mood of the first figure, to which all the other predicative syllogisms are reduced, would not give us any new information. From his point of view this would amount to saying that it would not be a syllogism.

Another interesting remark made in the passage concerns the view that the predicative syllogism can be constructed as an 'If – then' proposition where the two premisses of the predicative become the antecedent and its conclusion the consequent. As this and the succeeding passages show, any view we may hold as to the nature of the logical process in one of them, can be readily said of the other.

417, 10–15. The point made here is not directly relevant to the above discussion. Avicenna simply says that the implication of the consequent (conclusion) by the antecedent (the premisses) may not be evident but is shown by some proof. In such a case the implication will also be conclusive.

417, 15–16; 418 and 419. Here he seems to agree with the view that what is evidently implied by self-evident premiss(es) is self-evident. He says that in the proposition 'If A is B, then C is D', 'A is B' is self-evident and so is the implication. He adds that when 'A is B' comes to one's mind, it will come as a true assertion from which we will evidently reach 'C is D'. To assert 'A is B' again, he says, will not give us any new information. This applies also to the syllogism from predicative premisses. When we bring to our minds the premisses 'Every C is B' and 'Every B is A' they will lead us directly to the conclusion without asserting them again. The important question that one would raise here is whether he does not consider the "exceptive syllogism" as a syllogism. The answer to this will emerge from what follows.

420–24, 1–5. The question he assumes that one would raise is whether the second premiss in *any* syllogism is redundant. There are two kinds of redundant discourse, the passage explains. One can say that a statement is redundant (a) if it had been implicitly stated in what one said earlier; and so to state it again will be a repetition of the earlier statement. Or (b) when the verbal utterance is not needed though the meaning which the utterance expresses is. In this case the utterance will be called redundant. This happens, e.g. when one says 'Every B is C' and then concludes that 'Every B is A'. To be able to follow the argument, the hearer must bring to his mind the other concealed premiss, which is 'Every C is A', though he needs not utter it, for the utterance here is redundant. Avicenna then adds that the second premiss in a predicative syllogism can only be redundant in the sense (b); while the second premiss in the exceptive syllogism is redundant in the sense (a). But in the case of the exceptive syllogism this is so only if the antecedent of the 'If – then' premiss is self-evident. If not, then the assertion of the antecedent will be necessary to lead to the conclusion; and the argument formed from the 'If – then' proposition as a first premiss and the assertion of its antecedent as the second premiss will be conclusive. To Avicenna, the antecedent not being self-evident means that it is in need of a proof, and that proof must take the form of a conjunctive syllogism. Therefore, he concludes, the exceptive syllogism will be reduceable to the conjunctive!

424, 6–17, and 425. Just before the end of this passage Avicenna states clearly the point in all he says here and this is that the implication of the contradictory of the antecedent from the contradictory of the consequent does not become evident except by the one where we imply the consequent after asserting the antecedent. (See p. 271.) In the latter case the implication is self-evident, but not so in the first. Since it has been shown before that the latter is shown by the conjunctive, this will also be true of the first. There is no clear reason why the proposition in which we imply the contradictory of the antecedent from the contradictory of the consequent is not evident. At the beginning of the passage, however, it is said that these propositions are used in the *reductio ad absurdum* proofs. In such proofs the truth of the first part of the 'If – then' proposition (the contradictory of the consequent) is in question, i.e. not self-evident. Also, he adds the implication itself will not be evident but shown by using a conjunctive syllogism. (See p. 277.)

NOTE

[1] In the *Institutio Logica*, VIII, 2, Galen speaks of the case in which we assume the contradictory of the consequent and assert the contradictory of the antecedent, stating clearly that it is not primary and needs demonstration.

GLOSSARY

'aks. Conversion (of propositions) ἀντιστρέφειν . As in Aristotle's *Pr. An.* particularly 25a6, 8, 10, 28, 36b35–37a31, 53a7, 59a30. In Avicenna's text it also refers to the same operation when applied to conditional propositions, *shartiyya*, q.v. Cp. *rujūʿ*. See p. 267.

'alā 'l-iṭlāq. Unrestricted. Refers to the 'If – then' proposition when both its parts, *juzʾ*, q.v. are true regardless whether the first formally implies the second or not. See p. 12.

'alā 'l-taḥqīq. Restricted. Refers to the 'If – then' proposition when the antecedent, *muqaddam*, q.v. formally implies the consequent, *tālī*, q.v. Synonymous with *muttaṣila ḥaqīqiyya* (real connective). See p. 12.

ḍarb. Mood τρόπος. The term is used in the treatment of both the predicative, *ḥamlī*, q.v. and conjunctive-conditional, *iqtirānī*, q.v. syllogisms to differentiate in the various figures, *shakl*, q.v. the syllogisms according to the quality and quantity of the premisses. Avicenna extends its use to refer to arguments of the Chrysippian type, *istithnā*, q.v. as did Galen in *Inst. Log.*, Sextus in *Ag. the Log.* and Diogenes in *Lives.* See p. 274.

fī quwwati. Equivalent in force to, has the same force as. Possibly a translation of (Galen's *Inst. Log.*). See note 15 to Book V, Chapter One.

ḥadd. ὅρος . I translate it here as 'part' to avoid confusion. The original meaning of both the Greek and the Arabic words is 'limit'. In Aristotle's *Pr. An.* where predicative, *ḥamlī*, q.v. premisses and syllogisms are treated it means a 'term'. In this text it means 'term' as well as 'part', *juzʿ*, q.v. of a conditional premiss, *shartiyya*, q.v. that is a proposition. Cp. note 1 to Book VI, Chapter One.

ḥamlī. Predicative κατηγορικός. It refers to the syllogism whose premisses are all predicative propositions, *ḥamliyyāt*: 'A is B'. See pp. 216 and 219–20.

'ināad. Conflict μάχη. The relation expressed in an 'Either – or' proposition in which presence the antecedent, *muqaddam*, q.v. and the consequent, *tālī*, q.v. of that proposition cannot be both true. Such is also the definition given in Galen's *Inst. Log.* See pp. 222–23 and pp. 232–34.

'inād ghayr tāmm. Incomplete conflict. See *'inād nāqiṣ.*

'ināad nāqiṣ, opp. *'ināad tāmm*, q.v. Deficient conflict ἐλλιπής μάχη. The relation in which presence the antecedent, *muqaddam*, q.v. and the consequent, *tālī*, q.v. of an 'Either – or' proposition can be together false. See pp. 222–23. Synonymous with *'ināad ghayr tāmm* (incomplete conflict). Defined as such in Galen's *Inst. Log.*

'ināad tāmm, opp. *'ināad nāqiṣ*, q.v. Complete conflict τελεία μάχη . The relation in which presence the antecedent, *muqaddam*, q.v. and the consequent, *tālī*, q.v. of an 'Either – or' proposition can neither be true together nor can they be false together. See pp. 222–23. Same definition as in Galen's *Inst. Log.*

iqtirānī. Conjunctive. Refers to predicative, *ḥamlī*, q.v. and conditional syllogisms, *shartiyya*, q.v. to which the Aristotelian idea of the middle term is applied. It may be a translation of κατὰ πρόσληψιν. See note 110 to the Introduction and pp. 258–61. (*Al-Qiyās*, 295–357.)

istiqrāʾ. Induction ἐπαγωγή. As in Aristotle's *Pr. An.* It is compared in the text with what is called 'divided syllogism', *qiyās muqassam*, q.v. See pp. 264–65.

istithnāʾī. Exceptive. Refers to arguments of the same type as those attributed to Chrysippus.

Such as 'If *p*, then *q*; but *p*, therefore *q*'. Possibly a translation of κατὰ μετάληψιν. See note 110 to the Introduction. (*Al-Qiyās*, 389–407.)

ittibāʿ. Following ἀκολουθία? A general term used to designate the relation between the antecedent, *muqaddam*, q.v. and the consequent, *tālī*, q.v. of an 'If – then' proposition. It is divided into *luzūm*, q.v. and *ittifāq*, q.v. See p. 226.

ittifāq. Chance connection. A term used in the text to show that the subject-matter of the antecedent, *muqaddam*, q.v. and the consequent, *tālī*, q.v. of an 'If – then' proposition is not related in any way and that both parts, *juzʾ*, q.v. should be true propositions. See p. 226.

ittiṣāl nāqiṣ, opp. *ittiṣāl tāmm*, q.v. Deficient connection. It designates an 'If – then' proposition which is false when the antecedent, *muqaddam*, q.v. is true and the consequent, *tālī*, q.v. is false, and true otherwise. May be the same as what in the *Inst. Log.* Galen calls ἐλλιπής ἀκολοθία. See pp. 224 and 271. Synonymous with *ittiṣāl ghayr tāmm* (incomplete connection). Interchangeable with *luzūm nāqiṣ* (deficient implication) and *luzūm ghayr tāmm* (incomplete connection).

ittiṣāl tāmm, opp. *ittiṣāl nāqiṣ*, q.v. Complete connection. The same as the relation called by modern logicians 'equivalence' in which the connective proposition is true when both its parts are true or both are false, and false otherwise. See pp. 224 and 271. May be the same as what in the *Inst. Log.* Galen calls τελεία ἀκολουθία. Interchangeable with *luzūm tāmm* (complete implication).

jazāʾ. Apodosis. The second part, *juzʾ*, q.v. of an 'If – then' proposition which expresses what in modern logic is called 'formal implication', *luzūm*, q.v. Correlative with *sharṭ*, q.v. (see *tālī*). Interchangeable with *lāzim*, q.v. Cf. pp. 226–27 where an account of Greek terminology is given.

juzʾ. Part. Meaning the antecedent, *muqaddam*, q.v. or the consequent, *tālī*, q.v. of a conditional proposition, *sharṭiyya*, q.v. of any type. Also the subject and predicate of a predicative proposition, *ḥamlī*, q.v. See *ḥadd*. Cp. note 1 to Book VI, Chapter One, *al-Qiyās*, 232 and 255 ff.

lāzim. Implicate. Correlative with *malzūm*, q.v. Interchangeable with *jazāʾ*, q.v.

luzūm. Implication. Refers to the relation in an 'If – then' proposition when the subject-matter of its parts, *juzʾ*, q.v. is related. See p. 226.

luzūm ghayr tāmm. Incomplete implication. See *ittiṣāl nāqiṣ*.

luzūm nāqiṣ, opp. *luzūm tāmm*, q.v. Deficient implication. See *ittiṣāl nāqiṣ*.

luzūm tāmm, opp. *luzūm nāqiṣ*. Complete implication. See *ittiṣāl tāmm*.

malzūm. Implicant. Correlative with *lāzim*, q.v. Interchangeable with *sharṭ*, q.v.

mashhūr. Indemonstrable ἀναπόδεικτος? As in Sextus' *Ag. the Log.* when it refers to arguments or moods, *ḍarb*, q.v. But when it describes propositions *mashhūrāt*, it means widely-accepted. See pp. 274–75.

manfaṣila. A separative proposition διαιρετικαὶ προτάσις. A general term for the 'Either – or' proposition. Galen's *Inst. Log.* describes it as a Peripatetic term. See p. 234.

munfaṣila ghayr ḥaqīqiyya, opp. *munfaṣila ḥaqīqiyya*, q.v. Unreal separative proposition. A general term which describes the 'Either – or' proposition (a) when both its parts, *juzʾ*, q.v. are false παραπλήσια διεξευγμένοις and (b) when both its parts are true παραδιεξ-ευγμένον. Avicenna has no special names for (a) and (b) as we find in Galen's *Inst. Log.* for example. See p. 234.

munfaṣila ḥaqīqiyya, opp. *munfaṣila ghayr ḥaqīqiyya*, q.v. Real separative proposition διαιρετικαὶ προτάσις as, e.g. in Galen's *Inst. Log.* It refers to the 'Either – or' proposition which is true when one of its parts, *juzʾ*, q.v. is true and the other false, and false otherwise. See p. 234.

muqaddam. Antecedent. The first part, *juz'*, q.v. of a conditional proposition, *sharṭiyya*, q.v. of either type. Correlative with *tālī*, q.v. (see *sharṭ*.) Cf. pp. 226–27 where there is also an account of Greek terminology.

mushtarak. Shared. Designates the middle term or proposition in a syllogism, *qiyās*, q.v. Very likely a translation of ἀμφότερος which occurs in Galen's *Inst. Log.* See note 1 to Book VI, Chapter One. See also in particular *al-Qiyās*, 419, 3. See *yashtarik*.

muttaṣila. A connective proposition κατὰ συνέχειαν. A general term for the 'If – then' proposition. It is described in, e.g. Galen's *Inst. Log.* as a Peripatetic term. See p. 216.

muttaṣila ḥaqīqiyya. A real connective proposition. See *ʿala'l-taḥqīq*.

qaḍāyā mutaradidatu'l-aḥwāl. Indeterminable propositions. I.e. propositions which can be treated as conditional, *sharṭiyya*, q.v. or predicative, *ḥamlī*, q.v. See pp. 226 and 241–42.

qiyās. Syllogism συλλογισμός. Used in the text to refer to inferences which involve at least two premisses (apart from the conclusion). It applies not only to arguments in which the Aristotelian idea of the middle term is used, but also to arguments of the type attributed to Chrysippus, *istithnā'ī*, q.v. In so extending the use of the word 'syllogism' Avicenna is possibly following the footsteps of the Aristotelian commentators. See pp. 275 and 216–17.

qiyās kāmil. Perfect τέλειος syllogism. I.e., to which others (imperfect ones) are reduced, and which is itself not reduceable to any other syllogism. Apart from its use in Avicenna's treatment of predicative syllogism, *ḥamlī*, q.v. one finds it used in the sections dealing with conjunctive-conditional syllogisms, *iqtirānī*, q.v. and the exceptive syllogism, *istithnā'ī*, q.v. See p. 275.

qiyās muqassam. Divided syllogism. In it a middle term, *ḥadd*, q.v. joins an 'Either – or' premiss, whose parts, *juz'*, q.v. share, *yashtarik*, q.v. their subjects or predicates, with one or more premisses of any type. It is compared in the text with induction, *istiqrā'*, q.v. See pp. 262–65.

rujūʿ. Reduction. It is the process by which we infer, e.g. the proposition 'Always: when every A is B, then not every C is D' from 'Never: if every A is B, then every C is D'. In the Arabic translation of Aristotle's *Pr. An.* the word *rujūʿ* translates ἀντιστρέφειν in, among other places, 32a30 and 36b38, where the Greek word refers to a process like the one we mentioned. To avoid confusion we translated it 'reduction' and kept 'conversion' for *ʿaks*, q.v. See p. 267.

shakl. Figure σχῆμα. Used with the predicative syllogism, *ḥamlī*, q.v. (as in Aristotle's *Pr. An.*) as well as the conjunctive-conditional, *iqtirānī*, q.v. and the divided, *qiyās muqassam*, q.v. syllogisms, to differentiate the syllogisms, within each type, according to the placement of the middle part (term or proposition), *ḥadd*, q.v. It is not used, however, to refer to the Chrysippian type of arguments, as we find in Galen's *Inst. Log.* See *ḍarb*, also p. 274.

sharṭ. Protasis. Describes the first part, *juz'*, q.v. of an 'If – then' proposition when it expresses formal implication, *luzūm*, q.v. Correlative with *jazā'*, q.v. (see *muqaddam*). Cf. pp. 226–27 where there is an account of Greek terminology. Interchangeable with *malzūm*, q.v.

sharṭiyya. Conditional. Describes propositions: 'If – then' and 'Either – or', as well as syllogisms in which at least one premiss is a conditional proposition. See *waḍʿiyya*; also pp. 215–16 for the question of its Greek equivalent. Cf. also pp. 219–21.

sharṭiyya basīṭa, opp. *sharṭiyya murakkaba*, q.v. Simple conditional proposition in which the antecedent, *muqaddam*, q.v. and the consequent, *tālī*, q.v. are predicative, *ḥamlī*, q.v. propositions. See pp. 239–40.

sharṭiyya mukhtalaṭa, opp. *sharṭiyya ṣirfa*, q.v. Mixed conditional syllogisms. It is not clear whether it means syllogisms in which the premisses are a mixture of 'If – then' and 'Either – or' propositions or of a conditional, *sharṭiyya*, q.v. and a predicative, *ḥamlī*, q.v. proposition. See p. 217, also pp. 218–19 where it is compared with what a Greek scholium calls mixed μικτός hypothetical.

sharṭiyya murakkaba, opp. *sharṭiyya basīṭa*, q.v. Compound conditional proposition in which one or both parts, *juz'*, q.v. are conditional propositions, *sharṭiyya*, q.v. of either type. See pp. 239–40.

sharṭiyya ṣirfa, opp. *sharṭiyya mukhtalaṭa*, q.v. Pure conditional syllogisms. The text is not clear whether it means syllogisms made up of the same type of conditional propositions, *sharṭiyya*, q.v. or those which contain only conditional premisses to the exclusion of the predicatives, *ḥamlī*, q.v. See pp. 218–19 where it is compared with ἁπλῶς which occurs in a Greek scholium.

takāfu'. Equivalence. The antecedent, *muqaddam*, q.v. and the consequent, *tālī*, of a real separative proposition, *munfaṣila ḥaqīqiyya*, q.v. are said to be equivalent in the sense that they can interchange their positions without the truth-value (truth or falsity) of the whole proposition being changed. The word *takāfu'* is imported by Avicenna or his source from Aristotle's *Categories* where it is used to translate ἀντιστρέφειν. It should be noted that ἀντιστρέφειν in the *Categories* is used of terms which reciprocate. See p. 235.

talāzum. Equipollence or mutual implication. It is used only in the treatment of immediate inference. Two conditional, *sharṭiyya*, q.v. propositions are said to be equipollent if we can immediately infer the one from the other. See pp. 266–67.

tālī. Consequent. The second part, *juz'*, q.v. of a conditional, *sharṭiyya*, q.v. proposition of either type. Correlative with *muqaddam*, q.v. (see *jazā'*). Cf. pp. 226–27 where the Greek terminology is given.

waḍ'iyya. Hypothetical. Used in *Manṭiq al-Mashriqiyyīn*, p. 61 and in *al-Qiyās*, 423, 8 only to refer to the 'If – then' proposition. Some translators used it to refer to syllogisms as well. See pp. 215–16 where the question of its Greek equivalent is discussed.

yashtarik. Share κοινωνέω. As in Galen's *Inst. Log.*, it is said of coterminous propositions which share one of their parts, *juz'*, q.v. See note 3 to Book V, Chapter Three. Cp. *mushtarak*.

BIBLIOGRAPHY

TEXTS AND TRANSLATIONS

Alexander of Aphrodisias, *In Aristotelis Analyticorum Priorum Librum I Commentarium* (ed. by M. Wallies), *Commentaria in Aristotelem Graeca*, II, (I), Berlin 1883.

Alexander of Aphrodisias, *In Aristotelis Topicorum Libros Octo Commentaria* (ed. by M. Wallies), *Commentaria in Aristotelem Graeca*, II (II), Berlin 1881.

Ammonius, *In Aristotelis Analyticorum Priorum Librum I Commentarium* (ed. by M. Wallies), *Commentaria in Aristotelem Graeca*, IV (VI), Berlin 1899.

Aristotle, *Prior Analytics* (ed. and transl. into English by M. Tredennick), The Loeb Classical Library, London and Cambridge, Mass. 1938.

Aristotle, *Aristotle's Prior and Posterior Analytics*. A revised text with Introduction and Commentary by W. D. Ross, Oxford 1949.

Aristotle, *Topica* (ed. and transl. into English by E. S. Forster), The Loeb Classical Library, London and Cambridge, Mass. 1960.

Aristotle, *Aristotle's Categories and De Interpretatione*. A translation with notes and glossary by J. L. Ackrill Oxford 1963.

Aristotle, *see* A. Badawi.

Aristotle, *see* Khalil Georr.

Aristotle, *see* Isḥāq ibn Ḥunayn.

J. von Arnim, *Stoicorum Veterum Fragmenta*, Leipzig 1905–24, 4 Vols.

Al-Ashʿarī, *Maqālāt al-Islāmiyyīn* (ed. by H. Ritter), 2 Vols., Istanbul 1929–33.

Avicenna, *al-Shifāʾ, al-Madkhal* (ed. by G. C. Anawati and others), Cairo 1952.

Avicenna, *al-Shifāʾ, al-Maqūlāt* (ed. by G. C. Anawati and others), Cairo 1959.

Avicenna, *al-Shifāʾ, al-ʿIbāra*, British Museum MS. Or. 7500.

Avicenna, *al-Shifāʾ, al-Qiyās* (ed. by S. Zayed), Cairo 1964.

Avicenna, *al-Shifāʾ, al-Burhān* (ed. by A. Affifi), Cairo 1956.

Avicenna, *al-Shifāʾ, al-Jadal* (ed. by A. Ehwani), Cairo 1965.

Avicenna, *al-Shifāʾ, al-Safsaṭa* (ed. by A. Ehwani), Cairo 1958.

Avicenna, *al-Najāt*, 2nd ed., Cairo 1938.

Avicenna, *Avicenna's De Anima, Being the Psychological Part of Kitāb al-Shifāʾ* (ed. by F. Rahman), London 1959.

Avicenna, *La logique de fils de Sina communément appelé Avicenne* [a French translation of the logic of *al-Najat*], by P. Vattier, Paris 1658.

Avicenna, *Manṭiq al-Mashriqiyyīn*, Cairo 1910.

Avicenna, *al-Ishārāt waʾl-Tanbīhāt* (ed. by J. Forget), Leiden 1892.

Avicenna, *Livre des directives et remarques* [a French translation of *al-Ishārāt waʾl-Tanbīhāt*], by A. M. Goichon, Paris 1951.

Avicenna, *Livre des définitions* [an edition and a French translation with notes of *Kitāb al-Ḥudūd*], by A. M. Goichom, Cairo 1963.

Avicenna, *Le livre de science* [a French translation of *Danesh-Name*], by M. Achena and H. Massé, 2 Vols., Paris 1955–58.

Avicenna, *Avicenna's Treatise on Logic: Part One of Danesh-Name Alai* (ed. and transl. into English by Farhang Zabech), The Hague 1971.

Avicenna's Biography (transl. into English by A. J. Arberry), in *Avicenna on Theology*, London 1951.

Avicenna, see A. Badawi.

A. Badawi (ed.), *Manṭiq Arisṭū*, 3 Vols., Cairo 1948–52 [The Medieval Arabic translation of Aristotle's *Organon*].

A. Badawi (ed.), *Arisṭū ʿInda'l-ʿArab*, Cairo 1948. [Contains Avicenna's *Notes on the De Anima* and his letter to Abū Jaʿfar al-Kiyā].

Boethius, *Commentarii in Aristotelis* Aristotelis Librum 'Περὶ Ἑρμηνείας' (ed. by C. Meiser), Leipzig, 1877–80.

Diogenes Laertius, *Lives of Eminent Philosophers* (ed. with an English translation by R. D. Hicks), 2 Vols., London and Cambridge, Mass. 1925.

Euclid, *The Thirteen Books of Euclid's Elements*, translated with introduction and commentary, by T. L. Heath, New York 1956 (2nd ed.), Vol. 2.

Al-Fārābī *Sharḥ Kitāb al-ʿIbāra* (ed. by W. Kutsch and S. Marrow), Beyrouth 1960.

Al-Fārābī, 'Farabi'nin Bazi Mantik Eserleri' (ed. and transl. into Turkish by M. Türker), *Revue de la Faculté des langues, d'histoire et de géographie de l'Université d'Ankara* **XVI** (1958) 165–286.

Al-Fārābī, *Al-Fārābī's Short Commentary on Aristotle's Prior Analytics*, English translation by N. Rescher, Pittsburg 1963.

Al-Fārābī, *Al-Alfāẓ al-Mustaʿmala fī'l-Manṭiq* (ed. by M. Mahdi), Beyrouth 1968.

Al-Fārābī, *Al-Jamʿ bayna Raʾyayy al-Ḥakīmayn* (ed. by A. N. Nader), Beyrouth 1960.

Al-Fārābī, *Fārābī, Deux ouvrages inédits sur la réthorique* (ed. by J. Langhade and M. Grignaschi), Beyrouth 1971.

Al-Fārābī, see G. Vajda.

Galen, *Galeni Institutio Logica* (ed. by C. Kalbfleisch), Leipzig 1896.

Galen, *Galen's Institutio Logica*, English translation, Introduction and Commentary by J. S. Kieffer, Baltimore 1964.

Galen, *Einführung in die Logik* [German translation with commentary on *Institutio Logica*], by J. Mau, Berlin 1960.

Khalil Georr, *Les catégories d'Aristote dans leurs versions syro-arabes, edition des textes précédée d'une étude historique et critique et suivie d'un vocabulaire technique*, Beyrouth 1948.

Ḥunayn ibn Isḥāq, *Ḥunain ibn Isḥāq, Über die syrischen und arabischen Galen-Übersetzungen* [Arabic text and German translation], by G. Bergsträsser, Leipzig 1925.

Isḥāq ibn Ḥunayn, *Fī'l-Nafs*, ed. by A. Badawi, Cairo 1954 [medieval Arabic translation of Aristotle's *De Anima*].

Isḥāq ibn Ḥunayn, *Die Hermeneutik des Aristoteles in der arabischen Übersetzung des Ishāk Ibn Honain*, ed. by I. Pollak, Leipzig 1913.

Ibn al-Nadīm, *al-Fihrist* (ed. by G. Flügel), Leipzig 1871.

Philoponus, *In Aristotelis Analytica Priora Commentaria* (ed. by M. Wallies), *Commentaria in Aristotelem Graeca*, XIII (II), Berlin 1905.

Ibn al-Qifṭī, *Taʾrīkh al-Ḥukamāʾ*, J. Lippert, Leipzig 1903.

Sextus Empiricus, *Sextus Empiricus* (ed. and transl. into English by R. G. Bury), The Loeb Classical Library, 4 Vols., London and Cambridge, Mass. 1933.

Al-Shahrastānī, *al-Milal waʾl-Niḥal* (ed. by W. Cureton), Leipzig 1923.

Ibn Sina, see Avicenna.

Themistius, *In Aristotelis Analyticorum Priorum Librum I Paraphrasis* (ed. by M. Wallies), *Commentaria in Aristotelem Graeca*, XXIII (III), Berlin 1884.

Al-Ṭusī, *Sharḥ al-Ishārāt*, published by S. Dunya in his edition of *al-Ishārāt wa'l-Tanbīhāt*, 3 Vols., Cairo 1957–60.

Ibn Abī Uṣaybiʿa, *'Uyūn al-Anbā' fī Ṭabaqāt al-Aṭibbā'* (ed. by A. Müller), 2 Vols., Cairo - Königsberg 1882–84.

G. Vajda, 'Autour de la théorie de la connaissance chez Saadia', *Revue des Études Juives* **126** (1967) 375–97. [Contains a partial translation of an incomplete middle commentary by al-Fārābī on the *Topics*.]

Al-Yaʿqūbī, *Tārīkh* (ed. by M. Th. Houtsma), Vol. I, Leiden 1883.

STUDIES

S. M. Afnan, *Avicenna, His Life and Works*, London 1958.

S. M. Afnan, *Philosophical Terminology in Arabic and Persian*, Leiden 1964.

G. C. Anawati, *Mu'allafāt Ibn Sīnā*, Cairo 1950.

Paul Barth, *Die Stoa* (ed. by Goedeckmeyer), 6th ed., Stuttgart 1946.

C. Bergsträsser, *Neue Materialien zu Hunain Ibn Ishaqs Galen-bibliographie*, Leipzig 1932.

J. M. Bochenski, *A History of Formal Logic* (transl. and ed. by Ivo Thomas), Indiana 1961. [Contains extensive bibliographies on the history of logic.]

J. M. Bochenski, *La logique de Théophraste*, Fribourg 1947.

J. M. Bochenski, *Ancient Formal Logic*, Amsterdam 1951.

J. M. Bochenski, 'On the Categorical Syllogism', *Dominican Studies* **I**, (1948) 40–41.

Philotheus Boehner, *Medieval Logic*, Manchester 1952.

Lewis Carrol, 'What the Tortoise Said to Achilles', *Mind* (1895) 278–80.

J. Christensen, *An Essay on the Unity of Stoic Philosophy*, Copenhagen 1962.

Karl Dürr, *The Propositional Logic of Boethius*, Amsterdam 1951.

M. T. Fumagalli, *The Logic of Abelard*, Dordrecht, Holland 1970.

A. M. Goichon, *Lexique de la langue philosophique d'Ibn Sīnā*, Paris 1938.

A. M. Goichon, *Vocabulaire d'Aristote et d'Ibn Sīnā*, Paris 1939.

A. M. Goichon, 'Une logique moderne à l'époque mediévale, la logique d'Avicenne', *Archives d'histoire doctrinale et littéraire du moyen-âge* **16** (1948).

A. M. Goichon, 'La place de la définition dans la logique d'Avicenne', *La revue du Caire* (1951) 95–106.

V. Goldschmidt, *Le système stoïcien et l'idée de temps*, Paris 1958.

J. B. Gould, *The Philosophy of Chrysippus*, Albany, New York 1970.

G. E. von Grünebaum (ed.), *Logic in Classical Islamic Culture*, Wiesbaden 1970.

S. Horowitz, 'Über den Einfluss des Stoicismus auf die Entwicklung der Philosophie bei den Arabern', *Zeitschrift der Deutschen Morgenländischen Gesellschaft* **57** (1903) 177 ff.

Martha Hurst, 'Implication in the Fourth Century B.C.', *Mind* **44** (1935) 484–95.

Fehmi Jadaane, *L'influence du stoïcisme sur la pensée musulmane*, Beyrouth 1968.

Karl Kalbfleisch, *Über Galens Einleitung in die Logik*, Leipzig 1897.

E. Kapp, *Greek Foundations of Traditional Logic*, New York 1942.

W. and M. Kneale, *The Development of Logic*, Oxford 1962.

C. Lejewski, 'On Prosleptic Syllogisms', *Notre Dame Journal of Formal Logic* **II** (1961) 158–76.

C. I. Lewis, *A Survey of Symbolic Logic*, Berkeley 1918.

A. A. Long (ed.), *Problems in Stoicism*, London 1971.

J. Lukasiewicz, *Aristotle's Syllogistic from the Standpoint of Modern Formal Logic*, 2nd., enlarged, Oxford 1957.

I. Madkour, *L'Organon d'Aristote dans le monde arabe*, Paris 1934.

I. Madkour, 'Avicenne, le traité des catégories du *Shifā'*, *Mélanges de l'Institut dominicain d'études orientales du Caire* **5** (1958) 253–78.

Benson Mates, *Stoic Logic*, Berkeley 1961.

J. Mau, 'Stoische Logik', *Hermes* **85** (1957) 147–58.

Y. Mehdawi, *Bibliographie d'Ibn Sina*, Tehran 1954.

E. A. Moody, *Truth and Consequence in Medieval Logic*, Amsterdam 1953.

I. van Müller, *Über Galens Werk vom Wissenschaftlichen Beweis*, Munich 1895.

C. Nallino, *Arabian Astronomy, Its History During the Medieval Times*, Rome 1911 [Arabic]. *Storia dell'astronomia presso gli Arabi nel Medio Evo*, published in *Raccolta di soritti e inediti*, a cura di Maria Nallino, Vol. V, Rome 1944, pp. 88–329 [Italian].

G. Patzig, *Die Aristotelische Syllogistik*, 2nd ed., Göttingen 1963.

S. Pines, 'La "philosophie orientale" d'Avicenne et sa polémique contre les bagdadiens', *Archives d'histoire doctrinale et littéraire du moyen-âge* **19** (1952) 5–37.

M. Pohlenz, *Die Stoa*, Göttingen 1947.

C. Prantl, *Geschichte der Logic im Abendlande*, 4 Vols., Leipzig 1955–70.

A. N. Prior, *Formal Logic*, Oxford 1955.

W. V. Quine, *Philosophy of Logic*, Englewood Cliffs, New Jersey 1970.

N. Rescher, *Galen and the Syllogism*, Pittsburgh 1966.

N. Rescher, 'Some Arabic Technical Terms of Syllogistic Logic and their Greek Originals', *Journal of the American Oriental Society* **82** (1962) 203–04.

N. Rescher, *Studies in the History of Arabic Logic*, Pittsburgh 1963.

N. Rescher, *The Development of Arabic Logic*, Pittsburgh 1964.

L. M. de Rijk, *Logica Modernorum*, 2 Vols., Assen, Holland 1962–67.

Wilhelm Risse, *Bibliographia Logica, Verzeichnis der Druckschriften zur Logik mit Angabe ihrer Fundorte*, Band I, 1472–1800, Hildesheim 1965.

J. M. Rist, *Stoic Philosophy*, Cambridge 1969.

A. I. Sabra, ' A Twelfth Century Defence of the Fourth Figure of the Syllogism', *Journal of the Warburg and Courtauld Institutes* **28** (1965) 14–28.

A. I. Sabra, 'Review of N. Rescher's *al-Fārābī's Short Commentary on Aristotle's Prior Analytics', Journal of the American Oriental Society* **85** (1965) 241–43.

J. E. Sandys, *A History of Classical Scholarship*, 3rd ed., Vol. I, Cambridge 1921.

J. E. Saunders (ed.), *Greek and Roman Philosophy after Aristotle*, New York and London 1966.

Heinrich Scholz, *Geschichte der Logik*, Berlin 1931.

Heinrich Scholz, 'Review of J. W. Stakelum, *Galen and the Logic of Propositions', Deutsche Literaturzeitung*, nos. 37–38, 1941, cols. 866–69.

N. Shehaby, 'Review of N. Rescher's *Galen and the Syllogism', Philosophical Books* **VIII** (1967) 20–21.

J. W. Stakelum, *Galen and the Logic of Propositions*, Rome 1940.

M. Steinschneider, *Die arabischen Übersetzungen aus dem Griechischen*, Graz 1960.

Garra de Vaux, *Avicenne*, Paris 1900.

Richard Walzer, *Greek into Arabic*, Oxford 1962.

Gerard Watson. *The Stoic Theory of Knowledge*, Belfast 1966.

George Hendrik von Wright, *Logical Studies*, London 1957.

E. Zeller, *The Stoics, Epicureans and Sceptics* (trans by O. J. Reichel), London 1870.

INDEX

Ackrill, J. L., 229, 235, 255 nn.24, 27, 256 n.55
Yaḥyā ibn ʿAdiyy: his commentary on the *Topics* depends on Alexander's, 8, 10; and Ammonius', 25 n.37; wrote *On the Analysis of Syllogisms*, 10, 25 n.37
Affifi, A., 275 n.3
Alexander of Aphrodisias: described as 'the most excellent among later scholars', 6, 7, 8; a book on hypothetical syllogisms is attributed to, 7, 159–160; Avicenna's occupation at one time with works by, 8; commentaries on the *Prior Analytics* by, 8, 218; a partial commentary on the *Topics* by, 8; a commentary on the *De Interpretatione* by, 8; the differences between the Peripatetic and the Stoic approaches to logic as reported by, 14, 27 n.96, 28 n.110, 203; his report of Peripatetic and Stoic terminology for 'If – then' and 'Either – or' propositions, 216, 254 n.9, 255 nn.16, 22, 256 n.34; his report of Theophrastus' view on the equivalence between the *prosleptic* and the universal categorical propositions, 257 n.68; the Stoic indemonstrables are called 'syllogisms' by, 275; the reduction of the Stoic indemonstrables to predicative syllogisms as reported by, 278, 279
Ammonius, 25 n.37, 218, 255 n.16, 257 n.66
Anawati, C., 24 n.2, 170 n.1
Arberry, A. J., 26 n.51
Aristotle: Avicenna's reasons for not commenting on his works, 1; Avicenna's adoption of his method of presentation, 3; frequently referred to by Avicenna, 4; called 'the author of logic', 4; the reference to hypothetical syllogisms in his *Prior Analytics*, 5; references to a book on conditional syllogisms by, 5, 24 n.11, 190; the influence of his works in the Arab world, 6; Themistius' account of his views, 8; Arabic epitomes of and commentaries on *the Organon*, 9, 10; the two kinds of inferences he acknowledges, 16, 24 n.10, 26 n.59, 27 n.97, 28 n.110; his definition of *horos*, 99 n.1; references to the *Prior Analytics*, 203, 208, 211, 215, 218; his definition of a statement-making sentence, 220, 229, 221; his theory of opposition as a source for the idea of conflict, 223; his definition of terms which reciprocate, 235, 254 nn.1, 2, 255 nn.24, 27, 257 n.74, 258; his view on induction, 264, 267, 275 nn.7, 8
Al-Ashʿarī, 232, 256 n.58

Badawi, A., 24 nn.2, 9, 25 n.34, 192 n.7, 254 n.1
Baghdad, the School of, 8
Bergsträsser, 26 n.49, 254 n.6
Bukhārā, 7, 26 n.51
Al-Burhān of *al-Shifāʾ* by Avicenna, 275 n.3
Bury, R. G., 256 n.48, 276 n.10

Categorical. *See* Predicative
Christian translators and commentators, their attitude towards Greek philosophy, 3
Chrysippus: his indemonstrables, 5, 10, 16, 219, 223, 255 n.22, 273–75; what he says of 'a hypothetical' in his *Dialectical Definitions*, 229

Concomitance (*ma'iyya*), 40

Conflict: al-Fārābī's account of complete and defective, 10, 11; Avicenna's definition and distinction between complete and defective (incomplete), 12–13, 15, 36, 44ff., 61, 62, 80, 81, 83, 118ff., 174, 222, 232, 236, 242, 255 n.23, 273, 274

Conjunctive syllogism: favoured by Avicenna, 6, 16; description of, 18, 22, 27 n.98, 27 n.107, 28 n.110, 49, 52 n.9, 119, 183, 190, 203, 209, 270; 275 n.8; proposition, 239, 240

Connection, complete and incomplete (defective), 12, 19, 36, 40, 41, 46, 50, 56, 57, 61, 86, 93, 94, 95, 175, 189, 190, 216, 223–25, 250, 251, 271, 274

Conversion, 95, 96, 98, 108–10, 127, 129, 130–37, 142, 157, 174, 175, 179, 186, 187, 191, 267, 268, 269 n.2

Conversion per contrapositionem, 107, 180, 269

Conversion simpliciter, 180, 269

Coupling (*irtibāṭ*), 36

Cureton, W., 8

De Anima of *al-Shifā'* by Avicenna, 24 n.2

Abū 'Uthmān al-Dimashqī: translated Porphyry's *Isagoge*, 8, 254 n.1

Diogenes Laertius: his report on the different approaches to logic taken by the Peripatetics and the Stoics, 14; distinctions between hypothetical, inferential, and causal, 228, 229, 256 nn.48, 50, 52, 257 n.63, 275 n.2, 276 n.10

Divided syllogism, 16, 20–22, 152–160, 262–65

Dürr, Karl, 255 n.21

Ehwani, A. F., 275 n.4

Equipollence, 16, 17, 56, 163, 164, 165, 167, 169, 171, 173, 175, 178, 179, 266, 267

Equivalence. *See Takāfu'*

Euclid, 43 n.4

Exceptive syllogism, 5; disfavoured by Avicenna, 6; al-Fārābī's account of, 10, 16, 19, 22, 23, 27 n.98, 28 n.110, 49, 52 n.9, 183ff., 219, 275 n.8; premiss, 67, 75 n.6, 183ff., 270ff

Al-Fārābī: his criticism of Galen, 6; epitomized all of Aristotle's logical works, 9; the logical works of, 9–10; his exposition of conditional arguments, 10, 13, 23; his references to books by Aristotle on conditional syllogisms, 24 n.11, 25 n.12, 26 n.59, 28 n.114, 229, 256 n.56

Figurative proposition. *See Majāziyya*

Flügel, C., 25 n.36

Following, definition and distinction between two kinds of, 11–12, 15, 36–38, 41, 64, 65, 69, 70, 72, 73, 76–79, 85, 86, 222, 226, 242, 243, 247, 249, 255 n.23

Galen: 'excellent in medicine but weak in logic', 5, 6; criticism of his views on syllogisms from possible premisses, 6; Avicenna influenced by, 6; what the Arabs knew of his logical works, 9; his views on complete conflict when a proposition consists of more than two parts, 13; his reports regarding the differences between the Peripatetics and the Stoics, 14, 21–22, 25 nn.19, 21, 26 nn.49–50, 27 nn.84, 87, 59 n.3, 191; the different terminology used for the 'If – then' and 'Either – or' propositions by the Peripatetics and the Stoics as reported by, 216; his report on conflict and its possible source, 223, 224; his report on connection and separation, 225; his account of the paradisjunctive, 226; his use of *dunamai* which could be a source for *fī quwwati*, 43 n.15; what he says on the particles used with conditional propositions, 228; the three kinds of separatives as reported by, 234;

a book on *Hypothetical Syllogisms* by, 254 n.6, 255 nn.10, 11, 256 nn.43, 44, 51; the conversion and inversion of the 'If-then' proposition as given by, 269 n.2; his report on the indemonstrables, 273, 274, 275 n.2; the primacy of categorical syllogisms, 278, 281 n.1
Greek philosophy and logic: Arabic translations, commentaries... etc. of, 2, 3; Avicenna's attitude towards, 2; Avicenna's plan to discuss all that is important in, 6, 7, 22, 25 n.30; Greek philosophers, 215; Greek terminology for 'If – then' and 'Either – or' propositions and the syllogisms compounded of them, 216ff.; terminology for the antecedent and consequent, 227; the reduction of conjunctive propositions to the conditionals might have originated with Latin-Greek commentators, 239

Ḥabīb ibn Bahrīz: epitomized the *De Interpretatione*, 9
Heath, T. L., 43 n.4
Hicks, R. D., 256 nn.48, 52
Houtsma, M. T., 254 n.7
Ḥunayn ibn Isḥāq: epitomized the *De Interpretatione*, 9, 26 nn.49, 50, 254 n.6
Hypothetical syllogisms: a work by Galen on, 9, 26 n.50; Alexander's definition of, 27 n.96, 28 n.110; pure and mixed, 218, 219; hypothetical-connective propositions, 209, 216; Stoic and Peripatetic views on hypothetical propositions, 223, 225; hypothetical expressions, 228, 229

Al-ʿIbāra of *al-Shifāʾ* by Avicenna, 15, 27 n.90, 221, 255 n.30
Indemonstrables of Avicenna, 184, 185, 188, 189, 274, 275
Indemonstrables of Chrysippus. *See* Chrysippus
Indemonstrables of Galen. *See* Galen
Indeterminable propositions, 36, 56, 224, 226
Induction, 152, 264, 265
Isḥāq ibn Ḥunayn: epitomized the *De Interpretatione*, 9; his translation of the *De Interpretatione*, 28 n.110, 192 n.7
Al-Ishārāt waʾl-Tanbīhāt of Avicenna: later than *al-Shifāʾ*, 1; contains shorter accounts of conditionals, 1, 23–24 n.2

Al-Jadal of *al-Shifāʾ* by Avicenna, 275 n.4
Al-Jubbāʾī, gives a partial truth-functional analysis of the 'If – then' proposition, 232, 257 n.58
Al-Jūzjānī, describes the circumstances in which *al-Shifāʾ* was written, 1, 4, 24 n.4

Kalām, as a possible source for the objection-answer method, 24 n.8
Kalbfleisch, C., 27 n.84
M. el-Khodeiri, 25 n.17
Kieffer, J. S., 27 n.87, 28 n.110, 223, 256 n.37, 256 n.43, 273, 278
Al-Kindī: commented on the *Prior Analytics* and epitomized the *De Interpretatione*, 10
Abū Jaʿfar al-Kiyā, 8, 24 n.9
Kneale, W. and M., 255 n.14
Kutsch, W., 24 n.11, 26 n.60

Al-Lawāḥiq (a book Avicenna intended to write but most probably did not), 164, 179, 195, 257 n.75
Lejewski, C., 257 n.68
Liddell, H. G., 28 n.110

Lippert, J., 24 n.3

Al-Madkhal of *al-Shifā'* by Avicenna, 8, 24, 25 n.17, 27 n.88, 28 n.113, 170 n.1, 255 n.28, 256 n.49
Madkour, I., 7, 24 n.4, 25 n.28
Mahdi, M., 9
majāziyya proposition ('If-then'), 254 n.7
Manṭiq al-Mashriqiyyīn of Avicenna: gives a brief account of conditionals, 24 n.2, 170 n.1; its account for the reason why a conditional is so called, 215, 216; it gives the name *majāziyya* for the 'If-then' proposition, 254 n.7
Al-Maqūlāt of *al-Shifā'* by Avicenna, 25 n.17
Marrow, S., 24 n.11, 26 n.60
Mates, B., 255 n.13, 256 n.48, 273
Abū Bishr Mattā: commented on the *Prior Analytics*, *De Interpretatione*, and *Topics*, 9; wrote a book *On Conditional Syllogisms*, 9, 254 n.1; the translator of the *Posterior Analytic*, 254 n.1
Mau, J., 274
Modality, 74, 75 n.11, 99, 163, 253, 254
Al-Mubāḥathāt of Avicenna, 25 n.34
Müller, A., 25 n.44
Ibn al-Muqaffaʿ, epitomized the *De Interpretatione*, 9

Nader, A. N., 24 n.11
Ibn al-Nadīm, 4, 8, 9, 25 n.36, 254 n.1
Al-Najāt of Avicenna: belongs to the same period as *al-Shifā'*, 1; gives a short account of conditionals, 1, 23–4 n.2; refers to Alexander by name, 7; refers to Aristotle's commentaries, 8; gives an account of *reductio ad absurdum* proofs, 277
Nallino, C., 26 n.48
Abū ʿAbd Allāh al-Nātilī, 26 n.53
Nichomachus, 43 n.4
Notes to Aristotle's *De Anima* by Avicenna, 24 n.2

Objection-answer method, Avicenna's use of, 2, 3
The Orientals, 24 n.2, 254 n.7
Origen, his reference to the Stoic 'arguments from two conditionals', 217

Perfect syllogism, 91–92, 146, 185, 188, 276 n.8
Peripatetics: Avicenna sides with the, 5, 14, 25 n.17; their approach to logic, 14, 21; their role in diverting the attention of philosophers from Stoic logic, 22; the Stoic views in Avicenna come from their works, 23, 28 n.110; their terminology for the 'If – then' and 'Either – or' propositions, 216; their view on hypothetical propositions, 273; their terminology for the antecedent and consequent of an 'If – then' proposition, 234, 254 n.1, 256 n.42; commentators, 275
Philoponus, John: referred to as *shaykhuʾl naṣārā*, 8; Avicenna's occupation with the works of, 8; commentaries on the *Prior Analytics*, *De Interpretatione* and *Topics* by, 9; his reference to Theophrastus' conditional syllogism, 218, 256 n.48, 275
Pines, S., 24 n.2, 25 n.35
Plato, 228; his theory of Ideas (Forms), 37, 228, 238; his view on connection and separation in the *Sophist*, 256 n.42
Platonists, 256 n.42

Pollak, I., 28 n.110
Porphyry: several references to him in *al-Madkhal*, 8; the translation into Arabic of his *Isagoge*, 8; a commentary on the *De Interpretatione* by, 8
Prantl, C., 256 n.50
Predicative syllogisms, 5, 22, 23, 35, 66, 91, 95, 97, 99, 124, 133, 185, 203, 210, 211, 216, 275 n.8, 277, 280; propositions (premisses), 14, 16, 18, 35, 37, 39, 42, 46, 47, 52–58, 61–63, 70, 72, 73, 95, 124, 125ff., 133, 134, 149, 150, 152, 154, 229, 239, 240, 242, 243, 258, 261
Proximate conclusion, 196

Al-Qifṭī, 4, 8, 9, 24 nn.3, 4, 25 n.36
Quantifier, 15, 16, 62–64, 81, 242–44, 248, 249, 252
Quine, W. V., 220, 255 n.37
Quwayrī, commented on the *Prior Analytics* and the *De Interpretatione*, 10

Rahman, F., 24 n.2
Abū Bakr al-Rāzī: commented on the *Prior Analytics* and the *De Interpretatione*, 10; his works on logic, 10
Reductio ad absurdum proofs, 66, 70, 72, 79, 95ff., 141ff., 203ff., 209, 210, 246, 277, 278, 281
Reduction, 156, 159, 166, 187, 241, 260, 267
Rescher, N., 25 n.19, 26 n.50, 26 n.59
Ritter, H., 256 n.58
Ross, W. D., 267

Ibn al-Ṣalāḥ, 25 n.19, 26 n.50
Al-Sarakhsī: commented on the *Prior Analytics* and the *De Interpretatione*, 10
Ibn Sahlān al-Sāwī, 22
Scott, R., 28 n.110
Sextus Empiricus, his report on the differences between the Stoics and the Peripatetics approaches to logic, 14, 256 n.48, 257 n.63, 275, 275 nn.2, 6, 276 n.10
Al-Shahrastānī, 8
Quṭb al-Dīn al-Shīrāzī, 22
Situation-describing proposition (*qaḍiyya maḥalliyya*), 39
Stakelum, J. W., 223, 229, 256 n.35, 256 n.54
Stoics: their inference-schemas (indemonstrables), 5, 219; Avicenna's criticism of, 5, 190; Avicenna calls them 'literalists', 8; their approach to logic, 14; the destiny of their logic, 22; the source through which their views came to Avicenna, 23; Avicenna's criticism of their categories, 25 n.17; their terminology for the 'If – then' and 'Either – or' propositions, 216; Stoic arguments from two conditionals, 217; the Aristotelian theory of opposition as a possible source for their idea of conflict, 223; their conception of a hypothetical proposition, 223; their terminology for the antecedent and consequent of an 'If – then' proposition, 227; the names they give to separative propositions, 234, 255 n.19, 256 n.42

Tadhārī: the use of *sharṭiyya* as a translation of Aristotle's *ex hypotheseôs* by, 28 n.110; an early translation of the *Prior Analytics* by, 254 n.1
Takāfu', 46, 47, 51, 178, 235, 267
Abū al-Faraj ibn al-Ṭayyib: his criticism of the fourth figure in a commentary on Avicenna's *al-Qiyās*, 25 n.19
Thābit ibn Qurra: commented on the *Prior Analytics* and the *De Interpretatione*, 10

Themistius: Avicenna's reliance on, 8; the influence of his commentaries on the *Prior Analytics* and *Topics*, 9
Theon of Smyrna, 43 n.4
Theophrastus: his treatment of hypotheticals, 5, 218; referred to by Avicenna, 8; his commentary on the *De Interpretatione*, 257 n.68
Tredennick, H., 24 n.10
Türker, M., 26 n.59

Ibn Abī Uṣaybiʿa, 4, 8, 9, 25 n.44, 26 n.48

Wallies, M., 218, 254 n.9, 255 n.16, 256 n.48, 257 n.68
Walzer, R., 25 n.30, 254 n.1
Widely-accepted opinion, 57, 81, 82, 189, 257
Wright, G. H. von, 221, 255 n.31

Al-Yaʿqūbī, 254 n.7

Zayed, S., 23 n.1

SYNTHESE HISTORICAL LIBRARY

Texts and Studies
in the History of Logic and Philosophy

Editors:

N. KRETZMANN (Cornell University)
G. NUCHELMANS (University of Leyden)
L. M. DE RIJK (University of Leyden)

J. M. E. MORAVCSIK, *Patterns in Plato's Thought.* 1973, VIII + 212 pp.
JAN BERG (ed.), *Bolzano – Theory of Science.* 1973, XVI + 388 pp.
LEWIS WHITE BECK (ed.), *Proceedings of the Third International Kant Congress.* 1972, XI + 718 pp.
† KARL WOLF and PAUL WEINGARTNER (eds.), *Ernst Mally: Logische Schriften.* 1971, X + 340 pp.
† LEROY E. LOEMKER (ed.), *Gottfried Wilhelm Leibnitz: Philosophical Papers and Letters.* A Selection Translated and Edited, with an Introduction. 1969, XII + 736 pp.
† M. T. BEONIO-BROCCHIERI FUMAGALLI, *The Logic of Abelard.* Translated from the Italian. 1969, IX + 101 pp.

SYNTHESE LIBRARY

Monographs on Epistemology, Logic, Methodology,
Philosophy of Science, Sociology of Science and of Knowledge, and on the
Mathematical Methods of Social and Behavioral Sciences

Editors:

DONALD DAVIDSON (The Rockefeller University and Princeton University)
JAAKKO HINTIKKA (Academy of Finland and Stanford University)
GABRIËL NUCHELMANS (University of Leyden)
WESLEY C. SALMON (Indiana University)

ROLAND FRAÏSSÉ, *Course of Mathematical Logic. Vol. 1.* 1973, XVI + 186 pp.
I. NIINILUOTO and R. TUOMELA, *Theoretical Concepts and Hypothetico-Inductive Inference.*
1973, X + 254 pp.
RADU J. BOGDAN and ILLKA NIINILUOTO (eds.), *Logic, Language, and Probability.* 1973,
X + 323 pp.
GLENN PEARCE and PATRICK MAYNARD (eds.), *Conceptual Change.* XII + 282 pp.
M. BUNGE, *Exact Philosophy – Problems, Tools, and Goals.* 1973, X + 214 pp.
ROBERT S. COHEN and MARX W. WARTOFSKY (eds.), *Boston Studies in the Philosophy of
Science.* Volume IX: *A. A. Zinov'ev: Foundations of the Logical Theory of Scientific
Knowledge (Complex Logic).* Revised and Enlarged English Edition with an Appendix
by G. A. Smirnov, E. A. Sidorenka, A. M. Fedina, and L. A. Bobrova. 1973, XXII +
301 pp. (Also in paperback.)
K. J. J. HINTIKKA, J. M. E. MORAVCSIK, and P. SUPPES (eds.), *Approaches to Natural Lan-
guage. Proceedings of the 1970 Stanford Workshop on Grammar and Semantics.* 1973,
VIII + 526 pp. (Also in paperback.)
WILLARD C. HUMPHREYS, JR. (ed.), *Norwood Russell Hanson: Constellations and Conjec-
tures.* 1973, X + 282 pp.
MARIO BUNGE, *Method, Model and Matter.* 1973, VII + 196 pp.
MARIO BUNGE, *Philosophy of Physics.* 1973, IX + 248 pp.
LADISLAV TONDL, *Boston Studies in the Philosophy of Science.* Volume X: *Scientific Proce-
dures.* 1973, XIII + 268 pp. (Also in paperback.)
SÖREN STENLUND, *Combinators, λ-Terms and Proof Theory.* 1972, 184 pp.
DONALD DAVIDSON and GILBERT HARMAN (eds.), *Semantics of Natural Language.* 1972,
X + 769 pp. (Also in paperback.)
MARTIN STRAUSS, *Modern Physics and Its Philosophy. Selected Papers in the Logic, History,
and Philosophy of Science.* 1972, X + 297 pp.
†STEPHEN TOULMIN and HARRY WOOLF (eds.), *Norwood Russell Hanson: What I Do Not
Believe, and Other Essays.* 1971, XII + 390 pp.
†ROBERT S. COHEN and MARX W. WARTOFSKY (eds.), *Boston Studies in the Philosophy of
Science.* Volume VIII: *PSA 1970. In Memory of Rudolf Carnap* (ed. by Roger C. Buck
and Robert S. Cohen). 1971, LXVI + 615 pp. (Also in paperback.)
†YEHOSUA BAR-HILLEL (ed.), *Pragmatics of Natural Languages.* 1971, VII + 231 pp.

† ROBERT S. COHEN and MARX W. WARTOFSKY (eds.), *Boston Studies in the Philosophy of Science*. Volume VII: *Milič Čapek: Bergson and Modern Physics*. 1971, XV + 414 pp.

† CARL R. KORDIG, *The Justification of Scientific Change*. 1971, XIV + 119 pp.

† JOSEPH D. SNEED, *The Logical Structure of Mathematical Physics*. 1971, XV + 311 pp.

† JEAN-LOUIS KRIVINE, *Introduction to Axiomatic Set Theory*. 1971, VII + 98 pp.

† RISTO HILPINEN (ed.), *Deontic Logic: Introductory and Systematic Readings*. 1971, VII + 182 pp.

† EVERT W. BETH, *Aspects of Modern Logic*. 1970, XI + 176 pp.

† PAUL WEINGARTNER and GERHARD ZECHA (eds.), *Induction, Physics, and Ethics, Proceedings and Discussions of the 1968 Salzburg Colloquium in the Philosophy of Science*. 1970, X + 382 pp.

† ROLF A. EBERLE, *Nominalistic Systems*. 1970, IX + 217 pp.

† JAAKKO HINTIKKA and PATRICK SUPPES, *Information and Inference*. 1970, X + 336 pp.

† KAREL LAMBERT, *Philosophical Problems in Logic. Some Recent Developments*. 1970, VII + 176 pp.

† P. V. TAVANEC (ed.), *Problems of the Logic of Scientific Knowledge*. 1969, XII + 429 pp.

† ROBERT S. COHEN and RAYMOND J. SEEGER (eds.), *Boston Studies in the Philosophy of Science*. Volume VI: *Ernst Mach: Physicist and Philosopher*. 1970, VIII + 295 pp.

† MARSHALL SWAIN (ed.), *Induction, Acceptance, and Rational Belief*. 1970, VII + 232 pp.

† NICHOLAS RESCHER *et al.* (eds.), *Essays in Honor of Carl G. Hempel. A Tribute on the Occasion of his Sixty-Fifth Birthday*. 1969, VII + 272 pp.

† PATRICK SUPPES, *Studies in the Methodology and Foundations of Science. Selected Papers from 1911 to 1969*. 1969, XII + 473 pp.

† JAAKKO HINTIKKA, *Models for Modalities. Selected Essays*. 1969, IX + 220 pp.

† D. DAVIDSON and J. HINTIKKA (eds.), *Words and Objections: Essays on the Work of W. V. Quine*. 1969, VIII + 366 pp.

† J. W. DAVIS, D. J. HOCKNEY and W. K. WILSON (eds.), *Philosophical Logic*. 1969, VIII + 277 pp.

† ROBERT S. COHEN and MARX W. WARTOFSKY (eds.), *Boston Studies in the Philosophy of Science*. Volume V: *Proceedings of the Boston Colloquium for the Philosophy of Science 1966/1968*. VIII + 482 pp.

† ROBERT S. COHEN and MARX W. WARTOFSKY (eds.), *Boston Studies in the Philosophy of Science*. Volume IV: *Proceedings of the Boston Colloquium for the Philosophy of Science 1966/1968*. 1969, VIII + 537 pp.

† NICHOLAS RESCHER, *Topics in Philosophical Logic*. 1968, XIV + 347 pp.

† GÜNTHER PATZIG, *Aristotle's Theory of the Syllogism. A Logical-Philological Study of Book A of the Prior Analytics*. 1968, XVII + 215 pp.

† C. D. BROAD, *Induction, Probability, and Causation. Selected Papers*. 1968, XI + 296 pp.

† ROBERT S. COHEN and MARX W. WARTOFSKY (eds.), *Boston Studies in the Philosophy of Science*. Volume III: *Proceedings of the Boston Colloquium for the Philosophy of Science 1964/1966*. 1967, XLIX + 489 pp.

† GUIDO KÜNG, *Ontology and the Logistic Analysis of Language. An Enquiry into the Contemporary Views on Universals*. 1967, XI + 210 pp.

* EVERT W. BETH and JEAN PIAGET, *Mathematical Epistemology and Psychology*. 1966, XXII + 326 pp.

* EVERT W. BETH, *Mathematical Thought. An Introduction to the Philosophy of Mathematics*. 1965, XII + 208 pp.

† PAUL LORENZEN, *Formal Logic*. 1965, VIII + 123 pp.

† GEORGES GURVITCH, *The Spectrum of Social Time*. 1964, XXVI + 152 pp.

†A. A. Zinov'ev, *Philosophical Problems of Many-Valued Logic*. 1963, XIV + 155 pp.

†Marx W. Wartofsky (ed.), *Boston Studies in the Philosophy of Science*. Volume I: *Proceedings of the Boston Colloquium for the Philosophy of Science 1961/1962*. 1963, VIII + 212 pp.

†B. H. Kazemier and D. Vuysje (eds.), *Logic and Language. Studies dedicated to Professor Rudolf Carnap on the Occasion of his Seventieth Birthday*. 1962, VI + 256 pp.

*Evert W. Beth, *Formal Methods. An Introduction to Symbolic Logic and to the Study of Effective Operations in Arithmetic and Logic*. 1962, XIV + 170 pp.

*Hans Freudenthal (ed.), *The Concept and the Role of the Model in Mathematics and Natural and Social Sciences. Proceedings of a Colloquium held at Utrecht, The Netherlands, January 1960*. 1961, VI + 194 pp.

†P. L. Guiraud, *Problèmes et méthodes de la statistique linguistique*. 1960, VI + 146 pp.

*J. M. Bocheński, *A Precis of Mathematical Logic*. 1959, X + 100 pp.

Sole Distributors in the U.S.A. and Canada:

*GORDON & BREACH, INC., 440 Park Avenue South, New York, N.Y. 10016
†HUMANITIES PRESS, INC., 303 Park Avenue South, New York, N.Y. 10010